Lecture Notes in Computer Science   13197

More information about this subseries at https://link.springer.com/bookseries/7409

Pedro Ribeiro · Fernando Silva ·
José Fernando Mendes · Rosário Laureano (Eds.)

Network Science

7th International Winter Conference, NetSci-X 2022
Porto, Portugal, February 8–11, 2022
Proceedings

 Springer

Editors
Pedro Ribeiro (iD)
University of Porto
Porto, Portugal

José Fernando Mendes (iD)
University of Aveiro
Aveiro, Portugal

Fernando Silva (iD)
University of Porto
Porto, Portugal

Rosário Laureano (iD)
Iscte – Instituto Universitário de Lisboa
Lisbon, Portugal

ISSN 0302-9743   ISSN 1611-3349 (electronic)
Lecture Notes in Computer Science
ISBN 978-3-030-97239-4   ISBN 978-3-030-97240-0 (eBook)
https://doi.org/10.1007/978-3-030-97240-0

LNCS Sublibrary: SL3 – Information Systems and Applications, incl. Internet/Web, and HCI

This Springer imprint is published by the registered company Springer Nature Switzerland AG
The registered company address is: Gewerbestrasse 11, 6330 Cham, Switzerland

Preface

NetSci-X, the annual Network Science Society's signature winter conference, extends the popular NetSci conference series to provide an additional forum for a growing community of academics and practitioners working on networks. The series started in 2015. Its 7th edition, NetSci-X 2022, held in Porto from February 8 to February 11, 2022, was the first NetSci conference held in Portugal. The conference was jointly organized by the University of Porto, the University of Aveiro, and Iscte – Instituto Universitário de Lisboa and was hosted at the University of Porto, Faculty of Sciences, Computer Science Department. Previous NetSci-X conferences took place in Rio de Janeiro (Brazil), Wroclaw (Poland), Tel Aviv (Israel), Hangzhou (China), Santiago (Chile), and Tokyo (Japan). More information on the NetSci conference series and organization is available on the website at https://netscisociety.net.

The conference fosters interdisciplinary communication and collaboration in network science research across computer and information sciences, physics, mathematics, statistics, the life sciences, neuroscience, environmental sciences, social sciences, finance and business, and others. The conference aims to promote the dissemination of high-quality research as well as to engage researchers in their early career stages. Of special interest are applications which demonstrate the effectiveness of the main network science topics.

The call for papers attracted 163 submissions, representing 42 countries. The authors submitted their contributions to either the full papers track (19 submissions) or the extended abstract track. Each paper in both tracks was peer reviewed by at least two (typically three) independent reviewers from an international Program Committee. This proceedings volume is the collection of the 13 accepted full papers.

The great success of NetSci-X 2022 owes to these and other authors, who presented their work either in person in Porto or remotely. Needless to say, the success also owes to the keynote and invited speakers, who delivered impressive talks. Our keynote speakers were Jure Leskovec, Jurgen Kurths, Manuela Veloso, Stefano Boccaletti, Tijana Milenkovic, and Tiziana Di Matteo; our invited speakers were Angélica Sousa de Mata, Francisco Santos, Marcus Kaiser, Maria Angeles Serrano, Marta C. González, and Sune Lehmann.

As part of NetSci-X 2022, a school was held on February 8, dedicated to introducing young researchers to a diversity of fundamental topics in network science, including a tutorial about science communication. A poster session was also organized as part of the conference program to allow authors to briefly present their work and have the opportunity to be challenged with questions.

The 7th NetSci-X conference in Porto would not have been possible without the support of many individuals and organizations. We owe special thanks to the authors of all submitted papers, the members of the Program Committee, and the reviewers for their contributions to the success of the conference. We would also like to express our gratitude to the members of the organizing committee. Moreover, we are indebted to the members of the Network Science Society for their trust, guidance, and support. Finally, a number of institutional and industrial sponsors contributed to the organization of the conference. Their names and logos appear on the NetSci-X 2022 website at https://net scix.dcc.fc.up.pt.

It was a pleasure and an honor to organize and host NetSci-X 2022 in Porto. We hope that all participants enjoyed the technical program and the social events organized during the conference, as well as the city of Porto and Portugal.

February 2022

Pedro Ribeiro
Fernando Silva
José Fernando Mendes
Rosário Laureano

Organization

General Chairs

Fernando Silva — University of Porto, Portugal
José Fernando Mendes — University of Aveiro, Portugal
Rosário Laureano — Iscte – Instituto Universitário de Lisboa, Portugal

School Chair

Andreia Sofia Teixeira — University of Lisbon, Portugal

Local Organization

Carlos Ferreira — Polytechnic Institute of Porto, Portugal
Sylwia Bugla — CRACS/INESC TEC, Portugal
Mariana Barros — University of Porto, Portugal

Program Chair

Pedro Ribeiro — University of Porto, Portugal

Program Committee

Adilson Motter — Northwestern University, USA
Alberto Antonioni — Carlos III University of Madrid, Spain
Alessandro Pluchino — University of Catania, Italy
Alessio Cardillo — Universitat Oberta de Catalunya, Spain
Alexander Gates — Northeastern University, USA
Alexandre P. Francisco — University of Lisbon, Portugal
Alice Patania — Indiana University, USA
Andreia Sofia Teixeira — University of Lisbon, Portugal
Aric Hagberg — Los Alamos National Laboratory, USA
Balazs Lengyel — Corvinus University of Budapest, Hungary
Beom Jun Kim — Sungkyunkwan University, South Korea
Boleslaw Szymanski — Rensselaer Polytechnic Institute, USA
Brennan Klein — Northeastern University, USA
Byungjoon Min — Chungbuk National University, South Korea
Carlo Piccardi — Politecnico di Milano, Italy

Carolina Mattsson	Leiden University, The Netherlands
Claudio Castellano	Istituto dei Sistemi Complessi (ISC-CNR), Italy
Dan Braha	NECSI, USA
Daniel Figueiredo	UFRJ, Brazil
Deok-Sun Lee	Korea Institute for Advanced Study, South Korea
Dina Mistry	Northeastern University, USA
Emma Towlson	University of Calgary, Canada
Fabrizio De Vico Fallani	Inria - ICM, France
Federico Botta	University of Exeter, UK
Feng Xia	Federation University Australia, Australia
Filippo Radicchi	Northwestern University, USA
Ginestra Bianconi	Queen Mary University of London, UK
Giovanni Petri	ISI Foundation, Italy
Giulio Cimini	University of Rome Tor Vergata, Italy
Giulio Rossetti	University of Pisa, Italy
Giuseppe Mangioni	University of Catania, Italy
Gregorio D'Agostino	ENEA, Spain
Hang-Hyun Jo	Catholic University of Korea, South Korea
Haoxiang Xia	Dalian University of Technology, China
Hiroki Sayama	Binghamton University, USA
James Gleeson	University of Limerick, Ireland
Jianxi Gao	Rensselaer Polytechnic Institute, USA
Johannes Wachs	Central European University, Hungary
Jordi Duch	Universitat Rovira i Virgili, Italy
Jorge G. T. Zanudo	Pennsylvania State University, USA
José Fernando Mendes	University of Aveiro, Portugal
José Manuel Galán	Universidad de Burgos, Spain
Junming Huang	Princeton University, USA
Laura Maria Alessandretti	ENS Lyon, France
Leto Peel	Maastricht University, The Netherlands
Luca Pappalardo	University of Pisa, Italy
Lucas Lacasa	IFISC (CSIC-UIB), Spain
Luis E. C. Rocha	Ghent University, Belgium
M. Ángeles Serrano	Universitat de Barcelona, Spain
Manlio De Domenico	Fondazione Bruno Kessler, Italy
Marcella Tambuscio	Austrian Academy of Sciences, Austria
Marco Alberto Javarone	Centro Ricerche Enrico Fermi, Italy, and University College London, UK
Marco Tulio Angulo	National Autonomous University of Mexico, Mexico
Matúš Medo	University of Bern, Switzerland
Michele Tizzoni	ISI Foundation, Italy

Mikko Kivela	Aalto University, Finland
Márton Pósfai	Central European University, Hungary
Naoki Masuda	State University of New York at Buffalo, USA
Osnat Mokryn	University of Haifa, Israel
Paolo Bajardi	ISI Foundation, Italy
Pedro Ribeiro	University of Porto, Portugal
Per Sebastian Skardal	Trinity College Dublin, Ireland
Petter Holme	Tokyo Institute of Technology, Japan
Philipp Hoevel	University College Cork, Ireland
Radosław Michalski	Wrocław University of Science and Technology, Poland
Renaud Lambiotte	University of Oxford, UK
Riccardo Di Clemente	University of Exeter, UK
Rodolfo Baggio	Bocconi University, Italy, and Tomsk Polytechnic University, Russia
Rosa M. Benito	Universidad Politécnica de Madrid, Spain
Rosário Laureano	Iscte – Instituto Universitário de Lisboa, Portugal
Sandro Meloni	IFISC (CSIC-UIB), Spain
Sang Hoon Lee	Gyeongsang National University, South Korea
Satyam Mukherjee	Northwestern University, USA
Sean Cornelius	Ryerson University, Canada
Taro Takaguchi	LINE Corporation, Japan
Tatsuro Kawamoto	AIST, Japan
Teruyoshi Kobayashi	Kobe University, Japan
Tiago Peixoto	Central European University, Hungary
Tiziano Squartini	IMT School for Advanced Studies Lucca, Italy
Vedran Sekara	IT University of Copenhagen, Denmark
Xin Lu	Karolinska Institutet, Sweden
Yanqing Hu	Sun Yat-sen University, Taiwan
Yifang Ma	Southern University of Science and Technology, China
Yohsuke Murase	RIKEN, Japan
Zhihai Rong	UESTC, China
Zhong-Ke Gao	Tianjin University, China

Additional Reviewers

Ahmad Naser Eddin	Cátia Vaz	Qi Wang
Alberto Barbosa	Hengfang Deng	Robert Eyre
Andre Meira	Lu Zhong	Shuo Yu
Bernardo Monechi	Luciano Grácio	Vanessa Silva
Chao Fan	Pietro Coletti	Xiangyi Meng

NetSci-X Keynote Speakers

Jure Leskovec	Stanford University, USA
Jurgen Kurths	Humboldt University Berlin, Germany
Manuela Veloso	Carnegie Mellon University and J. P. Morgan, USA
Stefano Boccaletti	Institute for Complex Systems (ISC-CNR), Italy
Tijana Milenkovic	University of Notre Dame, USA
Tiziana Di Matteo	King's College London, UK

NetSci-X Invited Speakers

Angélica Sousa de Mata	Universidade Federal de Lavras, Brazil
Francisco Santos	University of Lisbon, Portugal
Marcus Kaiser	University of Nottingham, UK
Maria Angeles Serrano	University of Barcelona, Spain
Marta C. González	University of California, Berkeley, USA
Sune Lehmann	Technical University of Denmark and University of Copenhagen, Denmark

NetSci-X School Speakers

Eugenio Valdano	Sorbonne Université and iPLESP, France
Fernando P. Santos	University of Amsterdam, The Netherlands
Joana Cabral	University of Minho, Portugal
Marta Daniela Santos	University of Lisbon, Portugal

Contents

Using Localized Attacks
with Probabilistic Failures to Model
Seismic Events over Physical-Logical
Interdependent Networks

Ivana Bachmann[✉][iD] and Javier Bustos-Jiménez[iD]

NIC Labs, University of Chile, Santiago, Chile
`ivana@niclabs.cl`

Abstract. Natural catastrophes can affect different structures with varying intensities depending on the global and local characteristics of the event. For example, for earthquakes we have global characteristics such as the depth, magnitude, and type (interface or intraslab). Whereas soil conditions, and the hypocentral distance are local characteristics. Here we study the robustness against seismic events of physical-logical interdependent networks used to represent Internet-like systems. To do this we present a novel type of localized attack: Localized Attacks with Probabilistic Failures (LAPF). We use LAPF to model seismic events as Seismic Attacks (SA). We compare the effect of seismic attacks with the effect of localized attacks. To generate these seismic attacks we use real data from earthquakes registered in Chile. We find that seismic attacks can result in catastrophic system failure, and can cause more damage than localized attacks by damaging a smaller fraction of nodes in the physical network. The results also show that catastrophic damage can be prevented by simply adding more interlinks between the logical network and the physical network. We found that seismic attacks that resulted in the loss of more than half of the logical network are related to the removal of logical bridge nodes during the cascading failure, suggesting that the robustness of physical-logical interdependent networks may be improved by identifying and protecting these types of nodes.

Keywords: Localized attacks · Robustness · Interdependent networks · Spatially embedded networks

1 Introduction

Natural disasters such as floods, tsunamis, earthquakes, volcanic eruptions, etc. cause damages within a geographic area. Localized Attacks (LA) have been used to model this type of events as they affect a circular area of the physical space [5,6,23]. However, while localized attacks cause everything within its attack area to fail, natural disasters can cause different levels of damage for different infrastructures located in the same area. Thus, some elements may be fully

© Springer Nature Switzerland AG 2022
P. Ribeiro et al. (Eds.): NetSci-X 2022, LNCS 13197, pp. 1–14, 2022.
https://doi.org/10.1007/978-3-030-97240-0_1

functional even after being affected by the event. Here, the damage perceived by an infrastructure depends on the characteristics of the event, local geographical conditions, infrastructure characteristics, etc.

For tsunamis, the damage level perceived by an infrastructure will depend on variables such as the distance to the shore, the elevation at which the infrastructure was built, the tsunami characteristics, etc. In the case of earthquakes, the damage level perceived by an infrastructure will depend on local conditions: hypocentral distance, and soil characteristics, as well as global conditions: earthquake magnitude, earthquake type (interface or intraslab), depth, etc. Because of this, two infrastructures that are geographically close to each other can experience different damage levels despite being affected by the same event. Assimaki et al. [2] observed that, after the 2010 earthquake in Chile, two adjacent multistory buildings located in downtown Concepción suffered vastly different damage levels due to the soil conditions assumed when designing each building. Here, one of the buildings collapsed, whereas the other building only suffered minor damages. The distance between these buildings was approximately 20 m.

Differences as the ones observed by Assimaki et al. are not captured by localized attacks. To capture these differences we need to consider the specific characteristics that contribute to the damage caused by a natural disaster. Furthermore, since the damage caused by an earthquake cannot be modeled in the same way as the damage caused by a tsunami, flood, or tornado, we need to consider the characteristics specific to the type of natural disaster that we want to represent.

To have a more accurate representation of the damage caused by natural disasters over physical networks we propose a novel type of localized attack: Localized Attack with Probabilistic Failures (LAPF). Given an adverse event, LAPFs allow us to assign a different failure probability to each node according to the local and global characteristics of the event. That is, the failure probability distribution can be tailored to consider the specific characteristics that contribute to the damage caused by a particular natural catastrophe. To the best of our knowledge this is the first time that localized attacks have been used considering a probabilistic approach as they have been mostly modeled to be uniform within a certain radius [25].

Here, we use LAPFs to model seismic events as Seismic Attacks (SA). We test the effect of SA over physical-logical interdependent networks used to model Internet-like systems [5]. To generate these seismic attacks we use real data from earthquakes registered in Chile. We compare the effect of SA with the effect of LA. Our findings suggest that seismic attacks can reduce the functionality of physical-logical systems as much as localized attacks, despite damaging less physical nodes. It is shown that both seismic attacks, and localized attacks can result in total system failure. Our results also show that physical attacks causing higher damage can be prevented by increasing the number of interlinks between the logical network and the physical network.

This article is organized as follows: In Sect. 2 related work is presented. In Sect. 3 we define LAPF and seismic attacks. Section 4 presents the physical-logical interdependent network model used along with the networks tested. Results are presented in Sect. 5. In Sect. 6 we discuss the results, and in Sect. 7 the main conclusions are presented.

2 Related Work

In the literature we can find several ways to attack interdependent networks, such as random attacks, targeted attacks, and localized attacks [4]. The most common way to attack or damage a system is by using random attacks, that is, randomly removing a set nodes from the system [4,7,17,29]. Targeted attacks on the other hand, pick the network elements to attack according to some parameter associated with said element. These attacks can pick nodes or edges using centrality measures [8,10,14], system values such as loads [28], etc.

However, these attacks do not offer an accurate representation of adverse events with local physical conditions such as natural catastrophes. To represent these scenarios we have localized attacks. Given a network allocated into a space S, localized attacks damage all the nodes and/or links contained within an area of radius r and centered in $c \in S$ [6,23]. It has been shown that localized attacks cause substantially more damage than an equivalent random attack in interdependent lattices when measuring the damage using percolation methods [6], making these attacks especially interesting to test over systems that contain physically embedded networks.

Localized attacks have been used to measure the effect of natural catastrophes or man-made threats over power-grids [21], the Internet network [5,20], and more generic networks [6,23,26]. Although most of these studies consider that localized attacks affect a circular area, there are some exceptions that consider other geometrical shapes [20,25]. To the best of our knowledge none of these works have considered localized attacks that cause damage according to a failure probability described by the conditions affecting the network elements.

3 Localized Attacks with Probabilistic Failures

Consider a physical network $P = (V_P, E_P)$. We define a localized attack with probabilistic failures or (LAPF) as an attack that affects a circular area of radius $r \in [0, \infty)$, where each node $u \in V_P$ contained within the attack area has a failure probability given by the failure probability distribution F. In Fig. 1 we can see a visualization of a LAPF. Here we observe that different areas within the circular area affected by the LAPF have different failure probabilities.

The failure probability distribution F is defined as a function $F : X \longrightarrow [0, 1]$, where X is the set of network elements that can be affected by the attack. In order to capture the conditions affecting the failure probability of an element we define the function $g : X \longrightarrow \Gamma$ where Γ contains n-tuples that describe the necessary data to determine the failure probability of a node, and the function $\Phi : \Gamma \longrightarrow [0, 1]$ that determines the failure probability that an event induces given the conditions described by $\gamma \in \Gamma$. Using functions g and Φ we can define F as the function composition of Φ and g ($F = \Phi \circ g$).

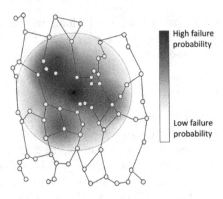

Fig. 1. LAPF graphic example.

3.1 Seismic Attacks

Given an infrastructure located at a geographic point x, the damage caused by an earthquake or seismic event over said infrastructure will depend on variables such as the event magnitude, the distance from the x to the epicenter, the depth of the event, the soil type at x, etc. Some of these variables are characteristics of the seismic event itself, such as the event magnitude and depth. Whereas other variables are related to local characteristics at point x, such as the soil type, and the hypocentral distance. Variations in the local properties of a point can lead to infrastructures located in different points to experience vastly different levels of damage. Thus, the same seismic event may have different effects over different nodes. To capture this behavior we model seismic events using localized attacks with probabilistic failures. Here, we will refer to a LAPF intended to model a seismic event as a Seismic Attack (SA). To model seismic attacks, we estimate the damage perceived by a node after a seismic event using the Ground Acceleration at the node's location. Then, we use this data to define the failure probability distribution F used by the LAPF.

The ground acceleration describes the acceleration perceived in a given location during an earthquake and it can be measured using instruments. This acceleration can be used to estimate how strong the shaking produced by an earthquake in a specific location is. In the literature we can find different Ground Motion Prediction Equations (GMPE) to estimate or predict the acceleration perceived in a given point in space given the local conditions [9,15,19,27]. In this work we aim to represent the conditions of Chile, thus we use the equations presented by Idini et al. [15] which were developed for the specific case of the Chilean subduction zone.

The equations presented by Idini et al. consider the contribution of the seismic source F_F, the path contribution F_D, and the local site effects F_S as follows.

$$log_{10}Y = F_F(M_w, H, F_{eve}) + F_D(R, M_w, F_{eve}) + F_S(V_{s30}, s_{T*})$$

Where Y is the ground acceleration, M_w is the moment magnitude of the event, F_{eve} is a variable representing whether the event is an interface event ($F_{eve} = 0$) or an intraslab event ($F_{eve} = 1$), H is the hypocentral depth, R is the hypocentral distance, V_{s30} is the average shear wave velocity down to 30 m depth, and s_{T*} is the site effect coefficient given by the local soil.

Using the GMPE provided by Idini et al. [15] we estimate the failure probability of a physical node after a seismic event. Here, $X = V_P$ is the set of physical nodes. The set Γ contains all the necessary data to calculate the ground acceleration. Thus, $\gamma \in \Gamma$ is a 6-tuple that contains the moment magnitude of the event M_w, the depth of the event H, the type of event F_{eve}, the hypocentral distance from the node to the event R, the average shear wave velocity down to 30 m depth V_{s30} at the node's location, and the site effect coefficient of the soil in which the node is located s_{T*}.

Given a physical node $v \in V_P$, and a seismic event ev, we have that the failure probability of node v during a seismic event ev is given by $F_{ev}(v) = \Phi(g_{ev}(v))$ where $g_{ev} : V_P \longrightarrow \Gamma$ is the function that returns the 6-tuple that contains all the necessary data to calculate the ground acceleration perceived by a node given the seismic event ev. Given $\gamma \in \Gamma$, we define the function $\Phi(\gamma) = \Phi_2(\Phi_1(\gamma))$ where Φ_1 corresponds to the equation provided by Idini et al. [15], that is, the equation that returns the ground acceleration associated to the conditions described by γ, and function Φ_2 gives us the failure probability given a ground acceleration value. Here, we define Φ_2 as follows.

$$\Phi_2(a) = \begin{cases} 0 & \text{if } a \leq c_1 \\ \phi(a) & \text{if } c_1 \leq a \leq c_2 \\ 1 & \text{if } a \geq c_2 \end{cases}$$

Where $a = \Phi_1(\gamma)$. Here, we assume that below c_1 node failure will not occur, and that above c_2 failure will always occur. Limits c_1 and c_2 have been selected based on the Japan Meteorological Agency (JMA) Seismic Intensity Scale [16]. The JMA Seismic Intensity Scale describes 10 intensity levels, with the lowest intensity level being 0 and the highest intensity level being 7. Each intensity level is associated to a seismic intensity defined by the JMA as I_{JMA}, with

$$I_{JMA} = 2log(a) + 0.94$$

where a is the ground acceleration measured in gal ($1gal = 0.01\,\text{m/s}^2$) at time period $\tau = 0.3\,\text{s}$ [16]. Thus, we set Φ_1 using the coefficients associated to $\tau = 0.3\,\text{s}$ as described in [15]. Using the JMA Seismic Intensity Scale as guideline we chose c_1 as the lowest ground acceleration for intensity 3 of the seismic scale ($c_1 = 0.06\,\text{m/s}^2$), and c_2 as the ground acceleration above which the seismic event is considered to have an intensity of 7 ($c_2 = 6\,\text{m/s}^2$). For simplicity in this application we define ϕ as a linear function with $\phi(c_1) = 0$ and $\phi(c_2) = 1$.

3.2 Seismic Data

For the data regarding the seismic event conditions we use the data set provided in the work of Idini et al. [15] which describes the moment magnitude M_w, depth H, and type F_{eve} of 103 seismic events registered in Chile. Here M_w ranges from

5.5 to 8.8. The average shear wave velocity down to 30 m depth V_{s30} at each node location was approximated from the image provided on Rauld et al. work [22]. We must note that the raw data used by Rauld et al. to generate this map is currently not available for public use, and efforts to gain access to this data were unsuccessful. Finally, since not enough data regarding the soil types as described in [15] is available, the soil type for the entire physical space has been approximated to s_{II} soil. Soil s_{II} was selected because it has been found to be present in similar proportions in both soil (55%) and rock (45%) [18].

4   Network Model

We model the Internet using a model presented in depth in our previous work [5]. Here, we have a logical network representing the BGP network, and a physical network representing the Internet Backbone. Consider $P = (V_P, E_P)$ the physical network, and $L = (V_L, E_L)$ the logical network. The interactions between both of these networks are modeled as a set I of bidirectional interlinks. The physical-logical interdependent network is described by the tuple (P, L, I). Here, the physical network must be spatially embedded, that is, each physical node $v \in V_P$ must be allocated into a physical space.

Each network contains provider nodes to represent ISPs, and consumer nodes that represent the users. A consumer node is considered to have Internet access if it has a path to a provider node. Physical nodes interconnected through an interlink with a logical provider node are considered to be provider nodes within the physical network. There are p_P physical provider nodes, and p_L logical provider nodes. Since each logical provider node must have at least one interlink we have that $p_P \geq p_L$.

This model is a multiple dependencies model [4], meaning that it supports many-to-many interdependencies and thus each node can have multiple interlinks. Here, a node u will remain functional if at least one of its interlinks is functional. Conversely, if all the interdependent nodes of a given node u fail, u will also fail. This condition is applied to physical nodes, and logical nodes. For each logical node u_L we add a total of $N_I(u_L)$ interlinks, with $N_I(u_L) \in \{1, \ldots, I_{max}\}$. For each logical consumer node u_L^c we randomly select a value $N_I(u_L^c)$ from the set $\{1, \ldots, I_{max}\}$ following a uniform distribution. Whereas for each logical provider node u_L^p we always add $N_I(u_L^p) = I_{max}$ interlinks.

4.1   Tested Networks

In this work we use a subset of the networks data set used in our previous work [5]. Since we use seismic data for seismic events registered in Chile, we use all the physical networks built using a long and narrow space shape with a width to length ratio of (1:25) as this space is based on Chile's continental geography. We also use the logical network used in this previous work. Each network in this data set starts with a single connected component.

In this data set the physical network can be model after Gabriel graphs (GG) [13], n-nearest neighbors (nNN) model with $n = 5$ [11], or Relative Neighborhood Graphs (RNG) [24]. These networks have been used because they heavily depend on physical conditions to be built. For each model $m \in \{$GG, 5NN, RNG$\}$ the network data set contains 10 different physical networks. Each of these networks is built using a different set of physical nodes allocations $loc_j(V_P, s)$ with $j \in \{1, \ldots, 10\}$, and $s = (1{:}25)$ the space shape. Thus, we generate each physical network as follows

$$P_j(m, s) = (V_P, E_P^m(loc_j(V_P, s)))$$

where $E_P^m(loc_j(V_P, s))$ is the set of links generated according to the physical model m, given the set of physical nodes allocations $loc_j(V_P, s)$.

As for the logical network we use a single instance of a scale-free network with $\lambda = 2.5$ [12]. This logical network $L = (V_L, E_L)$ is coupled with each physical network $P_j(m, s)$ to obtain each final system. We must note that since we use the same logical network used in [5], we observe that this network contains the bridge node u_L^b. A "bridge node" is a cut node that acts as a bridge between components with no provider nodes, and components with provider nodes. Although all bridge nodes are cut nodes, we have that if $p_L > 1$, then being a cut node is not sufficient to be a bridge node since it is possible to remove a cut node and end up with each connected component containing a provider node. For the case of the logical bridge node u_L^b we have that removing this node during the cascading failure process always results in a loss of half of the logical network [5]. Although in the present work we only test one logical network, we must note that other logical networks have been tested, and we have found that bridge nodes are a common occurrence in Scale-Free networks [3].

For the interlink set we generated interlinks using $I_{max} \in \{3, 10\}$. These interlinks sets differ from the ones tested in [5], since the interlink set tested in the present work assigns exactly I_{max} interlinks to logical provider nodes, that is $N_I(u_L^p) = I_{max}$ for each logical provider node u_L^p. Whereas in our previous work, given logical node u_L, we considered $N_I(u_L)$ to be selected at random from the set $\{1, \ldots, I_{max}\}$ regardless of whether u_L was a consumer node or not.

Since these systems are built using Chile as reference, parameters such as the number of physical nodes, the number of logical nodes, and the number of logical providers are set to simulate the conditions of this country. Thus, we have $p_L = 6$, $N_L = 300$ logical nodes, and $N_P = 2000$ physical nodes. Please note that as of the writing of this work the number of logical nodes for the case of Chile has increased to 378 [1].

5 Results

To test the effect of seismic attacks we measure the system's robustness as the fraction of functional logical nodes after a failure using the G_L index as defined in [5]:

$$G_L = \frac{N_L^f}{N_L}$$

where N_L is the initial number of functional logical nodes, and N_L^f is the number of functional logical nodes after the system has been damaged, and the cascading failure has stopped. Please note that, given the interdependent networks model used, it is possible to have up to p_L functional connected components on the logical network after an attack. Here we also test the effect of localized attacks (LA) to compare their effect over the robustness of physical-logical interdependent networks with the effect of SA. Both of these attacks can remove any physical node regardless of whether the node is a consumer node or a provider node. If a single attack removes all the provider nodes of either network during the cascading failure, then the attack will result in $G_L = 0$.

The localized attacks tested remove all physical nodes within a circular area of radius r in the physical network. We must notice that two LAs with the same radius but different centers may contain different fractions $(1 - p)$ of physical nodes within their attack areas.

5.1   Localized Attacks

Given space shape $s = (1:25)$ a set $C(s)$ of 100 uniformly spread centers were tested. On each center we perform a localized attack of radius $r = w_{ln}$, with w_{ln} the width of the (1:25) space. Figures in this section show each LA tested over each of the 30 interdependent systems considered for a given I_{max} value, thus each figure shows the effect of a total of 3000 LAs.

In Fig. 2 we see the comparison of G_L versus the fraction of failed physical nodes. Here, each point shows the effect of a single localized attack over an interdependent system. In Fig. 2 we can observe that there is not a clear correlation between $(1 - p)$ and the G_L value. Furthermore most localized attacks resulted in high G_L values, meaning that most logical nodes remained functional once the cascading failure stopped. However, we can also observe that for systems built using $I_{max} = 3$ there are localized attacks that result in a $G_L \leq 0.5$, meaning that at least half of the logical nodes failed during the cascading failure. Even more, some of these attacks resulted in the total loss of the logical network ($G_L = 0$). These attacks do not appear as a continuum, but rather as a distinct group that always damages at least half of the logical network.

Localized attacks that result in a $G_L \leq 0.5$ correspond to High Damage Localized Attacks (HDLAs) and are likely to be caused by logical bridge node u_L^b (see Sect. 4.1). Consider $CF(x)$ the set of nodes removed during the cascading failure caused by a localized attack x. In Fig. 3 we observe that HDLAs remove node u_L^b during the cascading failure process ($u_L^b \in CF$), whereas non-HDLAs do not.

We must note that only a small percentage of the localized attacks tested resulted in $G_L \leq 0.5$. Indeed, as we can see in Table 1 less than 4% of the localized attacks tested result in HDLA for systems built using $I_{max} = 3$. For the case of systems built using $I_{max} = 10$ we observe that there are no attacks that result in HDLA.

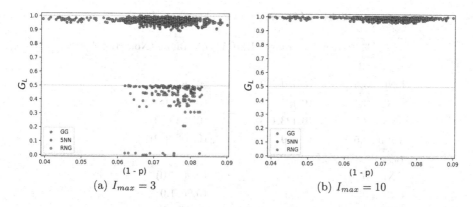

Fig. 2. Each localized attack G_L value versus $(1 - p)$.

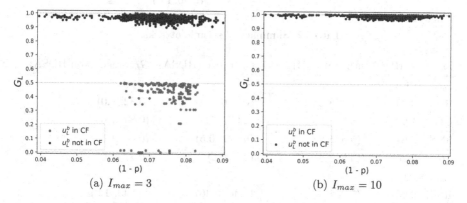

Fig. 3. Each localized attack G_L value versus $(1 - p)$. Red nodes correspond to LA x with $u_L^b \in CF(x)$. Black nodes correspond to LA x with $u_L^b \notin CF(x)$. (Color figure online)

5.2 Seismic Attacks

The considered seismic data set contains 103 different seismic events registered in Chile. Given an interdependent system, we perform a seismic attack for each pair (c, ev) with $c \in C(s)$ (see Sect. 5.1) and ev a seismic event. Figures in this section show each SA tested over each of the 30 interdependent systems considered for a given I_{max}, thus each figure shows a total of 309,000 SAs.

In Fig. 4 we can see the effect of each SA tested over each interdependent system. We can see that, similar to localized attacks, seismic attacks can cause High Damage Seismic Attacks (HDSAs): seismic attacks that result in $G_L \leq 0.5$. In Fig. 4 we can see that HDSAs occur on systems with $I_{max} = 3$ and $I_{max} = 10$. As we can see in Fig. 5, HDSAs remove the logical bridge node u_L^b described in Sect. 5.1. This suggests that, for seismic attacks, HDSAs are caused by the removal of the logical node u_L^b during the cascading failure process.

Table 1. Summary of localized attacks.

	% HDLA	G_L range (HDLA)	G_L range (Non-HDLA)
$I_{max} = 3$			
RNG	3.6	$(0.0, 0.459)$	$(0.893, 1.0)$
GG	3.4	$(0.4, 0.5)$	$(0.893, 1.0)$
5NN	3.5	$(0.423, 0.5)$	$(0.893, 1.0)$
Total	3.5	$(0.0, 0.5)$	$(0.893, 1.0)$
$I_{max} = 10$			
RNG	0	–	$(0.96, 1.0)$
GG	0	–	$(0.96, 1.0)$
5NN	0	–	$(0.96, 1.0)$
Total	0	–	$(0.96, 1.0)$

Table 2. Summary of seismic attacks.

m	% HDSA	M_w range (HDSA)	G_L range (HDSA)	G_L range (Non-HDSA)
$I_{max} = 3$				
RNG	3.26	$(5.5, 8.8)$	$(0.0, 0.487)$	$(0.82, 1.0)$
GG	1.9	$(5.5, 8.8)$	$(0.027, 0.5)$	$(0.84, 1.0)$
5NN	1.61	$(5.5, 8.8)$	$(0.027, 0.5)$	$(0.86, 1.0)$
Total	2.26	$(5.5, 8.8)$	$(0.0, 0.5)$	$(0.82, 1.0)$
$I_{max} = 10$				
RNG	0.0058	$(7.8, 8.8)$	$(0.46, 0.467)$	$(0.943, 1.0)$
GG	0.0029	$(7.8, 8.3)$	$(0.48, 0.48)$	$(0.95, 1.0)$
5NN	0.0010	$(8.8, 8.8)$	$(0.483, 0.483)$	$(0.95, 1.0)$
Total	0.0032	$(7.8, 8.8)$	$(0.46, 0.483)$	$(0.943, 1.0)$

Figure 6 shows the effect of each seismic attack tested over each of the physical-logical systems, and the moment magnitude M_w of the event associated with each seismic attack. Here we observe that for $I_{max} = 3$ the magnitude of the event is not correlated with the occurrence of HDSAs. However, we observe that for $I_{max} = 10$ HDSAs only occur with higher M_w events. This can be further observed in Table 2, here we can see the detailed information regarding the percentage that these HDSAs represent from the total, the M_w range associated to HDSAs, and the range of G_L values associated to HDSAs and non-HDSAs. In Table 2 we can see that HDSA represent a very small percentage of the total number of seismic attacks tested. For $I_{max} = 3$, all the HDSAs combined represent less than 3% of all the seismic attacks tested. For $I_{max} = 10$ this percentage drops to less than 0.004%.

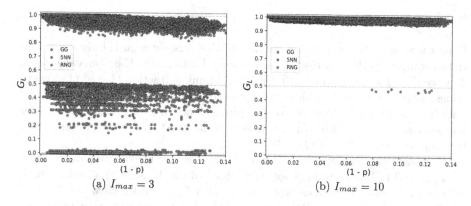

(a) $I_{max} = 3$ (b) $I_{max} = 10$

Fig. 4. Each seismic attack G_L value versus $(1 - p)$.

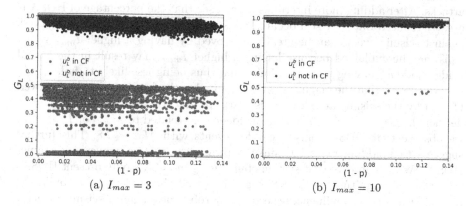

(a) $I_{max} = 3$ (b) $I_{max} = 10$

Fig. 5. Each seismic attack G_L value versus $(1 - p)$. Red nodes correspond to SA x with $u_L^b \in CF(x)$. Black nodes correspond to SA x with $u_L^b \notin CF(x)$. (Color figure online)

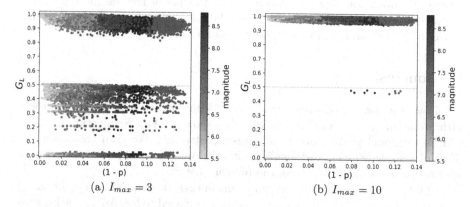

(a) $I_{max} = 3$ (b) $I_{max} = 10$

Fig. 6. Each seismic attack G_L value versus $(1-p)$. Colors show the moment magnitude M_w associated to the SA. (Color figure online)

6 Discussion

From the results shown in Sect. 5 we can see that seismic attacks have the potential to completely destroy the logical network. Particularly, they can cause more damage than localized attacks that remove a similar fraction $(1 - p)$ of physical nodes. This can be seen as high damage seismic attacks (HDSAs) can occur by initially removing less than 6% of the physical nodes (see Fig. 5), whereas for localized attacks at least 6% of the physical nodes must be removed for an attack to result in a $G_L \leq 0.5$ (see Fig. 3).

However, the percentage of HDSA is very low. In Table 2 we can see that, for $I_{max} = 3$ HDSAs represent less than 2.3% of all the seismic attacks tested. Whereas for localized attacks over systems with $I_{max} = 3$ we have that 3.5% of the LAs tested result in HDLAs (see Table 1). We also observe that increasing the I_{max} value results in no HDLA. This is not the case for high damage seismic attacks. After adding more interlinks we can see that the percentage of HDSA is greatly reduced but they still occur. This suggests that the system's robustness against seismic events can be greatly improved by having a higher I_{max} value. This may be explained because having a higher I_{max} may result in the logical bridge node u_L^b having more interlinks, and thus being less likely to fail.

We observe that the magnitude M_w is related to the fraction of nodes removed $(1 - p)$ by the seismic attack. We also observe that for systems with $I_{max} = 3$, neither the G_L value nor the HDSA incidence are related to M_w. For $I_{max} = 10$ we observe that HDSAs only occur for events with $M_w \geq 7.8$. This further suggests that adding more interlinks improves the system robustness against HDSA. We also observe that systems built using $m = 5NN$ only present HDSAs for events of magnitude $M_w = 8.8$, suggesting that the model used to build the physical network also influences the systems' robustness against seismic attacks.

Another interesting thing to note is that the fraction of nodes removed $(1-p)$ does not appear to be strictly correlated to the magnitude of the seismic attack (see Fig. 6). This can be explained because the ground acceleration that a node experiences does not only depend on the magnitude of the seismic event. The depth, and event type (interface or intraslab) can greatly impact the ground acceleration [15], and thus the failure probability of each physical node.

7 Conclusion

In this work we presented a novel way to model physical attacks: localized attacks with probabilistic failures (LAPF). Here, we show a LAPF application by using LAPFs to model seismic events as "seismic attacks". We then compared the effect of seismic attacks, and localized attacks over physical-logical interdependent networks designed to model the Internet network.

We found that seismic attacks can result in catastrophic damage by inducing failure on a small fraction of physical nodes. Compared to localized attacks, seismic attacks can cause catastrophic damage by damaging fewer physical nodes. However, we found that very few seismic attacks have the potential to lead to catastrophic events, and that their effect can be greatly mitigated by increasing the number of interlinks between the physical network and the logical network.

Our results show that logical bridge node u_L^b plays a key role over the robustness of physical-logical interdependent networks. We found that the failure of node u_L^b during the cascading process results in the loss of more than half of the logical network for both seismic attacks and localized attacks. This is consistent with previous findings [5]. This suggests that protecting these specific nodes might prove crucial to protect these types of systems against seismic events.

As for the future there are several types of events that can be modeled using LAPF, such is the case of other natural catastrophes (tsunamis, floods, volcanic eruptions, etc.), and man made threats (bombs, gas explosions, etc.). As for seismic attacks, it would be interesting to test the effect of seismic attacks over other physically embedded networks, such as the transportation network or the power grid network. Finally, the protective effect of increasing the number of interlinks of bridge nodes, changing the location of the physical nodes interconnected to it, or adding backup nodes to avoid its failure remains to be tested.

Acknowledgment. Work partially funded by CONICYT/ANID Doctorado Nacional 21170165, and supported by the supercomputing infrastructure of the NLHPC (ECM-02).

References

1. Number of autonomous system. https://www-public.imtbs-tsp.eu/~maigron/RIR_Stats/RIR_Delegations/World/ASN-ByNb.html. Accessed 15 Nov 2021
2. Assimaki, D., Ledezma, C., Montalva, G.A., Tassara, A., Mylonakis, G., Boroschek, R.: Site effects and damage patterns. Earthquake Spectra **28**(1_suppl1), 55–74 (2012)
3. Bachmann, I.: To appear. In: Methods Based on Interdependent Networks to Analyze the Internet Robustness. Ph.D. thesis (2022)
4. Bachmann, I., Bustos-Jiménez, J., Bustos, B.: A survey on frameworks used for robustness analysis on interdependent networks. Complexity **2020** (2020)
5. Bachmann, I., Valdés, V., Bustos-Jiménez, J., Bustos, B.: Effect of adding physical links on the robustness of the internet modeled as a physical-logical interdependent network using simple strategies. Int. J. Crit. Infrastruct. Prot. 100483 (2021)
6. Berezin, Y., Bashan, A., Danziger, M.M., Li, D., Havlin, S.: Localized attacks on spatially embedded networks with dependencies. Sci. Rep. **5** (2015)
7. Buldyrev, S.V., Parshani, R., Paul, G., Stanley, H.E., Havlin, S.: Catastrophic cascade of failures in interdependent networks. Nature **464**(7291), 1025–1028 (2010)
8. Chattopadhyay, S., Dai, H., Hosseinalipour, S., et al.: Designing optimal interlink patterns to maximize robustness of interdependent networks against cascading failures. IEEE Trans. Commun. **65**(9), 3847–3862 (2017)
9. Crouse, C.: Ground-motion attenuation equations for earthquakes on the Cascadia subduction zone. Earthq. Spectra **7**(2), 201–236 (1991)
10. Dong, G., Gao, J., Du, R., Tian, L., Stanley, H.E., Havlin, S.: Robustness of network of networks under targeted attack. Phys. Rev. E **87**(5), 052804 (2013)
11. Eppstein, D., Paterson, M.S., Yao, F.F.: On nearest-neighbor graphs. Discrete Comput. Geom. **17**(3), 263–282 (1997)

12. Faloutsos, M., Faloutsos, P., Faloutsos, C.: On power-law relationships of the internet topology. In: ACM SIGCOMM Computer Communication Review, vol. 29, pp. 251–262. ACM (1999)
13. Gabriel, K.R., Sokal, R.R.: A new statistical approach to geographic variation analysis. Syst. Zool. **18**(3), 259–278 (1969)
14. Huang, X., Gao, J., Buldyrev, S.V., Havlin, S., Stanley, H.E.: Robustness of interdependent networks under targeted attack. Phys. Rev. E **83**(6), 065101 (2011)
15. Idini, B., Rojas, F., Ruiz, S., Pastén, C.: Ground motion prediction equations for the Chilean subduction zone. Bull. Earthq. Eng. **15**(5), 1853–1880 (2017)
16. Japanese meteorological agency seismic intensity scale calculation method. https://www.data.jma.go.jp/svd/eqev/data/kyoshin/kaisetsu/calc_sindo.htm# gosei. Accessed 15 Nov 2021
17. Kotnis, B., Kuri, J.: Percolation on networks with antagonistic and dependent interactions. Phys. Rev. E **91**(3), 032805 (2015)
18. Leyton, F., Pastén, C., Ruiz, S., Idini, B., Rojas, F.: Empirical site classification of CSN network using strong-motion records. Seismol. Res. Lett. **89**(2A), 512–518 (2018)
19. Midorikawa, S.: Semi-empirical estimation of peak ground acceleration from large earthquakes. Tectonophysics **218**(1–3), 287–295 (1993)
20. Neumayer, S., Zussman, G., Cohen, R., Modiano, E.: Assessing the vulnerability of the fiber infrastructure to disasters. IEEE/ACM Trans. Network. **19**(6), 1610–1623 (2011)
21. Ouyang, M., Xu, M., Zhang, C., Huang, S.: Mitigating electric power system vulnerability to worst-case spatially localized attacks. Reliab. Eng. Syst. Saf. **165**, 144–154 (2017)
22. Rauld, R., Medina, F., Leyton, F., Ruiz, S.: Mapa de microzonificación sismo-geológica para chile. In: Congreso Geológico Chileno, pp. 106–109 (2015)
23. Shao, S., Huang, X., Stanley, H.E., Havlin, S.: Percolation of localized attack on complex networks. New J. Phys. **17**(2), 023049 (2015)
24. Toussaint, G.T.: The relative neighbourhood graph of a finite planar set. Pattern Recogn. **12**(4), 261–268 (1980)
25. Vaknin, D., Bashan, A., Braunstein, L.A., Buldyrev, S.V., Havlin, S.: Cascading failures in anisotropic interdependent networks of spatial modular structures. New J. Phys. **23**(11), 113001 (2021)
26. Vaknin, D., Gross, B., Buldyrev, S.V., Havlin, S.: Spreading of localized attacks on spatial multiplex networks with a community structure. Phys. Rev. Res. **2**(4), 043005 (2020)
27. Vipin, K., Anbazhagan, P., Sitharam, T.: Estimation of peak ground acceleration and spectral acceleration for south India with local site effects: probabilistic approach. Nat. Hazard. **9**(3), 865–878 (2009)
28. Zhao, Z., Zhang, P., Yang, H.: Cascading failures in interconnected networks with dynamical redistribution of loads. Physica A **433**, 204–210 (2015)
29. Zhou, D., Stanley, H.E., D'Agostino, G., Scala, A.: Assortativity decreases the robustness of interdependent networks. Phys. Rev. E **86**(6), 066103 (2012)

A Historical Perspective on International Treaties via Hypernetwork Science

Elie Alhajjar[✉][iD] and Ross Friar

Army Cyber Institute, West Point, NY 10996, USA
elie.alhajjar@westpoint.edu

Abstract. An alliance is a formal contingent commitment by two or more states to some future action. Alliances have been widely discussed in the international relations community because hundreds or perhaps thousands of interactions may take place between states in any given year, but few interactions create the impact intended by alliance formation. In this paper, we investigate the historical dynamics of international alliances from a hypernetwork science perspective. Exploring the Formal Alliances dataset from the Correlates of War Project, we focus on three time periods: pre-World War I, pre-World War II, and current day. By using centrality measures such as the notions of s-closeness, s-betweenness, s-eccentricity, and s-local clustering coefficient, we provide a rating benchmark to classify the impact of an alliance.

Keywords: Hypergraphs · Hypernetwork science · International treaties · Centrality measures

1 Introduction

Alliance theory was originally developed as an extension of balance of power theory; alliances were formed to make sure that the capabilities of major state coalitions remained relatively equal. Equality of power was believed to promote peace: alliances that "correctly" balance the system are supposed to lead to peace, while incorrect balancing makes war more likely [12].

Alliance commitments are also said to reduce the level of uncertainty in the system and minimize the likelihood of war that may result owing to misperception and miscalculation. These commitments can also reduce the chances of catastrophic shifts in the systemic balance of power. Some balance of power theorists claim that alliances are also necessary to avoid the most dangerous wars. A belligerent world power, seeking domination of the system, would likely restrain itself when confronted with an alliance system poised against it. Alliances, then, are an indispensable means of maintaining equilibrium in the system [4].

Balance of power theory can also support the existence of large, system-wide wars against potential dominance caused by alliance formation. These include the wars against Philip of Spain in the late sixteenth century, against Louis XIV

P. Ribeiro et al. (Eds.): NetSci-X 2022, LNCS 13197, pp. 15–25, 2022.
https://doi.org/10.1007/978-3-030-97240-0_2

in the late seventeenth century, against revolutionary and Napoleonic France a century later, and against Germany twice in the past century [7].

Based mostly on logical reasoning, historical anecdote, and often post hoc balance of power explanations, the traditional literature has not produced a convincing, consistent, theoretical explanation of the relationship between alliances and war. Not until the investigatory process turned empirical did researchers begin a process of accumulation that has provided many of the answers to the alliance-war puzzle. In this work, we aim at shedding some light on this interplay while relying on the newly emerging field of hypernetwork science.

In contrast with the traditional network science field based on the mathematical concept of graphs, higher-order network analysis uses the ideas of hypergraphs, simplicial complexes, multilinear and tensor algebra to study complex systems. We restrict our attention to hypergraphs, defined simply as a generalization of graph structures, where edges represent relationships among two or more entities. They are perhaps the most general representation of higher-order relationships, and were first discussed in the 1960's and 1970's (see [2] as an example).

The current paper is organized as follows. After this brief introduction, we give an overview of the field of hypernetwork science in Sect. 2. Section 3 describes the methodology used to calculate the centrality measures based on the hypergraphs created from international alliances. We explain the intuition as well as the technical details of our chosen methods. In Sect. 4, we record the results and discuss our findings to highlight the level of impact a treaty ought to have. We conclude our work in Sect. 5 and pose some open questions and future research directions.

2 Prerequisites

In this section, we give a brief introduction to the field of hypernetwork science as discussed in [6]. For more technical details, the reader is encouraged to consult [1] and the references therein.

The underlying objects of study in network science are graphs. For a finite set of elements V, denote by $V \times V$ the set of all ordered pairs $\{v_i, v_j\}$ of elements of V, where $\times$ denotes the Cartesian product. A relation on the set V is any subset $E \subseteq V \times V$. A *simple undirected graph*, or a graph, is a pair $G = (V, E)$, where V is a finite set of *nodes* (or *vertices*) and E is a relation on V such that $\{v_i, v_j\} \in E$ implies $\{v_j, v_i\} \in E$ and $v_i \neq v_j$, that is, G has no *loops*. The elements of E are called *edges* or *links*.

As abstract mathematical objects, graphs benefit from their simplicity but are limited to representing pairwise relationships between entities. Depicting group interactions is not possible in graphs natively, hence the concept of hypergraphs. A *hypergraph* is a pair $H = (V, E)$, where V is a finite set of vertices as above but E is now a set of subsets of V. More precisely, a *hyperedge* $e \in E$ is an arbitrary subset of V consisting of k vertices, thereby representing a k-way relationship for any integer $k > 0$. When $k = 2$ for all hyperedges, we recover the definition of graphs; hence hypergraphs are a generalization of graphs in this sense.

An example of a hypergraph is shown in Fig. 1. Multi-way relationships can be seen as follow: Ross, Mom, Dad, and grandparents are family members; Andrew, Ross, and Hailey are high school friends; Philip, Becky, Ross, and Hailey are college friends; while Ross and Hailey are a couple.

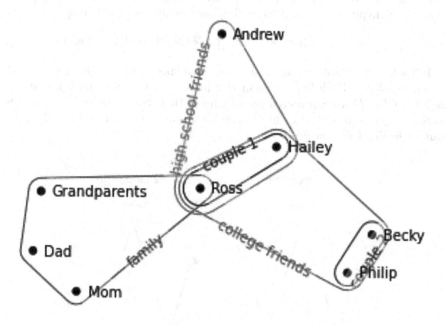

Fig. 1. An example of a hypergraph.

While *adjacency matrices* are generally used to represent graphs, the most common way to represent hypergraphs is incidence matrices. For a hypergraph $H = (V, E)$, where $V = \{v_1, \ldots, v_n\}$ is the set of vertices and $E = \{e_1, \ldots, e_m\}$ is the set of hyperedges, the *incidence matrix* S of H is a rectangular Boolean matrix defined by $S(i, j) = 1$ if $v_i \in e_j$ and 0 otherwise. Figure 2 shows the incidence matrix of the previous hypergraph.

	Andrew	Becky	Dad	Grandparents	Hailey	Mom	Philip	Ross
College friends	0	1	0	0	1	0	1	1
Couple 1	0	0	0	0	1	0	0	1
Couple 2	0	1	0	0	0	0	1	0
Family	0	0	1	1	0	1	0	1
High school friends	1	0	0	0	1	0	0	1

Fig. 2. Incidence matrix of the hypergraph.

In a graph $G = (V, E)$, a *walk* from a node v_i to a node v_j is a collection of ordered vertices $\{v_i, v_{i+1}, \dots, v_{j-1}, v_j\} \subseteq V$ and a collection of ordered edges $\{(v_i, v_{i+1}), (v_{i+1}, v_{i+2}), \dots, (v_{j-1}, v_j)\} \subseteq E$. The *length* of a walk is the number of edges traversed along the walk. A *shortest walk*, or a *geodesic walk*, from a node v_i to a node v_j, is a walk of shortest length. In the context of hypergraphs, this definition of a walk does not naturally extend since two hyperedges can intersect at any number of vertices, and two vertices can belong to any number of shared hyperedges. As such, for a positive integer s, an *s-walk* of length k between two hyperedges a and b is defined as a sequence of hyperedges

$$a = e_{i_0}, e_{i_1}, \dots, e_{i_k} = b, \text{ where } |e_{i_{j-1}} \cap e_{i_j}| \geq s \text{ for all } j = 1, \dots, k \text{ and } i_{j-1} \neq i_j.$$

To each hypergraph H, one can associate a special graph, the *s-line graph* $L_s(H)$, as follows. Each hyperedge in H represents a vertex in $L_s(H)$, and two vertices in $L_s(H)$ are connected by an edge if their corresponding hyperedges intersect in at least s vertices in H. The linegraphs for $s = 1$ and $s = 2$ of the example in Fig. 1 are shown in Fig. 3.

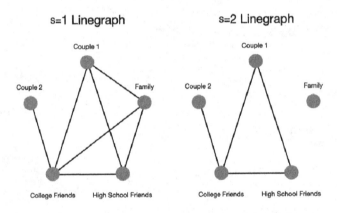

Fig. 3. Example of s-linegraphs for $s = 1, 2$.

For two hyperedges a and b of size greater than or equal to s, the *s-distance* $d_s(a, b)$ is the length of the shortest s-walk between a and b if such an s-walk exists, and ∞ otherwise. By letting E_s denote the set of hyperedges $e \in E$ such that $|e| \geq s$, one can define the following:

1. The *s-eccentricity* of a hyperedge e is $\max_{f \in E_s} d_s(e, f)$.
2. The *s-diameter* is the maximum s-eccentricity over all edges $e \in E_s$, while the *s-radius* is the minimum.
3. The *average s-distance* of H is $\binom{|E_s|}{2}^{-1} \sum_{e, f \in E_s} d_s(e, f)$.
4. The *s-closeness centrality* of a hyperedge e is $\dfrac{|E_s| - 1}{\sum_{f \in E_s} d_s(e, f)}$.

5. The *s-betweenness* centrality of a hyperedge $e \in E_s$ is equal to the betweenness centrality of the corresponding vertex in the *s*-linegraph. In a graph, the betweenness centrality of a vertex v is the ratio of the number of shortest paths between any pair of vertices in the graph that pass through v divided by the total number of shortest paths in the graph.
6. The *s-local clustering coefficient* of a hyperedge e is the number of closed *s*-paths of length three containing e divided by the number of *s*-paths of length two centered at e.
7. The *s-global clustering coefficient* of a hypergraph is triple the total number of *s*-paths of length three (i.e., *s-triangles*) divided by the total number of *s*-paths of length two (i.e., *s-wedges*).

3   Methodology

In this section, we give a technical description of the features in the dataset used in our experiments. We then explain the details of the techniques employed for finding hypernetwork science metrics. This leads to the layout of our computational setting.

3.1   The Dataset

The first dataset on international alliances was released in 1966 [9] and then updated in the next couple of years [10]; it established detailed coding criteria upon which all Correlates of War formal international alliance datasets have since been assembled. Implicit among such criteria are the effective dates of an alliance and its nature (defense, neutrality/non-aggression, or entente) [11].

The most current dataset contains 415 treaties involving 180 countries and dating back to the year 1648. Each data point contains the country name, one of the alliances it is a part of, the start and end dates of the alliance, the start and end dates of that country's entry and exit to/from the alliance, as well as other information about the treaty including whether it was a Type I: Defense Pact, Type II-a: Neutrality, Type II-b: Non-aggression, or Type III: Entente. Defense pacts commit states to intervene militarily if another partner is attacked. Neutrality and non-aggression pacts specify that parties remain militarily neutral if any cosignatory is attacked. Finally, ententes pledge consultation or cooperation during armed attacks [3].

For the sake of illustration, we mention two type I treaties of different time periods: the Peace of Westphalia and the North Atlantic Treaty Organization (NATO). The former has often been considered the beginning of the international state system as it was the first peace to recognize both territorial sovereignty and autonomy. The latter is a prime example of extended deterrence alliances, in which one state dominates bilaterally or a few states dominate multilaterally while the smaller states gain security against rivals or possible predatory states.

3.2   Methods

The dataset is divided into three main timelines: pre-World War I, pre-World War II, and current day status based on the alliance start and end dates. With this in mind, we create three hypergraphs in which vertices represent countries and hyperedges represent alliances. Each treaty is given a unique identification number, and different types of treaties are distinguished by different colors: red for type I, green for type II a-b, and blue for type III. All hypergraph calculations and visualizations in this paper were created using HyperNetX (HNX) [8], a recently released Python library echoing NetworkX [5] for exploratory hypergraph data analytics.

For each of the three hypergraphs, we compute the average s-distance, the s-diameter, and the s-global clustering coefficient. Moreover, we rank hyperedges within each hypergraph based on their s-closeness centrality, s-betweenness centrality, and s-local clustering coefficient. Finally, we measure the total impact of a treaty by combining several factors such as the (normalized) GDP of the countries involved, the length and the type of the treaty, the centrality metrics, and the fact of it being cross-continental or not. We use a weighted sum of these factors with weights adjusted to emphasize the importance of the GDP compared to the rest of the factors. The results of our experiments for several values of s are reported in the next section.

4   Results and Discussion

In this section, we adopt the following abbreviations: CC - closeness centrality, BC - betweenness centrality, E - eccentricity, LCC - local clustering coefficient, and P - weigthed sum.

4.1   World War I Results

World War I began in 1914 when Austria-Hungary attacked Serbia after Archduke Franz Ferdinand and his wife Sophie were assassinated. The first hypergraph includes 19 countries and 14 treaties as follows: 7 of type I, 3 type II, and 4 of type III. Figure 4 shows the dynamics of the international alliances in the final years leading to the war.

Due to the small size and the sparsity of the WWI hypergraph, $s = 1$ is the only significant value in this case. The average 1-distance is 1.8, the 1-diameter is 4, and the 1-global clustering coefficient is 0.49. The treaty that had the highest impact is the one between France, the United Kingdom, and Spain in 1907. Figure 5 records the five most impactful treaties in the early twentieth century, where P denotes the impact of a treaty as an aggregate sum of the factors previously mentioned.

Fig. 4. The hypergraph for WWI.

Treaty	Type	Countries	1-CC	1-BC	1-E	1-LCC	P
84	Type IIa: Non-Aggression Pact	Guatemala, Honduras, El Salvador, Nicaragua, Costa Rica	0	0.0	0	0.0	0.129
88	Type IIa: Non-Aggression Pact	Ecuador, Bolivia	0	0.0	0	0.0	0.069
1	Type I: Defense Pact	United Kingdom, Portugal	0.455	0.0	4	1.0	0.203
77	Type I: Defense Pact	United Kingdom, Japan	0.5	0.028	4	0.5	0.205
83	Type III: Entente	United Kingdom, France, Spain	0.625	0.061	3	0.6	0.224

Fig. 5. Top 5 treaties before WWI.

4.2   World War II Results

The second World War began when Germany invaded Poland in 1939. The induced hypergraph includes 50 countries and 46 international treaties: 16 of type I, 26 of type II, and 4 of type III. Figure 6 gives a rough idea of the complex set of interactions between countries in the 1930's.

The 1-diameter of the second hypergraph is 5, the average 1-distance is 1.87, and the 1-global clustering coefficient is 0.69. The most impactful treaty is the one that England signed with a handful of countries to deal with the large number of attacks on merchant vessels in the Mediterranean sea. Figure 7 indicates the top 5 treaties for the values $s = 1, 2$.

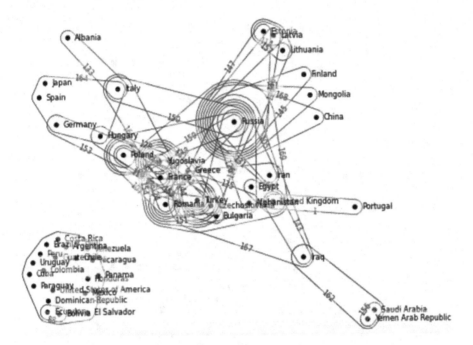

Fig. 6. The hypergraph for WWII.

Treaty	Type	Countries	1-CC	1-BC	1-E	1-LCC	2-CC	2-BC	2-E	2-LCC	P
88	IIa	Ecuador, Bolivia	1.0	0.0	1	0.0	1.0	0.0	1	0.0	0.05
1	I	United Kingdom, Portugal	0.483	0.0	3	1.0	0	0.0	0	0.0	0.061
143	I	United Kingdom, Iraq	0.5	0.016	3	0.5	0	0.0	0	0.0	0.039
163	I	United Kingdom, Egypt	0.483	0.0	3	1.0	0.52	0.0	2	0.0	0.044
169	I	United Kingdom, France, Yugoslavia...	0.843	0.285	3	0.324	1.0	0.069	1	0.064	0.111

Fig. 7. Top 5 treaties before WWII.

4.3   Current Day Results

As of 2021, there are 99 active treaties involving 145 countries: 37 are defense pacts, 54 are non-aggression pacts, and 8 are ententes. For the third hypergraph, the 1-diameter is 7, the average 1-distance is 2.78, and the 1-global clustering coefficient is 0.671. On the other hand, the 2-diameter is 3, the average 2-distance is 1.76, and the 2-global clustering coefficient is 0.26. It is not surprising that the most impactful treaty of our modern time is the North Atlantic Treaty Organization (NATO). Figures 8 and 9 summarize the current day status of the international alliances' picture.

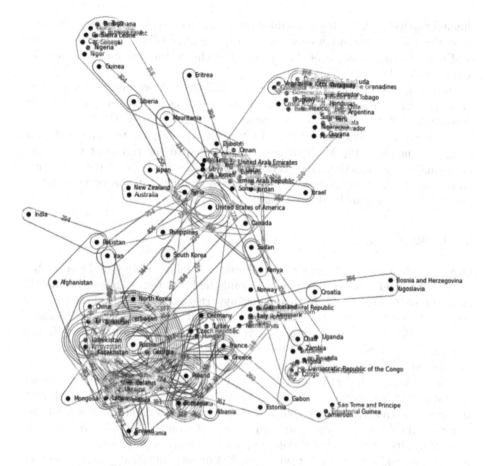

Fig. 8. The hypergraph for the current day status.

Treaty	Type	Countries	1-CC	1-BC	1-E	1-LCC	2-CC	2-BC	2-E	2-LCC	P
210	I	USA, Canada, Bahamas, Cuba, Haiti...	0.435	0.14	6	0.301	0.737	0.014	2	0.083	0.111
227	I	USA, Canada, United Kingdom, Netherlands, Belgium...	0.533	0.276	5	0.194	0.667	0.011	2	0.095	0.083
199	III	Mauritania, Somalia, Djibouti, Morocco, Algeria...	0.303	0.069	5	0.267	1.0	0.0	1	0.5	0.073
230	I	Somalia, Morocco, Algeria, Tunisia, Libya...	0.281	0.034	5	0.306	1.0	0.0	1	0.5	0.072
318	I	Cape Verde, Guinea-Bissau, Gambia, Mali, Senegal...	0.323	0.051	4	0.333	1.0	0.0	1	0.0	0.048

Fig. 9. Top 5 currently active treaties.

4.4 Discussion

Over a period of 100+ years, the average 1-distance increased, a fact that indicates the spread of treaties to involve almost all countries in the world. Regional pacts became more common after World War II and continue to evolve in some contentious areas more than others. This is also reflected in the increase of the 1-

diameter as well, which almost doubled over the same period of time. On another note, the 1-global clustering coefficient stabilized after WWII mainly due to the continuity of the main pacts signed after the end of the war and that remain active to this day.

Zooming in on some of the most influential treaties, we find that the three mentioned in the previous sections played a crucial role in dictating global power balance and affecting major world events. The treaty between the UK, France, and Spain was a game changer in WWI, while the one between the UK and several countries in the Mediterranean region shaped the course of WWII. At the moment, the NATO alliance is definitely considered the most dominant one on the international stage and we witness many smaller states working on many political levels to join the defense pact.

5   Conclusion

One of the first empirical tests of the alliance-war relationship found that states ranking high on alliance activity also rank high on war engagement, initiation, and battle deaths [9]. In this paper, hypernetwork science techniques were employed to validate this correlation. In particular, we focused on the alliances leading to WWI, the ones leading to WWII, and the ones currently active. Using centrality measures, we identified the most impactful treaties and provided a "big picture" view of the world dynamics in each of the three time phases.

Measuring the impact of an alliance is a non-trivial task and pinpointing all the factors that contribute to such a task is difficult. Besides the length and the size of a treaty, its geographical bound, and the economical power of the countries involved in it, one can study the evolution of a treaty over time to understand its growing or shrinking impact regionally or internationally. There is no guaranteed way to predict future conflict or war, but alliances are definitely a major player in shaping balance around the world. In an upcoming paper, we intend to use the toolkit developed herein to investigate the trade pacts all over the globe with the hope of devising methods to measure the economical impact of such pacts and their influence on international relations.

Acknowledgment. The first author would like to thank the Network Science Center at the United States Military Academy for their support during the project. The second author would like to thank the Intelligent Cyber-Systems and Analytics Research Lab (ICSARL) at the Army Cyber Institute (ACI) in West Point, NY for their hospitality. Most of the work was done during his summer research stay at the institute.

References

1. Aksoy, S.G., Joslyn, C., Ortiz Marrero, C., Praggastis, B., Purvine, E.: Hypernetwork science via high-order hypergraph walks. EPJ Data Sci. **9**(1), 1–34 (2020). https://doi.org/10.1140/epjds/s13688-020-00231-0
2. Berge, C.: Graphs and Hypergraphs. North-Holland Publishing Company, Amsterdam (1973)

3. Gibler, D.M.: International Military Alliances, 1648–2008. CQ Press, Washington, D.C. (2009)
4. Gulick, E.V.: Europe's Classical Balance of Power. Norton, New York (1982)
5. Hagberg, A., Swart, P., Chult, D.S.: Exploring network structure, dynamics, and function using networkx. Technical report, Los Alamos National Lab (LANL), Los Alamos, NM, USA (2008)
6. Joslyn, C.A., et al.: Hypernetwork science: from multidimensional networks to computational topology. In: Kaufman, L., et al. (eds.) ICCS 2020. SPC, pp. 377–392. Springer, Cham (2021). https://doi.org/10.1007/978-3-030-67318-5_25
7. Levy, J.: The causes of war: a review of theories and evidence. In: Tetlock, P.E., et al. (eds.) Behavior, Society, and Nuclear War, vol. 1, pp. 209–333. Oxford University Press, New York (1989)
8. Praggastis, B., Arendt, D., Joslyn C., Purvine, E., Aksoy S., Monson K.: Hyper-NetX (2019). https://github.com/pnnl/HyperNetX
9. Singer, J.D., Melvin, S.: Formal alliances, 1815–1939: a quantitative description. J. Peace Res. **3**(1), 1–32 (1966)
10. Singer, J.D., Melvin, S.: Alliance aggregation and the onset of war, 1815–1945. In: Singer, J.D. (ed.) Quant. Int. Polit. Insight Evid., pp. 247–286. Free Press, New York (1968)
11. Singer, J.D., Melvin, S.: The Wages of War, 1816–1965: A Statistical Handbook. Wiley, New York (1972)
12. Walt, S.: The Origins of Alliance. Cornell University Press, Ithaca (1987)

On the Number of Edges of the Fréchet Mean and Median Graphs

Daniel Ferguson and François G. Meyer[✉][iD]

Applied Mathematics, University of Colorado at Boulder, Boulder, CO 80309, USA
fmeyer@colorado.edu
https://francoismeyer.github.io/

Abstract. The availability of large datasets composed of graphs creates an unprecedented need to invent novel tools in statistical learning for graph-valued random variables. To characterize the average of a sample of graphs, one can compute the sample Frechet mean and median graphs. In this paper, we address the following foundational question: does a mean or median graph inherit the structural properties of the graphs in the sample? An important graph property is the edge density; we establish that edge density is an hereditary property, which can be transmitted from a graph sample to its sample Frechet mean or median graphs, irrespective of the method used to estimate the mean or the median. Because of the prominence of the Frechet mean in graph-valued machine learning, this novel theoretical result has some significant practical consequences.

Keywords: Frechet mean and median graphs · statistical network analysis

1 Introduction

We consider the set $\mathcal{G}$ formed by all undirected unweighted simple labeled graphs with vertex set $\{1, \dots, n\}$. We equip $\mathcal{G}$ with a metric d to measure the distance between two graphs.

We characterize the "average" of a sample of graphs $\{G^{(1)}, \dots, G^{(N)}\}$, which are defined on the same vertex set $\{1, \dots, n\}$, with the sample Fréchet mean and median graphs, [6].

Definition 1. *The sample Fréchet mean graphs are solutions to*

$$\widehat{\boldsymbol{\mu}}_N[G] = \operatorname*{argmin}_{G \in \mathcal{G}} \frac{1}{N} \sum_{k=1}^{N} d^2(G, G^{(k)}), \tag{1}$$

and the sample Fréchet median graphs are solutions to

$$\widehat{\boldsymbol{m}}_N[G] = \operatorname*{argmin}_{G \in \mathcal{G}} \frac{1}{N} \sum_{k=1}^{N} d(G, G^{(k)}). \tag{2}$$

This work was supported by the National Science Foundation, CCF/CIF 1815971.

P. Ribeiro et al. (Eds.): NetSci-X 2022, LNCS 13197, pp. 26–40, 2022.
https://doi.org/10.1007/978-3-030-97240-0_3

Solutions to the minimization problems (1) and (2) always exist, but the minimizers need not be unique. All our results are stated in terms of any of the elements in the set of minimizers of (1) and (2).

Because the focus of this work is not the computation of the Fréchet mean or median graphs, but rather a theoretical analysis of the properties that these graphs inherit from the graph sample, we assume that the graphs in the sample are defined on the same vertex set.

The vital role played by the Fréchet mean as a location parameter [9,10,13], is exemplified in the works of [1,14], who have created novel families of random graphs by generating random perturbations around a given Fréchet mean graph.

1.1 Our Main Contributions

We consider a set of N unweighted simple labeled graphs, $\{G^{(1)}, \ldots, G^{(N)}\}$, with vertex set $\{1, \ldots, n\}$. In this paper, we address the following foundational question: does a mean or median graph inherit the structural properties of the graphs in the sample? Specifically, we establish that edge density is an hereditary property, which can be transmitted from a graph sample to its sample Fréchet mean or median.

Because sparse graphs provide prototypical models for real networks, our theoretical analysis is significant since it provides a guarantee that this structural property is preserved when computing a sample mean or median. In a similar vein, the authors in [8] construct a sparse median graph, which provides a more interpretable summary, from a set of graphs that are not necessarily sparse.

Our work answers the question raised by the author in [7]: "does the average of two sparse networks/matrices need to be sparse?" Specifically, we prove the following result: the number of edges of the Fréchet mean or median graphs of a set of graphs is bounded by the sample mean number of edges of the graphs in the sample. We prove this result for the graph Hamming distance, and the spectral adjacency pseudometric, using different arguments.

2 Preliminary and Notations

We denote by $\mathcal{S}$ the set of $n \times n$ adjacency matrices of graphs in $\mathcal{G}$,

$$\mathcal{S} = \left\{ \boldsymbol{A} \in \{0,1\}^{n \times n}; \text{where } a_{ij} = a_{ji}, \text{and } a_{i,i} = 0;\ 1 \leq i < j \leq n \right\}. \quad (3)$$

For a graph $G \in \mathcal{G}$, we denote by $\boldsymbol{A}$ its adjacency matrix, and by $e(\boldsymbol{A})$ the number of edges – or *volume* – of G,

$$e(\boldsymbol{A}) = \sum_{1 \leq i < j \leq n} a_{ij}. \quad (4)$$

We denote by $\boldsymbol{\lambda}(\boldsymbol{A}) = [\lambda_1(\boldsymbol{A}) \cdots \lambda_n(\boldsymbol{A})]$, the vector of eigenvalues of $\boldsymbol{A}$, with the convention that $\lambda_1(\boldsymbol{A}) \geq \ldots \geq \lambda_n(\boldsymbol{A})$.

2.1   Distances Between Graphs

In this work, we consider two metrics: the Hamming distance and the spectral adjacency pseudometric. We briefly recall the definitions of these.

Definition 2. *Let $G, G' \in \mathcal{G}$ be two unweighted graphs with known vertex correspondence and with adjacency matrix $\boldsymbol{A}$ and $\boldsymbol{A}'$ respectively. We define the Hamming distance between G and G' as*

$$d_H(\boldsymbol{A}, \boldsymbol{A}') \overset{def}{=} \sum_{1 \leq i < j \leq n} |a_{ij} - a'_{ij}| = e(\boldsymbol{A}) + e(\boldsymbol{B}) - 2 \sum_{1 \leq i < j \leq n} a_{ij} b_{ij}. \tag{5}$$

The Hamming distance is very sensitive to fine scale fluctuations of the graph connectivity. In contrast, a metric based on the eigenvalues of the adjacency matrix can quantify configurational changes that occur on a graph at many more scales [5, 17].

Definition 3. *Let $G, G' \in \mathcal{G}$ with adjacency matrix $\boldsymbol{A}$ and $\boldsymbol{A}'$ respectively. We define the adjacency spectral pseudometric as the ℓ_2 norm between the vectors of eigenvalues $\boldsymbol{\lambda}(\boldsymbol{A})$ and $\boldsymbol{\lambda}(\boldsymbol{A}')$ of $\boldsymbol{A}$ and $\boldsymbol{A}'$ respectively,*

$$d_\lambda(\boldsymbol{A}, \boldsymbol{A}') = ||\boldsymbol{\lambda}(\boldsymbol{A}) - \boldsymbol{\lambda}(\boldsymbol{A}')||_2. \tag{6}$$

The pseudometric d_λ satisfies the symmetry and triangle inequality axioms, but not the identity axiom. Instead, d_λ satisfies the reflexivity axiom, $\forall G \in \mathcal{G}$, $d_\lambda(G, G) = 0$. We note that the adjacency spectral pseudometric does not require node correspondence.

3   Main Results

In the following, we consider a set of N unweighted simple labeled graphs, $\{G^{(1)}, \ldots, G^{(N)}\}$, with vertex set $\{1, \ldots, n\}$. We denote by $\boldsymbol{A}^{(k)}$ the adjacency matrix of graph $G^{(k)}$. We equip the set $\mathcal{G}$ of all unweighted simple graphs on n nodes with a pseudometric, or a metric, d. The Fréchet mean and median graphs encode two notions of centrality (1) and (2) that minimise the following dispersion function, also called the Fréchet function.

Definition 4. *We denote by $\widehat{F}_q(\boldsymbol{A})$ the sample Fréchet function associated with a sample Fréchet median $(q = 1)$ or mean $(q = 2)$,*

$$\widehat{F}_q(\boldsymbol{A}) = \frac{1}{N} \sum_{k=1}^{N} d^q(\boldsymbol{A}, \boldsymbol{A}^{(k)}). \tag{7}$$

To quantify the connectivity of the graph sample, $\{G^{(1)}, \ldots, G^{(N)}\}$, we define the sample mean and variance of the number of edges.

Definition 5. *The sample mean and variance of the number of edges are defined by*

$$\bar{e}_N = \frac{1}{N} \sum_{k=1}^{N} e(A^{(k)}), \quad and \quad \sigma_N^2(e) = \frac{1}{N} \sum_{k=1}^{N} \left[e(A^{(k)})\right]^2 - [\bar{e}_N]^2. \quad (8)$$

We now turn our attention to the main problem. We consider the following question: if the graphs $G^{(1)}, \ldots, G^{(N)}$ all have a similar edge density, can one determine the edge density of the sample Fréchet mean or median graphs? and does that number of edges depend on the choice of metric d in (1) and (2)? We answer both questions in the following theorem.

Theorem 1. *Let $\{G^{(1)}, \ldots, G^{(N)}\}$ be a sample of unweighted simple labeled graphs with vertex set $\{1, \ldots, n\}$. Let $\widehat{\mu}_N[A]$ be the adjacency matrix of a sample Fréchet mean graph, and let $\widehat{m}_N[A]$ be the adjacency matrix of a sample Fréchet median graph. Let $e_{\widehat{\mu}}$ and $e_{\widehat{m}}$ be the number of edges of $\widehat{\mu}_N[A]$ and $\widehat{m}_N[A]$ respectively.*

If the Fréchet mean and median graphs are computed using the Hamming distance, then

$$e_{\widehat{\mu}} < 2\bar{e}_N + \frac{\sigma_N(e)}{\sqrt{2}}, \quad and \quad e_{\widehat{m}} < 2\,\bar{e}_N, \quad (9)$$

and if the Fréchet mean and median graphs are computed using the adjacency spectral pseudometric, then

$$e_{\widehat{\mu}} < 9\,\bar{e}_N, \quad and \quad e_{\widehat{m}} < 9\bar{e}_N. \quad (10)$$

Proof. The proof is a direct consequence of Lemmata 6 and 12.

Remark 1. When the graph $G^{(k)}$ are sampled from the inhomogeneous Erdős-Rényi random graph probability space $\mathcal{G}(n, P)$ [3], and if the distance on $\mathcal{G}$ is the Hamming distance, then $\widehat{\mu}_N[A] = \widehat{m}_N[A]$ with high probability [15]. In this case, a tight bound on $e_{\widehat{\mu}}$ or $e_{\widehat{m}}$ in (9) is $2\bar{e}_N$, which – unlike (9) – does not involve $\sigma_N(e)$.

The fact that we overestimate the bound on $e_{\widehat{\mu}}$ by the addition of the term $\sigma_N(e)/\sqrt{2}$ comes from our technique of proof, which relies on an estimate of the Fréchet function. As explained in Remark 4, our estimate of the Fréchet function is almost tight; it does include the term $\sigma_N(e)$, as it should.

Finally, the following corollary answers the question raised by the author in [7]: "does the average of two sparse networks/matrices need to be sparse?"

Corollary 1. *Let $\{G^{(1)}, \ldots, G^{(N)}\}$ be a sample of unweighted simple labeled graphs with vertex set $\{1, \ldots, n\}$. We assume that the number of edges of each $G^{(k)}$ satisfies*

$$e(A^{(k)}) = o\,(n^2), \quad but\ e(A^{(k)}) = \omega(n). \quad (11)$$

Then the sample Fréchet mean and median graphs – computed according to either the Hamming distance or the adjacency spectral pseudometric – are sparse, as defined by (11).

Proof of Corollary 1. *The corollary is a direct consequence of Theorem 1.*

4   Proofs of the Main Result

We give in the following the proof of Theorem 1. The key observation is that it is relatively easy to derive tight bounds on the number of edges of the sample Fréchet median graph. Inspired by the results in [15] that show that for large classes of random graphs the sample Fréchet median and mean graphs are identical, we prove that the bounds derived for the Fréchet median graphs also hold for the Fréchet mean graphs.

Our analysis begins in Subsect. 4.1 with the sample median graphs computed using the Hamming distance, we then move to the sample mean graphs in Subsect. 4.2. In Subsects. 4.4 and 4.5, we extend these results to the sample mean and median graphs computed with the adjacency spectral pseudometric.

When possible, we use the probability space $\mathcal{G}(n, \boldsymbol{P})$ of inhomogeneous Erdős-Rényi random graphs [3], equipped with the Hamming distance to test the tightness of our results [15].

4.1   The Median Graphs Computed Using the Hamming Distance

The Hamming distance, by nature, promotes sparsity [5,17], and we therefore expect that the volumes of the sample Fréchet mean and median graphs computed with this distance be similar to the sample mean number of edges.

When the distance is the Hamming distance, the sample Fréchet median graphs can in fact be characterized analytically.

Lemma 1. *The adjacency matrix $\widehat{\boldsymbol{m}}_N[\boldsymbol{A}]$ of a sample median graph $\widehat{\boldsymbol{m}}_N[G]$ is given by the majority rule,*

$$\left[\widehat{\boldsymbol{m}}_N[\boldsymbol{A}]\right]_{ij} = \begin{cases} 0 & \text{if } \sum_{k=1}^{N} a_{ij}^{(k)} < N/2, \\ 1 & \text{otherwise.} \end{cases} \quad \forall i, j \in \{1, \dots, n\}. \tag{12}$$

Proof of Lemma 1. *The result is classic and we omit the proof, which can be found for instance in [4].*

In the following lemma, we derive an upper bound on the number of edges of a Fréchet median graph, $e_{\widehat{m}}$.

Lemma 2. *Let $\bar{e}_N$ be the sample mean number of edges, given by (8). Then the number of edges of a Fréchet median graph $\widehat{\boldsymbol{m}}_N[G]$ is bounded by*

$$e_{\widehat{m}} \leq 2\bar{e}_N. \tag{13}$$

Remark 2. The bound (13) is tight for large N. Indeed, consider a sample of $2N$ graphs, where

$$G^{(k)} = \begin{cases} \text{the complete graph } K_n & \text{if } 1 \leq k \leq N+1, \\ \text{the empty graph} & \text{if } N+2 \leq k \leq 2N. \end{cases} \tag{14}$$

A Fréchet median graph $\widehat{m}_N[A]$, given by the majority rule (12) is K_n, and thus $e_{\widehat{m}} = n(n-1)/2$. On the other hand, the sample mean number of edges is $\bar{e}_N = e_{\widehat{m}}/2 + e_{\widehat{m}}/(2N)$. As the sample size N goes to infinity, we have

$$\lim_{N \longrightarrow \infty} e_{\widehat{m}} = 2\bar{e}_N, \tag{15}$$

which proves that the bound (13) is asymptotically tight.

Proof of Lemma 2. *Let* $\mathcal{E}_{\widehat{m}} = \{(i,j), \ i < j, \ [\widehat{m}_N[A]]_{ij} = 1\}$ *be the set of edges of* $\widehat{m}_N[G]$. *We have* $|\mathcal{E}_{\widehat{m}}| = e_{\widehat{m}}$. *Now,*

$$\sum_{k=1}^{N} e\left(A^{(k)}\right) = \sum_{1 \le i < j \le n} \sum_{k=1}^{N} a_{ij}^{(k)} = \sum_{i,j \in \mathcal{E}_{\widehat{m}}} \sum_{k=1}^{N} a_{ij}^{(k)} + \sum_{i,j \in \mathcal{E}_{\widehat{m}}^c} \sum_{k=1}^{N} a_{ij}^{(k)}. \tag{16}$$

Neglecting the edges (i,j) *not in* $\mathcal{E}_{\widehat{m}}$, *we have*

$$\sum_{k=1}^{N} e\left(A^{(k)}\right) \ge \sum_{i,j \in \mathcal{E}_{\widehat{m}}} \sum_{k=1}^{N} a_{ij}^{(k)} > \sum_{i,j \in \mathcal{E}_{\widehat{m}}} \frac{N}{2} = \frac{N}{2} e_{\widehat{m}},$$

whence we conclude

$$e_{\widehat{m}} \le \frac{2}{N} \sum_{k=1}^{N} e\left(A^{(k)}\right) = 2\bar{e}_N. \tag{17}$$

$\square$

4.2   The Mean Graphs Computed Using the Hamming Distance

First, we recall the following lower bound on the Hamming distance.

Lemma 3. *Let* A *and* B *be the adjacency matrices of two unweighted graphs with number of edges* $e(A)$ *and* $e(B)$ *respectively. Then*

$$|e(A) - e(B)| \le d_H(A, B). \tag{18}$$

Proof of Lemma 3. *The proof is elementary and is skipped.*

Next, we derive an upper bound on the deviation of the volume of a Fréchet mean, $e_{\widehat{\mu}}$, away from the sample average volume, $\bar{e}_N$, given by (8).

Lemma 4. *Let* $\widehat{\mu}_N[A]$ *be the adjacency matrix of a sample Fréchet mean computed using the Hamming distance, with* $e_{\widehat{\mu}}$ *edges. Let* $\bar{e}_N$ *be the sample mean number of edges. Then*

$$\left[e_{\widehat{\mu}} - \bar{e}_N \right]^2 < \frac{1}{N} \sum_{k=1}^{N} d_H^2(\widehat{\mu}_N[A], A^{(k)}) = \widehat{F}_2(\widehat{\mu}_N[A]). \tag{19}$$

Remark 3. This bound is not tight. We consider again the probability space of inhomogeneous Erdős-Rényi random graphs equipped with the Hamming distance. In that case, one can show that the population Fréchet mean and median coincide [15], and the adjacency matrix of the population Fréchet mean graph, $\mu[A]$, is given by the majority rule,

$$\left[\mu[A]\right]_{ij} = \begin{cases} 1 & \text{if } p_{ij} > 1/2, \\ 0 & \text{otherwise.} \end{cases} \tag{20}$$

Also, the population Fréchet function, F_2, evaluated at $\mu[A]$ is given by [15]

$$F_2(\mu[A]) = \left[\sum_{1\le i<j\le n} p_{ij} - \sum_{(i,j)\in\mathcal{E}(\mu[A])} (2p_{ij}-1)\right]^2 + \sum_{1\le i<j\le n} p_{ij}(1-p_{ij}), \tag{21}$$

where $\mathcal{E}(\mu[A])$ is the set of edges of the population Fréchet mean, $\mu[A]$. We claim that the lower bound on $\widehat{F}_2(\widehat{\mu}_N[A])$ in (19),

$$\left[\bar{e}_N - e_{\widehat{\mu}}\right]^2, \tag{22}$$

can be identified with the first term of $F_2(\mu[A])$ in (21),

$$\left[\sum_{1\le i<j\le n} p_{ij} - \sum_{(i,j)\in\mathcal{E}(\mu[A])} (2p_{ij}-1)\right]^2. \tag{23}$$

Indeed, the first sum inside (23) is the population mean number of edges, $\mathbb{E}[e]$, which matches the sample mean $\bar{e}_N$ in (22). Also, the second sum in (23) is bounded by $e(\mu[A])$, the number of edges of the population Fréchet mean,

$$0 < \sum_{(i,j)\in\mathcal{E}(\mu[A])} (2p_{ij}-1) < \sum_{(i,j)\in\mathcal{E}(\mu[A])} 1 = e(\mu[A]). \tag{24}$$

The number of edges $e(\mu[A])$ matches the sample estimate, $e_{\widehat{\mu}}$, in (22). In summary, the first term (23) of the population Fréchet function (21) matches the corresponding sample estimate (22).

However, the second term, $\sum_{1\le i<j\le n} p_{ij}(1-p_{ij})$ in (21), which accounts for the variance of the $n(n-1)/2$ independent Bernoulli edges, is not present in the lower bound on in $F_2[\mu[A]]$ given by (19), confirming that the lower bound in (19) is missing a variance term, and is therefore not tight.

Proof of Lemma 4. *Because of Lemma 3, we have*

$$\left|e(A^{(k)}) - e_{\widehat{\mu}}\right|^2 \le d_H^2(\widehat{\mu}_N[A], A^{(k)}). \tag{25}$$

Now, the function

$$x \longmapsto (e_{\widehat{\mu}} - x)^2 \tag{26}$$

is strictly convex so,

$$\left|\bar{e}_N - e_{\widehat{\mu}}\right|^2 = \left|\frac{1}{N}\sum_{k=1}^{N} e(A^{(k)}) - e_{\widehat{\mu}}\right|^2 < \frac{1}{N}\sum_{k=1}^{N}\left|e(A^{(k)}) - e_{\widehat{\mu}}\right|^2, \qquad (27)$$

and substituting (25) for each k in (27), we get the advertised result. □

Finally, we compute an upper bound on the Fréchet function evaluated at a sample Fréchet median graph, $\widehat{F}_2(\widehat{m}_N[A])$.

Lemma 5. *Let $\bar{e}_N$ and $\sigma_N^2(e)$ be the sample mean and variance of the number of edges (see (8)). Then the Fréchet function $\widehat{F}_2(\widehat{m}_N[A])$ evaluated at a Fréchet median graph is bounded by*

$$\widehat{F}_2(\widehat{m}_N[A]) \leq 2[\bar{e}_N]^2 + \sigma_N^2(e). \qquad (28)$$

Remark 4. As explained in Remark 3, when the graphs $G^{(k)}$ are sampled from $\mathcal{G}(n, P)$, then the population Fréchet mean and median graphs coincide, $\mu[G] = m[G]$. Also, the population Fréchet function $F_2(m[A])$ evaluated at a population Fréchet median graph is given by

$$F_2[m[A]] = \left[\sum_{1\leq i<j\leq n} p_{ij} - \sum_{(i,j)\in\mathcal{E}(m[A])} (2p_{ij} - 1)\right]^2 + \sum_{1\leq i<j\leq n} p_{ij}(1 - p_{ij}), \qquad (29)$$

where the term $\sum_{(i,j)\in\mathcal{E}(m[A])}(2p_{ij} - 1)$ is always positive (since the median graphs are constructed using the majority rule (12)). Therefore, we have

$$F_2[m[A]] \leq \left[\sum_{1\leq i<j\leq n} p_{ij}\right]^2 + \sum_{1\leq i<j\leq n} p_{ij}(1 - p_{ij}). \qquad (30)$$

The term $\sum_{1\leq i<j\leq n} p_{ij}$ is the expectation of the number of edges, whereas $\sum_{1\leq i<j\leq n} p_{ij}(1 - p_{ij})$ is the variance of the number of edges. In summary, we have the following bound on the population Fréchet function,

$$F_2(m[A]) \leq [\mathbb{E}[e]]^2 + \operatorname{var}[e], \qquad (31)$$

where e denotes the number of edges in graphs sampled from $\mathcal{G}(n, P)$. If we replace $\mathbb{E}[e]$ and $\operatorname{var}[e]$ by their respective sample estimates, $\bar{e}_N$ and $\sigma_N^2(e)$, then the bound (28) is only slightly worse (by a factor 2 in front of $\bar{e}_N$) than the population bound, (31). Interestingly, the variance of the number of edges is present in both expressions.

Proof of Lemma 5. *From (5), one can derive the following expression for the Hamming distance from a Fréchet median graph $\widehat{m}_N[G]$ to a graph $G^{(k)}$,*

$$d_H(\widehat{m}_N[A], A^{(k)}) = e_{\widehat{m}} + e(A^{(k)}) - 2\sum_{(i,j)\in\mathcal{E}_{\widehat{m}}} a_{ij}^{(k)}, \qquad (32)$$

where we recall that $\mathcal{E}_{\widehat{m}} = \left\{ (i,j),\ i < j,\ \left[\widehat{m}_N[A]\right]_{ij} = 1 \right\}$ *is the set of edges of* $\widehat{m}_N[G]$. *Taking the square of the Hamming distance given by (32), and summing over all the graphs, yields*

$$\widehat{F}_2\big(\widehat{m}_N[A]\big) = \frac{1}{N} \sum_{k=1}^{N} \left\{ \left[e_{\widehat{m}} + e\big(A^{(k)}\big) \right]^2 + 4 \left[\sum_{(i,j)\in\mathcal{E}_{\widehat{m}}} a_{ij}^{(k)} \right]^2 \right.$$
$$\left. - 4\big(e_{\widehat{m}} + e\big(A^{(k)}\big)\big) \left[\sum_{(i,j)\in\mathcal{E}_{\widehat{m}}} a_{ij}^{(k)} \right] \right\}.$$

Expanding all the terms, and using the definition of $\sigma_N^2(e)$ *and* $\bar{e}_N$ *in (8), we get*

$$\widehat{F}_2\big(\widehat{m}_N[A]\big) = \left[e_{\widehat{m}}\right]^2 + 2e_{\widehat{m}}\,\bar{e}_N + \sigma_N^2(e) + \left[\bar{e}_N\right]^2 + \frac{4}{N}\sum_{k=1}^{N} \left[\sum_{(i,j)\in\mathcal{E}_{\widehat{m}}} a_{ij}^{(k)} \right]^2$$
$$- \frac{4}{N}\sum_{k=1}^{N} e\big(A^{(k)}\big)\left[\sum_{(i,j)\in\mathcal{E}_{\widehat{m}}} a_{ij}^{(k)}\right] - 4e_{\widehat{m}}\left[\sum_{(i,j)\in\mathcal{E}_{\widehat{m}}} \frac{1}{N}\sum_{k=1}^{N} a_{ij}^{(k)}\right]$$
$$= \left[e_{\widehat{m}} + \bar{e}_N\right]^2 + \sigma_N^2(e) + 4\frac{1}{N}\sum_{k=1}^{N} \left[\sum_{(i,j)\in\mathcal{E}_{\widehat{m}}} a_{ij}^{(k)} \right]^2$$
$$- \frac{4}{N}\sum_{k=1}^{N} e\big(A^{(k)}\big)\left[\sum_{(i,j)\in\mathcal{E}_{\widehat{m}}} a_{ij}^{(k)}\right] - 4e_{\widehat{m}}\left[\sum_{(i,j)\in\mathcal{E}_{\widehat{m}}} \frac{1}{N}\sum_{k=1}^{N} a_{ij}^{(k)}\right]. \quad (33)$$

Now, because of the definition of the median graphs (12), we have the following upper bound

$$- 4e_{\widehat{m}}\left[\sum_{(i,j)\in\mathcal{E}_{\widehat{m}}} \frac{1}{N}\sum_{k=1}^{N} a_{ij}^{(k)}\right] \leq -2\left[e_{\widehat{m}}\right]^2. \quad (34)$$

Because $e\big(A^{(k)}\big) \geq \sum_{(i,j)\in\mathcal{E}_{\widehat{m}}} a_{ij}^{(k)}$, *we get the following upper bound,*

$$- 4\sum_{k=1}^{N} e\big(A^{(k)}\big) \sum_{(i,j)\in\mathcal{E}_{\widehat{m}}} a_{ij}^{(k)} \leq -4\sum_{k=1}^{N} \left[\sum_{(i,j)\in\mathcal{E}_{\widehat{m}}} a_{ij}^{(k)} \right]^2. \quad (35)$$

Finally, after substituting (34) and (35) into (33), we get the bound announced in the lemma,

$$\widehat{F}_2\big(\widehat{m}_N[A]\big) \leq \left[e_{\widehat{m}} + \bar{e}_N\right]^2 - 2\left[e_{\widehat{m}}\right]^2 + \sigma_N^2(e) = -\left[e_{\widehat{m}} - \bar{e}_N\right]^2 + 2\left[\bar{e}_N\right]^2 + \sigma_N^2(e)$$
$$\leq 2\left[\bar{e}_N\right]^2 + \sigma_N^2(e). \qquad \square$$

4.3   The Number of Edges of $\widehat{m}_N[G]$ and $\widehat{\mu}_N[G]$ when $d = d_H$

The following lemma provides the bounds given by Theorem 1 when d is the Hamming distance.

Lemma 6. *Let $\{G^{(1)}, \ldots, G^{(N)}\}$ be a sample of unweighted simple labeled graphs with vertex set $\{1, \ldots, n\}$. Let $\widehat{\boldsymbol{\mu}}_N[\boldsymbol{A}]$ be the adjacency matrix of a sample Fréchet mean graph, and $\widehat{\boldsymbol{m}}_N[\boldsymbol{A}]$ be the adjacency matrix of a sample Fréchet median graph, computed according to the Hamming distance. Then*

$$e\left(\widehat{\boldsymbol{\mu}}_N[\boldsymbol{A}]\right) < 2\bar{e}_N + \frac{\sigma_N(e)}{\sqrt{2}}, \quad \text{and} \quad e\left(\widehat{\boldsymbol{m}}_N[\boldsymbol{A}]\right) \leq 2\bar{e}_N. \tag{36}$$

Proof of Lemma 6. *The bound on $e\left(\widehat{\boldsymbol{m}}_N[\boldsymbol{A}]\right)$ is a straightforward consequence of Lemma 4. Indeed, (13) and (8) yield the bound in (36),*

$$e\left(\widehat{\boldsymbol{m}}_N[\boldsymbol{A}]\right) \leq \frac{2}{N} \sum_{k=1}^{N} e\left(\boldsymbol{A}^{(k)}\right) \leq 2\bar{e}_N.$$

We now move to $e\left(\widehat{\boldsymbol{\mu}}_N[\boldsymbol{A}]\right)$. We use $\widehat{\boldsymbol{m}}_N[\boldsymbol{A}]$ to derive an upper bound on the Fréchet function computed at $\widehat{\boldsymbol{\mu}}_N[\boldsymbol{A}]$. By definition of the sample Fréchet mean graphs, we have

$$\frac{1}{N} \sum_{k=1}^{N} d_H^2\left(\widehat{\boldsymbol{\mu}}_N[\boldsymbol{A}], \boldsymbol{A}^{(k)}\right) \leq \frac{1}{N} \sum_{k=1}^{N} d_H^2\left(\widehat{\boldsymbol{m}}_N[\boldsymbol{A}], \boldsymbol{A}^{(k)}\right). \tag{37}$$

Using (19) as a lower bound and (28) as an upper bound in (37), we get

$$\left[e_{\widehat{\mu}} - \bar{e}_N\right]^2 < 2\left[\bar{e}_N\right]^2 + \sigma_N^2(e),$$

and thus

$$\left|e_{\widehat{\mu}} - \bar{e}_N\right| \leq \sqrt{2\left[\bar{e}_N\right]^2 + \sigma_N^2(e)} \leq \frac{1}{\sqrt{2}}\left\{\sqrt{2}\bar{e}_N + \sigma_N(e)\right\} = \bar{e}_N + \frac{\sigma_N(e)}{\sqrt{2}}, \tag{38}$$

from which we get the advertised bound on $e_{\widehat{\mu}}$. $\qquad\square$

4.4   The Mean Graphs Computed Using the Adjacency Spectral Pseudometric

The technical difficulty in defining the sample Fréchet mean and median graphs according to the adjacency spectral pseudometric stems from the fact that the sample Fréchet function, $\widehat{F}_q(\boldsymbol{A})$, is defined in the spectral domain, but the domain over which the optimization takes place is the matrix domain. This leads to the definition of the set, Λ, of real spectra that are realizable by adjacency matrices of unweighted graphs (elements of $\mathcal{S}$, defined by (3)) [11],

$$\Lambda = \left\{\boldsymbol{\lambda}(\boldsymbol{A}) = \left[\lambda_1(\boldsymbol{A}) \cdots \lambda_n(\boldsymbol{A})\right]; \text{where } \boldsymbol{A} \in \mathcal{S}\right\}. \tag{39}$$

Let $\{G^{(1)}, \ldots, G^{(N)}\}$ be a sample of unweighted simple labeled graphs with vertex set $\{1, \ldots, n\}$. Let $\boldsymbol{A}^{(k)}$ be the adjacency matrix of graph $G^{(k)}$, and let

$\boldsymbol{\lambda}(\boldsymbol{A}^{(k)})$ be the spectrum of $\boldsymbol{A}^{(k)}$. The adjacency matrix, $\widehat{\boldsymbol{\mu}}_N[\boldsymbol{A}]$, of a sample Fréchet mean graph computed according to the adjacency spectral pseudometric, has a vector of eigenvalues, $\boldsymbol{\lambda}(\widehat{\boldsymbol{\mu}}_N[\boldsymbol{A}]) \in \Lambda$, that satisfies

$$\boldsymbol{\lambda}(\widehat{\boldsymbol{\mu}}_N[\boldsymbol{A}]) = \operatorname*{argmin}_{\boldsymbol{\lambda} \in \Lambda} \sum_{k=1}^{N} ||\boldsymbol{\lambda} - \boldsymbol{\lambda}(\boldsymbol{A}^{(k)})||^2. \tag{40}$$

Similarly, the adjacency matrix, $\widehat{m}_N[\boldsymbol{A}]$, of a sample Fréchet median computed according to the adjacency spectral pseudometric, has a vector of eigenvalues, $\boldsymbol{\lambda}(\widehat{m}_N[\boldsymbol{A}]) \in \Lambda$, that satisfies

$$\boldsymbol{\lambda}(\widehat{m}_N[\boldsymbol{A}]) = \operatorname*{argmin}_{\boldsymbol{\lambda} \in \Lambda} \sum_{k=1}^{N} ||\boldsymbol{\lambda} - \boldsymbol{\lambda}(\boldsymbol{A}^{(k)})||. \tag{41}$$

We recall the following result that expresses the number of edges as a function of the ℓ^2 norm of the spectrum of the adjacency matrix.

Lemma 7. *Let $G \in \mathcal{G}$ with adjacency matrix $\boldsymbol{A}$. Let $\lambda_1(\boldsymbol{A}) \geq \ldots \geq \lambda_n(\boldsymbol{A})$ be the eigenvalues of $\boldsymbol{A}$. Then*

$$2e(\boldsymbol{A}) = \sum_{i=1}^{n} \lambda_i^2(\boldsymbol{A}) = ||\boldsymbol{\lambda}(\boldsymbol{A})||_2^2. \tag{42}$$

Proof of Lemma 7. *The result is classic; see for instance [2, 16].*

We derive the following lower bound on the sample mean number of edges.

Lemma 8. *Let $\widehat{\mathbb{E}}_N[\boldsymbol{\lambda}(\boldsymbol{A})] = \frac{1}{N} \sum_{k=1}^{N} \boldsymbol{\lambda}(\boldsymbol{A}^{(k)})$ be the sample mean spectrum. Then*

$$\frac{1}{2}\left|\left|\widehat{\mathbb{E}}_N[\boldsymbol{\lambda}(\boldsymbol{A})]\right|\right|^2 \leq \bar{e}_N, \tag{43}$$

where $\bar{e}_N$ is the sample mean number of edges, given by (8).

Proof of Lemma 8. *The result is a straightforward consequence of the convexity of the norm combined with (42).*

If Λ were to be a convex set, then the spectrum of a sample Fréchet mean graph would simply be the sample mean spectrum, which would minimize (40). Unfortunately, Λ is not convex [12]. We can nevertheless relate the spectrum of a sample Fréchet mean graph, $\boldsymbol{\lambda}(\widehat{\boldsymbol{\mu}}_N[\boldsymbol{A}])$, to the mean spectrum $\widehat{\mathbb{E}}_N[\boldsymbol{\lambda}(\boldsymbol{A})]$. We take a short detour to build some intuition about the geometric position of the spectrum of $\widehat{\boldsymbol{\mu}}_N[\boldsymbol{A}]$ with respect to $\boldsymbol{\lambda}(\boldsymbol{A}^{(1)}), \ldots, \boldsymbol{\lambda}(\boldsymbol{A}^{(N)})$.

Warm-Up: The Sample Mean Spectrum. Let $\{G^{(1)}, \ldots, G^{(N)}\}$ be a sample of unweighted simple labeled graphs with vertex set $\{1, \ldots, n\}$. Let $\boldsymbol{A}^{(k)}$ be the adjacency matrix of graph $G^{(k)}$, and let $\boldsymbol{\lambda}(\boldsymbol{A}^{(k)})$ be the spectrum of $\boldsymbol{A}^{(k)}$.

Lemma 9. *Let* $\widehat{\mathbb{E}}_N[\lambda(A)]$ *be the sample mean spectrum. Then* $\exists\ k_0 \in \{1,\dots,N\}$ *such that*

$$\|\lambda(A^{(k_0)})\| \le \|\widehat{\mathbb{E}}_N[\lambda(A)]\|. \tag{44}$$

Proof of Lemma 9. *A proof by contradiction is elementary.*

Using the characterization of a sample Fréchet mean graph, $\widehat{\mu}_N[A]$, given by (40), we can extend the above lemma to $\lambda(\widehat{\mu}_N[A])$, and derive the following result.

Lemma 10. *Let* $\lambda(\widehat{\mu}_N[A])$ *be the spectrum of a sample Fréchet mean graph. Let* $\overline{e}_N$ *be the sample mean number of edges of the graphs* $G^{(1)},\dots,G^{(N)}$. *Then*

$$\|\lambda(\widehat{\mu}_N[A])\| \le 3\sqrt{2\overline{e}_N}. \tag{45}$$

Proof of Lemma 10. *Because of Lemma 9,*

$$\exists\ k_0 \in \{1,\dots,N\},\ \|\lambda(A^{(k_0)})\| \le \|\widehat{\mathbb{E}}_N[\lambda(A)]\|. \tag{46}$$

Now, because of Lemma 8, (46) implies that

$$\|\lambda(A^{(k_0)})\| \le \sqrt{2\overline{e}_N}. \tag{47}$$

Because the vector $\lambda(A^{(k_0)})$ *is in* Λ *(defined by (39)), we have*

$$\frac{1}{N}\sum_{k=1}^{N}\|\lambda(\widehat{\mu}_N[A]) - \lambda(A^{(k)})\|^2 \le \frac{1}{N}\sum_{k=1}^{N}\|\lambda(A^{(k_0)}) - \lambda(A^{(k)})\|^2.$$

Expanding the norms squared on both sides yields

$$\|\lambda(\widehat{\mu}_N[A])\|^2 - 2\langle\lambda(\widehat{\mu}_N[A]),\widehat{\mathbb{E}}_N[\lambda(A)]\rangle + \frac{1}{N}\sum_{k=1}^{N}\|\lambda(A^{(k)})\|^2$$

$$\le \|\lambda(A^{(k_0)})\|^2 - 2\langle\lambda(A^{(k_0)}),\widehat{\mathbb{E}}_N[\lambda(A)]\rangle + \frac{1}{N}\sum_{k=1}^{N}\|\lambda(A^{(k)})\|^2. \tag{48}$$

Subtracting $\frac{1}{N}\sum_{k=1}^{N}\|\lambda(A^{(k)})\|^2$ *and adding* $\|\widehat{\mathbb{E}}_N[\lambda(A)]\|^2$ *on both sides we get*

$$\|\lambda(\widehat{\mu}_N[A]) - \widehat{\mathbb{E}}_N[\lambda(A)]\|^2 \le \|\lambda(A^{(k_0)}) - \widehat{\mathbb{E}}_N[\lambda(A)]\|^2,$$

and therefore

$$\|\lambda(\widehat{\mu}_N[A])\| \le \|\lambda(A^{(k_0)})\| + 2\|\widehat{\mathbb{E}}_N[\lambda(A)]\|. \tag{49}$$

Finally, using Lemma 8 and (47) in the equation above, we obtain

$$\|\lambda(\widehat{\mu}_N[A])\| \le 3\sqrt{2\overline{e}_N}, \tag{50}$$

which completes the proof of the bound on the spectrum of the Fréchet mean. □

4.5   The Median Graphs Computed Using the Adjacency Spectral Pseudometric

We finally consider the computation of the median graphs. We have the following bound on the norm of the spectrum of $\widehat{m}_N[A]$.

Lemma 11. *Let* $\lambda(\widehat{m}_N[A])$ *be the spectrum of a sample Fréchet median graph. Let* $\bar{e}_N$ *be the sample mean number of edges of the graphs* $G^{(1)}, \dots, G^{(N)}$. *Then,*

$$\|\lambda(\widehat{m}_N[A])\| \leq 3\sqrt{2\bar{e}_N}. \tag{51}$$

Proof of Lemma 11. *The function* Φ,

$$\Phi : \mathbb{R}^n \longrightarrow [0, \infty)$$
$$x \longmapsto \Phi(x) = \|\lambda(\widehat{m}_N[A]) - x\|$$

is strictly convex, and therefore

$$\Phi\big(\widehat{\mathbb{E}}_N[\lambda(A)]\big) = \Phi\left(\frac{1}{N}\sum_{k=1}^N \lambda(A^{(k)})\right) \leq \frac{1}{N}\sum_{k=1}^N \Phi\big(\lambda(A^{(k)})\big). \tag{52}$$

Now, the right-hand side of (52) is the Fréchet function evaluated at one of its minimizers. Thus $F_1(\lambda(\widehat{m}_N[A]))$, *is smaller than* $F_1(\lambda(A^{(k_0)}))$, *where* $A^{(k_0)}$ *is defined in Lemma 9, and (52) becomes*

$$\|\lambda(\widehat{m}_N[A]) - \widehat{\mathbb{E}}_N[\lambda(A)]\| \leq \frac{1}{N}\sum_{k=1}^N \|\lambda(A^{(k_0)}) - \lambda(A^{(k)})\|. \tag{53}$$

Also, because of Lemma 8 and (47), we get

$$\frac{1}{N}\sum_{k=1}^N \|\lambda(A^{(k_0)}) - \lambda(A^{(k)})\| \leq \|\lambda(A^{(k_0)})\| + \sqrt{2\bar{e}_N} \leq 2\sqrt{2\bar{e}_N}. \tag{54}$$

Combining (53) and (54), and using Lemma 8 we conclude that

$$\|\lambda(\widehat{m}_N[A])\| \leq \|\widehat{\mathbb{E}}_N[\lambda(A)]\| + 2\sqrt{2\bar{e}_N} \leq 3\sqrt{2\bar{e}_N}.$$

This completes the proof of the bound on the spectrum of a Fréchet median. □

4.6   The Number of Edges of $\widehat{m}_N[G]$ and $\widehat{\mu}_N[G]$ when $d = d_\lambda$

The following lemma provides the bounds given by Theorem 1 when d is the spectral adjacency pseudometric.

Lemma 12. *Let* $\{G^{(1)}, \dots, G^{(N)}\}$ *be a sample of unweighted simple labeled graphs with vertex set* $\{1, \dots, n\}$. *We consider a sample Fréchet mean,* $\widehat{\mu}_N[A]$, *and a sample Fréchet median,* $\widehat{m}_N[A]$, *computed according to the spectral adjacency pseudometric. Then*

$$\max\big\{e(\widehat{\mu}_N[A]), e(\widehat{m}_N[A])\big\} \leq 9\,\bar{e}_N, \tag{55}$$

where $\bar{e}_N$ *is the sample mean number of edges given by (8).*

Proof of Lemma 12. *We first analyse the case of a sample Fréchet mean graph; a sample Fréchet median graph is handled in the same way. From lemmata 10 and 11, we have*

$$\|\lambda(\widehat{\boldsymbol{\mu}}_N[\boldsymbol{A}])\|^2 \leq 18 \, \overline{e}_N. \tag{56}$$

Now, from (42) we have $e\big(\widehat{\boldsymbol{\mu}}_N[\boldsymbol{A}]\big) = \frac{1}{2}\|\lambda(\widehat{\boldsymbol{\mu}}_N[\boldsymbol{A}])\|^2$, *and therefore*

$$e\big(\widehat{\boldsymbol{\mu}}_N[\boldsymbol{A}]\big) \leq 9 \, \overline{e}_N,$$

which completes the proof of the lemma.   □

References

1. Banks, D., Constantine, G.: Metric models for random graphs. J. Classif. **15**(2), 199–223 (1998)
2. Bapat, R.B.: Graphs and Matrices. UTX, vol. 27. Springer, London (2010). https://doi.org/10.1007/978-1-84882-981-7
3. Bollobás, B., Janson, S., Riordan, O.: The phase transition in inhomogeneous random graphs. Random Struct. Algorithms **31**(1), 3–122 (2007)
4. Devroye, L., Györfi, L., Lugosi, G.: A Probabilistic Theory of Pattern Recognition, vol. 31. Springer Science & Business Media (2013)
5. Donnat, C., Holmes, S.: Tracking network dynamics: a survey using graph distances. Ann. Appl. Stat. **12**(2), 971–1012 (2018)
6. Fréchet, M.: Les espaces abstraits et leur utilité en statistique théorique et même en statistique appliquée. Journal de la Société Française de Statistique **88**, 410–421 (1947)
7. Ginestet, C.E., Li, J., Balachandran, P., Rosenberg, S., Kolaczyk, E.D.: Hypothesis testing for network data in functional neuroimaging. Ann. Appl. Stat. **11**(2), 725–750 (2017)
8. Han, F., Han, X., Liu, H., Caffo, B., et al.: Sparse median graphs estimation in a high-dimensional semiparametric model. Ann. App. Stat. **10**(3), 1397–1426 (2016)
9. Jain, B.J.: On the geometry of graph spaces. Discret. Appl. Math. **214**, 126–144 (2016)
10. Jain, B.J., Obermayer, K.: Learning in Riemannian orbifolds. arXiv preprint arXiv:1204.4294 (2012)
11. Johnson, C.R., Marijuán, C., Paparella, P., Pisonero, M.: The NIEP. In: Operator Theory, Operator Algebras, and Matrix Theory. OTAA, vol. 267, pp. 199–220. Springer, Cham (2018). https://doi.org/10.1007/978-3-319-72449-2_10
12. Knudsen, C., McDonald, J.: A note on the convexity of the realizable set of eigenvalues for nonnegative symmetric matrices. Electron. J. Linear Algebra **8**, 110–114 (2001)
13. Kolaczyk, E.D., Lin, L., Rosenberg, S., Walters, J., Xu, J., et al.: Averages of unlabeled networks: geometric characterization and asymptotic behavior. Ann. Stat. **48**(1), 514–538 (2020)
14. Lunagómez, S., Olhede, S.C., Wolfe, P.J.: Modeling network populations via graph distances. J. Am. Stat. Assoc. **116**(536), 2023–2040 (2021)

15. Meyer, F.G.: The Fréchet mean of inhomogeneous random graphs. In: Benito, R.M., Cherifi, C., Cherifi, H., Moro, E., Rocha, L.M., Sales-Pardo, M. (eds.) COMPLEX NETWORKS 2021. SCI, vol. 1015, pp. 207–219. Springer, Cham (2022). https://doi.org/10.1007/978-3-030-93409-5_18
16. Van Mieghem, P.: Graph Spectra for Complex Networks. Cambridge University Press, Cambridge (2010)
17. Wills, P., Meyer, F.G.: Metrics for graph comparison: a practitioner's guide. PLOS ONE **15**(2), 1–54 (2020). https://doi.org/10.1371/journal.pone.0228728

Core But Not Peripheral Online Social Ties is a Protective Factor Against Depression: Evidence from a Nationally Representative Sample of Young Adults

Sofia Dokuka[✉], Elizaveta Sivak, and Ivan Smirnov

Institute of Education, HSE University, Moscow, Russia
{sdokuka,esivak,ibsmirnov}@hse.ru

Abstract. As social interactions are increasingly taking place in the digital environment, online friendship and its effects on various life outcomes from health to happiness attract growing research attention. In most studies, online ties are treated as representing a single type of relationship. However, our online friendship networks are not homogeneous and could include close connections, e.g. a partner, as well as people we have never met in person. In this paper, we investigate the potentially differential effects of online friendship ties on mental health. Using data from a Russian panel study ($N = 4,400$), we find that - consistently with previous research - the number of online friends correlates with depression symptoms. However, this is true only for networks that do not exceed Dunbar's number in size ($N \leq 150$) and only for core but not peripheral nodes of a friendship network. The findings suggest that online friendship could encode different types of social relationships that should be treated separately while investigating the association between online social integration and life outcomes, in particular well-being or mental health.

Keywords: social network · digital traces · depression

1 Introduction

Individual's mental health is known to be associated with their position within the social network. One of the most well-established relationships is the association between social integration and depressive symptoms [3,8,18,29,49]. Generally, social integration is understood as a structural aspect of people's relationships, that indicates how those relationships are patterned or organized [50]. However, in most of the studies, social integration is simply defined as the number of social contacts.

1.1 Social Integration and Depression

Longitudinal studies demonstrate that the association between social integration and depression might be explained by the protective role of social connections

© Springer Nature Switzerland AG 2022
P. Ribeiro et al. (Eds.): NetSci-X 2022, LNCS 13197, pp. 41–53, 2022.
https://doi.org/10.1007/978-3-030-97240-0_4

that serve as a stress buffer mitigating the depressive symptoms [22,26,50], or by the changes in friendship formation and interactions of individuals with depressive symptoms (i.e. such individuals tend to withdraw from existing contacts or create fewer new connections) [11,39]. Based on the National Longitudinal Study of Adolescent Health data (Add Health, $N = 11,023$), Ueno studied the association between the depressive symptoms and a variety of ego-network patterns [52]. He concluded that the number of friends was the strongest predictor of depressive symptoms. Although other variables generally showed significant correlations with depressive symptoms in the expected directions, the associations were very weak, especially when controlling for the number of friends. Employing the same longitudinal dataset Shaefer et al. [45] analyzed the role of depressive symptoms in the evolution of friendship networks and demonstrated that depressed persons withdrew from friendships over time, leaving them with fewer friends. Depressed individuals were also less likely to be selected as friends by others because they tend to occupy peripheral network positions. Negriff [39] found that higher levels of depressive symptoms led to smaller, less connected networks with fewer friends in the largest connected component of the network two years later. She concluded that individuals with depressive symptoms lack the social skills needed to form and maintain close relationships, which leads to the dissolution of friendship ties.

Previously reported results on the relationship between social network structure and depressive symptoms were mostly obtained for complete networks based on self-reported data [18,45], e.g. by asking school students to nominate their friends. Having information about the whole network structure allows controlling for a variety of network effects. However, it limits the generalizability of the findings as it is not clear if they are specific to particular schools or could be generalized to a large population. As a result, the association between depressive symptoms and ego network structure is not well understood at the population level. Self-reports on social networks can also be biased [32] which makes it essential to search for more objective measures of social interactions.

1.2   Online Social Integration

In the past decade, a significant fraction of social interactions migrated online, for example to social media platforms [33,57]. This process was accelerated in 2020 due to the COVID-19 pandemic and associated restrictions on face-to-face meetings, making social media and other digital platforms one of the key communication tools for a large part of the population. Given the central role that social media plays in interpersonal communication, it is important to understand the relationship between the online social environment of an individual and their depressive symptoms.

Empirical results for online networks largely agree with studies of offline networks. Users suffering from depression have smaller networks [39,42,54] with densely clustered pockets and less frequently explicitly mention their network partners compared to the non-depressed users [54]. Individuals with suicide ideation and depressive symptoms also have less clustered personal social networks and tend to connect with individuals similarly oriented toward suicide and depression [37].

Existing literature on the association between online networks and depressive symptoms mostly does not differentiate online friends, although online networks are known to consist of multiple layers, which differ in both emotional closeness with alters [15] and levels of support [9]. Moreover, network studies based on data on offline networks highlight the distinct impact of different ties on personal well-being [17, 25, 50]. This can also apply to online networks. For instance, Lup et al. [34] showed that the association between Instagram use and depressive symptoms is moderated by the number of strangers followed: more Instagram use is related to greater depressive symptoms only for those at highest levels of strangers followed, and for those at lower levels, Instagram use and depressive symptoms are unrelated.

In this paper, we investigate the potentially differential effect of online friendship ties on mental health, based on the survey data and data from a social networking site in a sample of young adults.

2 Methods

2.1 Survey Data

We used data from an ongoing Russian Longitudinal Panel Study of Educational and Occupational Trajectories (TrEC) [36] that tracks 4,399 students from 42 Russian regions who participated in the Programme for International Student Assessment (PISA) [40] in 2012. The initial TrEC sample was nationally representative for one age cohort (14–15 years old in 2012).

In the 2018 wave, the eight-item Patient Health Questionnaire depression scale (PHQ-8) [31] was included in the survey to measure depressive symptoms of participants. PHQ-8 asks individuals to self-rate the frequency of various depressive symptoms over the past 2 weeks using a 4-point verbal scale: "not at all," "several days," "more than half the days," and "nearly every day." Depression symptoms are scored as the sum of all items, ranging from 0 to 24. The depression questionnaire was filled by 2,554 participants.

The PHQ-8 scale has been shown to be a valid tool in detecting depression across various cultures [6, 19, 23, 44, 51] in both clinical and population-based studies.

2.2 Data on Online Friendship

In addition to survey data, the data set includes information on the online friendship of respondents on VK. VK was created in 2006 as a clone of Facebook and became the most popular Russian social networking site with more than 97, 000, 000 monthly active users. It is particularly popular among young adults: more than 90% of 18–24 years old use it regularly [43].

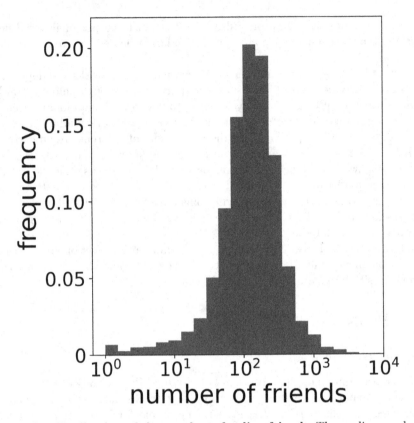

Fig. 1. The distribution of the number of online friends. The median number of friends is 132, the majority of users (56%) have between 50 and 200 friends, however, some users have as many as 4,476 online friends.

VK provides an application programming interface (API) that enables the downloading of information systematically from the site. The public API could be used for research purposes according to the VK team.

In 2018, publicly available information from VK was collected for TrEC participants. This online data is available only for those respondents who provided consent to use their VK data for research purposes (79%). Information on non-participant was anonymized, i.e. VK ID's of participants' friends were removed. The VK data collection procedure was approved by the Institutional Review Board.

For the purposes of this study, we have analyzed the structure of 1.5 radius ego networks, i.e. the networks that include friends of a participant on VK and friendship connections between them.

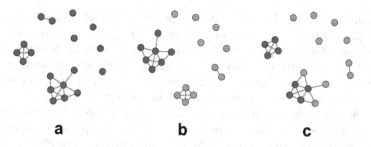

Fig. 2. Different approaches to identifying the core friends. Core (red) and periphery (grey) nodes of an empirical ego network without the ego. Core friends include (a) all nodes of the network, (b) only the nodes in the largest connected component, (c) only the nodes in 3-core. (Color figure online)

2.3 Network Size

Typically to empirical social networks [1,53], there is a large variability in the number of users' friends: while the majority (56%) has between 50 and 200 friends, some users have more than 2,000 connections (see Fig. 1). Such large networks cannot represent meaningful social ties indicating that users employ different strategies when accepting or sending friend requests on social media. While for some, online friendship might indicate relatively close social connections, others probably indiscriminately accept or send requests resulting in thousands of online "friends". To account for that, we consider separately those who have an unreasonably large number of friends and everyone else. We choose Dunbar's number ($N = 150$) as a threshold to separate these two groups as it is thought to be a soft upper limit of the personal social network size [14] and was empirically confirmed in both offline and online settings [24,27,41,55].

The exact Dunbar's number is to a certain degree an arbitrary threshold as it is not fixed for every individual but rather is an approximate estimate. However, we find that in our particular case this choice is reasonable based on empirical observations (see Results).

2.4 Core

We further assume that even for users with reasonably sized networks not all connections are necessarily equally important. One way to identify meaningful connections is to look at the cohesive structures within the ego networks. Borgatti and Everett [4] argue that networks tend to follow the core-periphery model. It means that the network consists of two classes of nodes, namely a cohesive subgraph (the core) in which actors are connected to each other in some maximal sense and a class of actors that are loosely connected to the cohesive subgraph (the periphery). Core-periphery structures are often analyzed with respect to complete networks. For example, differences between the core and peripheral nodes were studied in motion industry [7], metabolic networks [12], and liner shipping network [30]. These two different structural types of social connections might also play different roles in network functioning on an individual level [25]. Cohesive network connections of the ego network are more likely to provide emotional support and resource exchange, whereas periphery ties do not have these properties as they serve different functions (e.g. binding groups together or provide information) [21,25]. In the case of VK, isolated friends are also more likely to be bots or accounts with fake information [47].

For that reason, we separate online connections of the individuals into core and periphery nodes on the ego network level. For comparison, we use three different approaches. First, we include all friends in the core, Fig. 2a. Second, we include in the core only the nodes that are part of the largest connected component [56], Fig. 2b. Finally, we consider only friends that belong to the network k-core ($k = 3$), Fig. 2c, where k-core is a subgraph in which each node is adjacent to at least a minimum number, k, of the other nodes in this subgraph [46,56]. We choose $k = 3$ as it is the largest nontrivial value for our data, i.e. for $k \geq 4$ the size of k-core is zero for a large fraction of networks.

3   Results

3.1   Depressive Symptoms and Size of the Network Core

The prevalence of depression (PHQ-8 $\geq$ 10) is 16.6% in our sample ($N = 2,554$). The average PHQ-8 score is 5.3 ($SD = 4.7$). Similar depression rates have been previously found in samples of students and young adults [16,17,38]. The prevalence of depression among men (51.3% of a sample) is lower than among women: 11.5% for men vs 21.9% for women ($p - value = 2.8 \cdot 10^{-9}$, χ^2-test). This is expected given that prevalence of depression among women is approximately two times larger than among men [5,35].

The mean number of friends on VK is 190, the median is 132, similar to other online social networks [24,53]. The average size of the largest connected component is 112 nodes (the median is 70). The mean size of the network k-core is 117 (the median is 76).

We find no association between the number of online friends and depressive symptoms for the whole sample: the correlation between PHQ-8 scores and total number of friends is Pearson's $r = -0.01$, $p - value = 0.51$, for the size of the largest connected component, $r = -0.02$, $p - value = 0.43$, and for the core size, $r = -0.02$, $p - value = 0.36$.

3.2   Role of the Network Size

We then compared the relationship between depressive symptoms and network size separately for smaller ($N \leq 150$) and larger networks ($N > 150$) using a bootstrap test. For that purpose, we repeatedly drew a sample of networks from both groups with replacement and computed Pearson correlation coefficient between the size of the largest connected component and PHQ-8 scores. The results of simulations are presented in Fig. 3. The median value of correlation

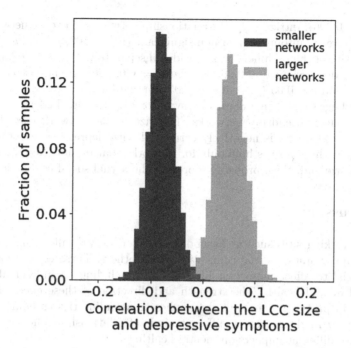

Fig. 3. The effect of network size on association between depressive symptoms and the size of network core. The distribution of the correlations between network core size (largest connected component) and depressive symptoms for smaller ($N \leq 150$) and larger ego networks ($N > 150$). The distributions are from 10,000 bootstrap simulations.

over 10,000 simulations for smaller networks is -0.08 and for larger networks is 0.05, the difference is significant with $p - value < 10^{-3}$.

We then check for the robustness of this result with respect to changing the threshold, N. For that purpose we have computed the correlation between network size and depression score for networks of various sizes. We, first, computed the correlation for the smallest 30% of all networks, i.e. networks whose size is between the 0th and 30th percentile. We then repeated the procedure by sliding the network size thresholds with a one percent step, i.e. computing correlation for networks lying between the 1st and 31st percentile, between the 2nd and 32nd, etc. The results (see Fig. 4) suggest that the relationship of interest is indeed different for smaller and larger networks. While there is a consistent significantly negative correlation for smaller networks, for larger networks it consistently does not differ from zero. Curiously, the change in the pattern seems to approximately correspond to Dunbar's number.

For the sample of networks that are smaller or equal than 150 nodes ($N = 1,382$), we find statistically significant associations between the size of the largest connected component and depressive symptoms (Pearson's $r = -0.08$, $p - value = 0.003$), and size of k-core and depressive symptoms ($r = -0.07$,

$p-value = 0.006$). Intriguingly, the relationship between the overall network size and depressive symptoms remain non-significant ($r = -0.02$, $p-value = 0.39$). When the size of the periphery was considered separately it even correlated positively with depression: $r = 0.06$ ($p-value = 0.02$) for the largest connected component and $r = 0.05$ ($p-value = 0.05$) for the k-core.

Our findings suggest that depressive symptoms of an individual are associated with their online friendship networks. The size of the network core, but not the network periphery, is negatively correlated with depressive symptoms. We also find that these results hold only for networks that do not exceed Dunbar's number in size and, thus, probably represent the actual social connections.

4 Discussion

Social networking sites such as Facebook, Twitter, or VK, allow their users to establish and maintain social connections with others. These connections have the potential to affect important life outcomes including an individual's well-being and mental health. The strength and direction of these effects are still not clear. In particular, most of the studies treat online ties as homogeneous, although they might represent different kinds of relationships and as a consequence have different impacts on mental health.

In our study, we examine the relationship between the structure of online ego networks and depressive symptoms in a nationally representative sample of young adults. The results could potentially be generalized to a population level, albeit for one age cohort. We find that the size of the network is negatively associated with depressive symptoms, however, this is true only for core but not peripheral nodes. The size of the periphery is positively correlated with depression. Social comparison theory provides one possible explanation of this association. Peripheral ties may represent people we do not know personally. Previous research has shown that Facebook users with more friends who are strangers are more likely to exhibit attribution error toward those users they do not know, i.e. to attribute the positive content presented on Facebook to others' personality, rather than situational factors [10]. Thus these users are more vulnerable to social media's positivity bias, which can lead to negative social comparison, and, in turn, emotional distress and depression [2,20,34,48].

We also find that some users have a very large number of online friends. These online ties are unlikely to represent meaningful social connections and, perhaps not surprisingly, for users with such large networks, the size of their core network is not associated with depressive symptoms.

These findings further support the notion that online friendship could represent different types of social relationships and, thus, online ties should be treated deferentially while investigating the association between online social integration and mental health.

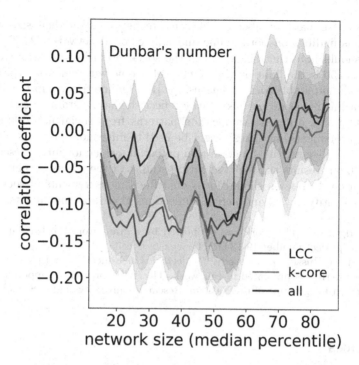

Fig. 4. The relationship between the network size and depressive symptoms. The change in the strength of correlation between the number of friends and depression depending on the network size. For smaller networks, there is a consistent significantly negative correlation between the size of the network core and depressive symptoms but not for the size of the whole network. For larger networks, the correlation consistently does not differ from zero. The 90% confidence intervals are computed via bootstrap.

4.1 Limitations and Further Research

Our study is limited by the cross-sectional nature of the data and does not allow exploring the causal relationships between the structure of online ego networks and depressive symptoms. Furthermore, the online friendship networks are relatively stable: once added friends are rarely removed while the manifestation of depressive symptoms is typically limited in time. This might explain the weakness of found relationships. The small effect sizes should be taken into account when considering future research as it does not allow detecting potentially differential effects for different groups, e.g. depending on users' gender, ethnicity, or socio-economic status. One potential solution is to collect data on specific groups of users, for example, those who might benefit most from online integration.

Further research might also go beyond the information on friendship networks and consider other types of communication information, such as comments, direct messages, or likes. This might serve as a better proxy for social integration, see, for example, [28].

We used Dunbar's number to differentiate networks on their size, following previous findings on both online and offline social networks [24,27,41,55]. Still, we should note that according to the social brain hypothesis introduced by Dunbar, 150 is the limit on the number of people with whom a typical person can maintain stable social relationships [13]. Online friendship ties that we consider in this paper do not necessarily reflect the actual stable social connections. Potentially, other communication patterns from social networking sites (e.g. posts, comments, and likes) might be used to infer more precise social relationships. We suggest this direction as a potential avenue for future research.

Overall, our results suggest that future studies of the effects of online social integration on depression should focus on refined measurements of social integration to identify *actual* and *active* connections at several time points.

Acknowledgment. This work was supported by a grant from the Russian Science Foundation (project number 19-18-00271).

The data of the Russian panel study "Trajectories in Education and Career" (TrEC http://trec.hse.ru/) is presented in this work. The TrEC project is supported by the Basic Research Programme of the National Research University Higher School of Economics.

References

1. Albert, R., Barabási, A.L.: Statistical mechanics of complex networks. Rev. Mod. Phys. **74**(1), 47 (2002)
2. Appel, H., Gerlach, A.L., Crusius, J.: The interplay between Facebook use, social comparison, envy, and depression. Curr. Opin. Psychol. **9**, 44–49 (2016)
3. van Beljouw, I.M., Verhaak, P.F., Cuijpers, P., van Marwijk, H.W., Penninx, B.W.: The course of untreated anxiety and depression, and determinants of poor one-year outcome: a one-year cohort study. BMC Psychiatry **10**(1), 1–10 (2010)
4. Borgatti, S.P., Everett, M.G.: Models of core/periphery structures. Soc. Netw. **21**(4), 375–395 (2000)
5. Brody, D.J., Pratt, L.A., Hughes, J.P.: Prevalence of depression among adults aged 20 and over: United states, 2013–2016. NCHS Data Brief **303**, 1–8 (2018)
6. Burdzovic Andreas, J., Brunborg, G.S.: Depressive symptomatology among Norwegian adolescent boys and girls: the patient health questionnaire-9 (PHQ-9) psychometric properties and correlates. Front. Psychol. **8**, 887 (2017)
7. Cattani, G., Ferriani, S.: A core/periphery perspective on individual creative performance: social networks and cinematic achievements in the hollywood film industry. Organ. Sci. **19**(6), 824–844 (2008)
8. Choi, K.W., et al.: An exposure-wide and mendelian randomization approach to identifying modifiable factors for the prevention of depression. Am. J. Psychiatry **177**(10), 944–954 (2020)
9. Choi, M., Aiello, L.M., Varga, K.Z., Quercia, D.: Ten social dimensions of conversations and relationships. In: Proceedings of the Web Conference 2020, pp. 1514–1525 (2020)
10. Chou, H.T.G., Edge, N.: "They are happier and having better lives than I am": the impact of using Facebook on perceptions of others' lives. Cyberpsychol. Behav. Soc. Netw. **15**(2), 117–121 (2012)

11. Coyne, J.C.: Depression and the response of others. J. Abnorm. Psychol. **85**(2), 186 (1976)
12. Da Silva, M.R., Ma, H., Zeng, A.P.: Centrality, network capacity, and modularity as parameters to analyze the core-periphery structure in metabolic networks. Proc. IEEE **96**(8), 1411–1420 (2008)
13. Dunbar, R.I.: Neocortex size as a constraint on group size in primates. J. Hum. Evol. **22**(6), 469–493 (1992)
14. Dunbar, R.I.: The social brain hypothesis. Evol. Anthropol. Issues News Rev. **6**(5), 178–190 (1998)
15. Dunbar, R.I., Arnaboldi, V., Conti, M., Passarella, A.: The structure of online social networks mirrors those in the offline world. Soc. Netw. **43**, 39–47 (2015)
16. Eisenberg, D., Gollust, S.E., Golberstein, E., Hefner, J.L.: Prevalence and correlates of depression, anxiety, and suicidality among university students. Am. J. Orthopsychiatry **77**(4), 534–542 (2007)
17. Elmer, T., Boda, Z., Stadtfeld, C.: The co-evolution of emotional well-being with weak and strong friendship ties. Netw. Sci. **5**(3), 278–307 (2017)
18. Elmer, T., Stadtfeld, C.: Depressive symptoms are associated with social isolation in face-to-face interaction networks. Sci. Rep. **10**(1), 1–12 (2020)
19. Fatiregun, A., Kumapayi, T.: Prevalence and correlates of depressive symptoms among in-school adolescents in a rural district in Southwest Nigeria. J. Adolesc. **37**(2), 197–203 (2014)
20. Feinstein, B.A., Hershenberg, R., Bhatia, V., Latack, J.A., Meuwly, N., Davila, J.: Negative social comparison on Facebook and depressive symptoms: rumination as a mechanism. Psychol. Pop. Media Cult. **2**(3), 161 (2013)
21. Fingerman, K.L.: Consequential strangers and peripheral ties: the importance of unimportant relationships. J. Family Theory Rev. **1**(2), 69–86 (2009)
22. Fiore, J., Becker, J., Coppel, D.B.: Social network interactions: a buffer or a stress. Am. J. Community Psychol. **11**(4), 423 (1983)
23. Ganguly, S., Samanta, M., Roy, P., Chatterjee, S., Kaplan, D.W., Basu, B.: Patient health questionnaire-9 as an effective tool for screening of depression among Indian adolescents. J. Adolesc. Health **52**(5), 546–551 (2013)
24. Gonçalves, B., Perra, N., Vespignani, A.: Modeling users' activity on Twitter networks: validation of Dunbar's number. PLoS ONE **6**(8), e22656 (2011)
25. Granovetter, M.S.: The strength of weak ties. Am. J. Sociol. **78**(6), 1360–1380 (1973)
26. Hays, J.C., Steffens, D.C., Flint, E.P., Bosworth, H.B., George, L.K.: Does social support buffer functional decline in elderly patients with unipolar depression? Am. J. Psychiatry **158**(11), 1850–1855 (2001)
27. Hill, R.A., Dunbar, R.I.: Social network size in humans. Hum. Nat. **14**(1), 53–72 (2003)
28. Hobbs, W.R., Burke, M., Christakis, N.A., Fowler, J.H.: Online social integration is associated with reduced mortality risk. Proc. Natl. Acad. Sci. **113**(46), 12980–12984 (2016)
29. Kawachi, I., Berkman, L.F.: Social ties and mental health. J. Urban Health **78**(3), 458–467 (2001)
30. Kojaku, S., Xu, M., Xia, H., Masuda, N.: Multiscale core-periphery structure in a global liner shipping network. Sci. Rep. **9**(1), 1–15 (2019)
31. Kroenke, K., Strine, T.W., Spitzer, R.L., Williams, J.B., Berry, J.T., Mokdad, A.H.: The PHQ-8 as a measure of current depression in the general population. J. Affect. Disord. **114**(1–3), 163–173 (2009)

32. Latkin, C.A., Edwards, C., Davey-Rothwell, M.A., Tobin, K.E.: The relationship between social desirability bias and self-reports of health, substance use, and social network factors among urban substance users in Baltimore, Maryland. Addict. Behav. **73**, 133–136 (2017)
33. Liu, S., et al.: Online mental health services in China during the Covid-19 outbreak. Lancet Psychiatry **7**(4), e17–e18 (2020)
34. Lup, K., Trub, L., Rosenthal, L.: Instagram# instasad?: exploring associations among Instagram use, depressive symptoms, negative social comparison, and strangers followed. Cyberpsychol. Behav. Soc. Netw. **18**(5), 247–252 (2015)
35. Luppa, M., et al.: Age-and gender-specific prevalence of depression in latest-life-systematic review and meta-analysis. J. Affect. Disord. **136**(3), 212–221 (2012)
36. Malik, V.: The Russian panel study 'trajectories in education and careers'. Longitudinal Life Course Stud. **10**(1), 125–144 (2019)
37. Masuda, N., Kurahashi, I., Onari, H.: Suicide ideation of individuals in online social networks. PLoS ONE **8**(4), e62262 (2013)
38. Mikolajczyk, R.T., et al.: Prevalence of depressive symptoms in university students from Germany, Denmark, Poland and Bulgaria. Soc. Psychiatry Psychiatr. Epidemiol. **43**(2), 105–112 (2008)
39. Negriff, S.: Depressive symptoms predict characteristics of online social networks. J. Adolesc. Health **65**(1), 101–106 (2019)
40. OECD: PISA 2012 Results: What Students Know and Can Do. Student Performance in Mathematics, Reading and Science. OECD Publishing (2014)
41. Overgoor, J., Adamic, L.A., et al.: The structure of US college networks on Facebook. In: Proceedings of the International AAAI Conference on Web and Social Media, vol. 14, pp. 499–510 (2020)
42. Park, S., Lee, S.W., Kwak, J., Cha, M., Jeong, B.: Activities on Facebook reveal the depressive state of users. J. Med. Internet Res. **15**(10), e217 (2013)
43. Public Opinion Foundation: Online practices of Russians: social networks (2016). http://fom.ru/SMI-i-internet/12495. Accessed 09 Sep 2021
44. Richardson, L.P., et al.: Evaluation of the patient health questionnaire-9 item for detecting major depression among adolescents. Pediatrics **126**(6), 1117–1123 (2010)
45. Schaefer, D.R., Kornienko, O., Fox, A.M.: Misery does not love company: network selection mechanisms and depression homophily. Am. Sociol. Rev. **76**(5), 764–785 (2011)
46. Seidman, S.B.: Network structure and minimum degree. Soc. Netw. **5**(3), 269–287 (1983)
47. Smirnov, I., Sivak, E., Kozmina, Y.: In search of lost profiles. Educ. Stud. Moscow **4**, 106–122 (2016)
48. Steers, M.L.N., Wickham, R.E., Acitelli, L.K.: Seeing everyone else's highlight reels: how Facebook usage is linked to depressive symptoms. J. Soc. Clin. Psychol. **33**(8), 701–731 (2014)
49. Taylor, H.O., Taylor, R.J., Nguyen, A.W., Chatters, L.: Social isolation, depression, and psychological distress among older adults. J. Aging Health **30**(2), 229–246 (2018)
50. Thoits, P.A.: Mechanisms linking social ties and support to physical and mental health. J. Health Soc. Behav. **52**(2), 145–161 (2011)
51. Tsai, F.J., Huang, Y.H., Liu, H.C., Huang, K.Y., Huang, Y.H., Liu, S.I.: Patient health questionnaire for school-based depression screening among Chinese adolescents. Pediatrics **133**(2), e402–e409 (2014)

52. Ueno, K.: The effects of friendship networks on adolescent depressive symptoms. Soc. Sci. Res. **34**(3), 484–510 (2005)
53. Ugander, J., Karrer, B., Backstrom, L., Marlow, C.: The anatomy of the Facebook social graph. arXiv preprint arXiv:1111.4503 (2011)
54. Vedula, N., Parthasarathy, S.: Emotional and linguistic cues of depression from social media. In: Proceedings of the 2017 International Conference on Digital Health, pp. 127–136 (2017)
55. Wang, Q., Gao, J., Zhou, T., Hu, Z., Tian, H.: Critical size of ego communication networks. EPL (Europhys. Lett.) **114**(5), 58004 (2016)
56. Wasserman, S., Faust, K., et al.: Social Network Analysis: Methods and Applications. Cambridge University Press, Cambridge (1994)
57. Wiederhold, B.K.: Connecting through technology during the coronavirus disease 2019 pandemic: avoiding "Zoom Fatigue". Cyberpsychol. Behav. Soc. Netw. **23**(7), 437–438 (2020)

Deep Topological Embedding
with Convolutional Neural Networks
for Complex Network Classification

Leonardo Scabini[1]([⊠]), Lucas Ribas[2], Eraldo Ribeiro[3], and Odemir Bruno[1]

[1] São Carlos Institute of Physics, University of São Paulo,
PO Box 369, São Carlos, SP 13560-970, Brazil
{scabini,bruno}@ifsc.usp.br
[2] Institute of Mathematics and Computer Science, University of São Paulo,
Avenida Trabalhador São-Carlense, 400, Centro, 13566-590 São Carlos, SP, Brazil
lucasribas@usp.br
[3] Department of Computer Science, Florida Institute of Technology, Florida, USA
eribeiro@fit.edu

Abstract. The classification of complex networks allows us to compare sets of networks based on their topological characteristics. By being able to compare sets of known networks to unknown ones, we can analyze real-world complex systems such as neural pathways, traffic flow, and social relations. However, most network-classification methods rely on vertex-level measures or they characterize single fixed-structure networks. Also, these approaches can be computationally costly when analyzing a large number of networks, as they need to learn the network embeds. To address these issues, we propose a hand-crafted embedding method called *Deep Topological Embedding (DTE)* that builds multidimensional and deep embeddings from networks, based on the joint distribution of vertex centrality, that combined represents the global structure of the network. The DTE can be approached as a two or three-dimensional visual representation of complex networks. In this sense, we present a convolutional architecture to classify DTE representations of different topological models. Our method achieves improved classification accuracy compared to related methods when tested on three benchmarks.

Keywords: Complex Networks · Neural Networks · Convolutional Neural Networks

1 Introduction

Complex networks are ideal computational tools for modeling many real-world phenomena especially those consisting of systems of various inter-related processes and interacting components, e.g., COVID-19 contagion [16,25], urban crime dynamics [20], neural connectivity [23], and texture analysis in computer vision [24]. These complex systems are only particular examples of a great class

© Springer Nature Switzerland AG 2022
P. Ribeiro et al. (Eds.): NetSci-X 2022, LNCS 13197, pp. 54–66, 2022.
https://doi.org/10.1007/978-3-030-97240-0_5

of evolving networks [8] which cannot be properly analyzed based only on knowledge of the system's individual components [2]. However, network analysis allows us to model the structure and functioning of connected phenomena by combining tools from graph theory, physics, and statistics.

A promising network-analysis tool is *supervised classification*, which distinguishes between types of networks [1] by learning topological characteristics from a set of known networks. In the sense of large-scale datasets and models, deep learning is the predominant approach lately, especially with artificial neural networks. However, graphs and Complex Networks are non-Euclidean data that cannot be directly inputted into most neural network architectures. There is a class of Machine Learning techniques, usually referred to as Geometric Deep Learning [6], which focus on generalizing deep neural networks to such data. Various models have been proposed for graphs into this paradigm, such as Graph Neural Networks [26], Graph Kernels [21], and Graph Convolutional Networks [13].

However, most of the mentioned models characterize vertex-level information or describe single networks instead of groups of them. The process of mapping networks into an Euclidean space can be costly, as all embeddings must be learned (i.e., needing a consistent number of parameters). In addition, such methods are often limited to fixed network structures. Hand-crafted embeddings (or feature extraction) from complex networks is an alternative to learned embeddings which is useful to reduce the computational cost, or when there is not sufficient data to properly learn the embeds. This approach, combined with supervised learning from sets of networks, has been explored by [17,18,22], who embed networks based on the dynamics of the life-like automaton. One limitation of automaton methods is that the cost of automaton's rule selection, which is performed during the network embedding, can become prohibitive for large network samples.

Convolutional Neural Networks (CNN) combined with a global network embedding has been used for complex network classification. Xin et al. [29] uses a random walk-based embedding to map a complex network into a 2-D image which is then input to a CNN. The image results from performing principal-component analysis on the high-dimensional random-walk data. While Xin et al.' method is a direct application of image-based CNNs to classify complex networks, the method is a good step towards applying CNN to complex networks. One limitation of such an approach is that random walks are non-deterministic and a considerable number of repetitions should be performed to achieve robust embeddings.

In this work, we propose a new model for complex network classification combining centrality measures and CNNs. Our main contribution is a hand-crafted technique called *deep topological embedding (DTE)* that builds visual representations of complex networks by combining the distribution of centrality measures into two or three-dimensional matrices (Sect. 3). This approach works on networks with varying properties and sizes. The DTE is input to a CNN that learns to distinguish networks. In this sense, the network embedding is done through a hand-crafted technique (DTE), based on known network properties, rather than learned from random weights. We tested our method on complex network datasets and compared the results with similar methods (Sect. 4), achieving promising classification accuracy.

2   Theoretical Background

2.1   Complex Networks

A complex network can be defined by a graph $G = (V, E)$, where $V = \{v_1, \ldots, v_n\}$ is the set of its n vertices and $E = \{e(v_i, v_j)\}$ are the edges (or connections) between vertex pairs. In this paper, we consider complex networks with undirected, unweighted edges, i.e., $e(v_i, v_j) = 1$ if v_i and v_j are linked (0 otherwise), and $e(v_i, v_j) = e(v_j, v_i)$, respectively. Given its graph representation, we can quantify the topology of a complex network by calculating different metrics [7]. Next, we summarize the two types of networks that we will classify in this paper, i.e., scale-free networks and small-world networks.

Scale-Free Networks. A classical metric is the degree of a vertex v_i, i.e., $k(v_i) = \sum_j a(v_i, v_j)$. Its value represents the number of edges linked to v_i. The degree is a type of *centrality* measure, which ranks the topological importance of nodes within the network. The network's degree distribution underpins several properties, such as the scale-free networks [3]. These networks' degree distribution follows a power law $P(k) \approx k^{-\gamma}$, where γ varies according to the network structure. Scale-free networks usually contain hubs, i.e., some vertices have a large degree and in turn, play a critical role in the network's internal functioning.

Small-World Networks. These networks allow for efficient spreading of information [28], as they have a small average shortest-path distance where vertices are reached easily. Small-world networks also have high clustering coefficient, which describes the degree of interconnectivity between neighboring vertices. This measure counts the fraction of triangles (i.e., fully connected triple) that occurs between a vertex v_i and its neighbors, and is given by $c(v_i) = \frac{2\bigtriangledown(v_i)}{k(v_i)(k(v_i)-1)}$, where $\bigtriangledown(v_i)$ is the number of triangles in which v_i participates, or simply the number of edges between the neighbors of v_i.

Other Network-Characterization Measures. In addition to vertex degree, the classification method proposed uses the following centrality measures to characterize complex networks (See [7] for a survey of measures):

- **Eigenvector centrality** [4] computes vertex centrality based on the centrality of its neighbors:

$$ev(i) = \lambda_1^{-1} \sum_j^n A_{ij} ev(j), \tag{1}$$

where A represents the network's adjacency matrix, and u_j is an eigenvector of A corresponding to the eigenvalue λ_j.

- **Current Flow betweenness** [5] quantifies the importance of vertices inspired by the electric flow in circuits, flowing through all possible paths:

$$CF_b(i) = \frac{\sum\limits_{a}^{n} \sum\limits_{b=a+1}^{n} U_i^{(a,b)}}{(n-1)(n-2)}, \tag{2}$$

where current is injected at a source a and drained at a target vertex b. The Laplacian matrix $L = D - A$ is computed, where D is the degree matrix, and then a new matrix Y is obtained by setting the first row and column of the inverse Laplacian L^{-1} as zero. Then, the matrix $U = YB$ [5] is obtained, where B is a vector that indicates the input and output current in each vertex i for the source-drain pair a and b, i.e., all its elements are zero except for the source and drain vertices.

- **Current Flow closeness** [5] measures the vertex's average distance to all other vertices through all possible paths:

$$CF_c(i) = \frac{n-1}{\sum\limits_{j \neq i}^{n} U_i^{(i,j)} - U_j^{(i,j)}}. \tag{3}$$

Under the electric-network analogy, this is equivalent to computing the effective resistance between vertices.

- **Subgraph centrality** [9] is the sum of weighted closed walks (as weights decrease with path length) of all lengths starting and ending at a given vertex:

$$sg(i) = \sum\limits_{j}^{n} (u_j^i)^2 e^{\lambda_j}. \tag{4}$$

2.2 Convolutional Neural Networks

The main contribution of this paper is a novel complex network embedding based on centrality measures that can be employed for classification tasks with neural networks. One neural network architecture that attracted notorious visibility lately is the deep CNN [14]. This kind of model focuses on multidimensional data with spatial/temporal relations such as time series, images, and videos. Since then, the growth performance of these models has motivated many successful applications [19]. We can identify two well-defined components in a CNN: (i) the feature extraction part and (ii) the classification part. The latter component is usually organized into one or more sequential fully-connected layers (all neurons of a layer connect to all neurons from the previous and next layers). On the other hand, the feature extraction part has evolved throughout the years, with several innovative architectural properties and modules. In this work, we focus on architectures with standard sequential convolutional layers.

The input of a CNN layer in the feature extraction part consists of a set of $M_z^d = [A_1, ..., A_i, ..., A_z]$ 2-D matrices of equal size, where z indicates the layer's depth, d the layer position and A_i represents the i-th input matrix. In the case of convolutional layers, the trainable weights are organized into a set of $(1 \leq j \leq n)$ filters $W = [f_j(x, y, z)]$, where x and y are its width and height, respectively. The weights are randomly initialized, usually considering optimized techniques such as the Glorot Normal Initialization [10]. The set of weights, also known as the filter bank, is in charge of computing the layer's output M_n^{d+1} by convolving M_z^d with every filter f_j. An activation function $\phi(M_n^{d+1})$ is applied, which intends to project the inputs in nonlinear space. In deep CNNs, this is usually done using the Rectifier-Linear-Unit [11] function $(\phi(M_n^{d+1}) = max(0, M_n^{d+1})$.

Another common practice is to use pooling layers that summarize the input matrix dimensions by combining a neuron window (usually 2×2) into a single neuron in the next layer, typically by computing the maximum or average value. After all convolutional and pooling layers, the last output matrix is flattened to fit in the activation step's first fully-connected layer. As we focus on a supervised classification problem, the last layer of the CNN is then fully connected, with its number of neurons corresponding to the number of classes the network will address. In this scenario, the CNN can then be trained, for instance, using Stochastic Gradient Descent (SGD) [27].

3   Proposed Method

Our goal is to manually embed complex networks and use CNNs to learn to classify them. This requires the network graph to be embedded in an Euclidean space. Thus, we propose to create network embeds from vertex-centrality measures. Consider a network $G = (V, E)$ with $|V| = n$ nodes, and some local measure $f(v_x)$ computed at node v_x. Measures calculated at each vertex are then combined into a feature vector $\varphi_f = [f(v_1), \ldots, f(v_n)]$ to form a network descriptor for a given measure f.

However, the size of vector φ_f varies with the number of vertices in the network. To obtain a set of descriptors of same size, we perform vector quantization (i.e., a bag-of-features approach) to create frequency histograms of fixed bin size, and then normalize them into probability functions. Consider $P(\varphi_f)$ as the frequency vector for a given network and measure f, where $|P(\varphi_f)| = b$ is the chosen bin size. To compute the histogram, we consider a discretization with bins $i \in [min(\varphi_f), max(\varphi_f)]$, divided into b equal-width bins. The frequency is then obtained by dividing each bin occurrence by the sum of total occurrences, i.e., the number of nodes n. Let us rewrite $P(\varphi_f)$ as $\varphi_{b,f}$, a one-dimensional vector representing the distribution of a given local complex network measure f and a bin size b

$$\varphi_{b,f}(i) = \frac{1}{n} \sum_{\forall v_x \in V} \delta(f(v_x), i), \tag{5}$$

where δ is the Kronecker's delta, that returns 1 when $f(v_x) = i$, and 0 otherwise.

3.1   Creating Higher-Dimensional Complex Network Representations

We combine two or more topological measures into higher-dimensional combinatorial histograms, obtaining arrays of two or three dimensions. Consider two measures $f1$ and $f2$ computed to each network node. Instead of computing their individual frequencies $\varphi_{b,f1}$ and $\varphi_{b,f2}$, we propose a new feature representation $\varphi_{b,f1,f2}(i,j) \in \mathbb{R}^{b \times b}$, a 2-D matrix of order b that represents the combinatorial frequency of the pairs $(f1(v_x), f2(v_x)), \forall v_x \in V$. The matrix indexes are the bins of each measure, thus $i \in [\min(\varphi_{b,f1}), \max(\varphi_{b,f1})]$ and $j \in [\min(\varphi_{b,f2}), \max(\varphi_{b,f2})]$. In other words, each cell $\varphi_{b,f1,f2}(i,j)$ represents the normalized occurrence (frequency) of nodes with measures $f1(v_x) = i$ and $f2(v_x) = j$

$$\varphi_{b,f1,f2}(i,j) = \frac{1}{n} \sum_{\forall v_x \in V} \delta(f1(v_x), i)\delta(f2(v_x), j). \tag{6}$$

The proposed matrix $\varphi_{b,f1,f2}$ can be built using any given pair of complex network local measures. By considering more than two measures, it is possible to obtain different matrices. For instance, using 3 measures $f1$, $f2$, and $f3$, it is possible to obtain matrices $\varphi_{f1,2}$, $\varphi_{f1,3}$, and $\varphi_{f2,3}$. This allows us to stack-up them to compose a 2-D or 3-D matrix $\varphi_{f1,f2,f3}$. When concatenating the three matrices, the resulting feature representation is similar to traditional color images composed of $z = 3$ channels. This approach also allows matrices with a higher number of channels according to an order-2 combinatorial of m measures, thus $z = \frac{m!}{2!(m-2)!}$. Let us define the new matrix as Φ_z, according to the resulting number of matrices z obtained with a set of m complex network measures, and then we can also rewrite the 2-D matrix $\varphi_{f1,f2} = \Phi_1$. Later we will define the order to combine measures when constructing Φ_z (see Sect. 4.2). Therefore, given a set of m measures and a bin number b, we can obtain a complex network embedding (DTE) $\Phi_{b,z} \in \mathbb{R}^{b \times b \times z}$ as a stack of one or more 2-D matrices, as shown in Fig. 1(a).

The resulting complex network embeds $\Phi_{b,z}$ represents the network topology and is invariant to the number of nodes n, as we normalize the histograms. We name this technique as Deep Topological Embedding (DTE), as it may be built with different depths (z value), given sufficient topological measures. To visualize how the matrices $\Phi_{b,z}$ are spatially organized, we compute them for a set of known complex network models and convert the results into images by changing the real space to 8-bit pixel values; the results are shown in Fig. 1. These spatial patterns summarize the studied CN, a wide range of structural information mapped into a b-by-b-by-z space. The patterns show that the DTE changes when the CN's internal parameters change (k) but varies more when analyzing a different model. Thus, DTE is robust to within-class variations and can detect between-class differences.

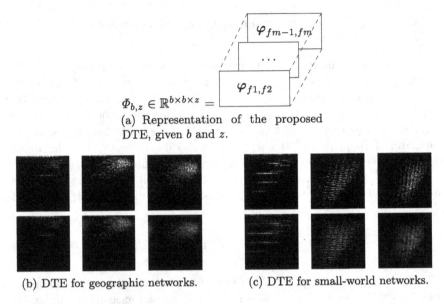

$$\Phi_{b,z} \in \mathbb{R}^{b \times b \times z} =$$

(a) Representation of the proposed DTE, given b and z.

(b) DTE for geographic networks.   (c) DTE for small-world networks.

Fig. 1. The structure of the proposed DTE method $\Phi_{b,z}$ (a). DTE representations are then obtained ($b = 56$) to different topological classes (b–c), with varying average degree (columns represent $k = 2, 10, 16$). The images (b–c) are obtained by normalizing the frequency values into 8-bit pixels (grayscale for $z = 1$, top row, and RGB for $z = 3$, bottom row).

3.2 Learning Complex Network Properties from DTE

Finally, we can employ the DTE representation $\Phi_{b,z}$, approached as an image, for pattern recognition through convolutional neural networks. Figure 2 shows the details of the deeper architecture we propose (5 convolutional and 4 fully-connected layers). We also consider a shallower model with 3 convolutional and 3 fully-connected layers, and two variants from these models: The "large" variant of each architecture uses double-layer width, e.g., instead the layer sizes $(8, 32, 128, 256)$ of the "shallow" model, the "shallow large" model uses $(16, 64, 256, 512)$. For the deep model, the thinner architecture uses half layer sizes of deep-large, i.e., $(8, 16, 32, 64, 128, 256, 128)$. In all cases, we flatten the output of the last convolutional layer using Global Average Pooling [15]. To mitigate overfitting, we apply a 50% dropout regularization [14] (a.k.a. dilution, randomly omitting half the weights) at the fully-connected layers during training.

3.3 DTE Computational Complexity

The computational cost for building DTEs $\Phi_{b,z}$ for a given network is directly related to the cost of the employed centrality measures f (which depends on the number of nodes n and edges m). For instance, one of the most costly centrality measures is the current flow betweenness CF_b, which has computational

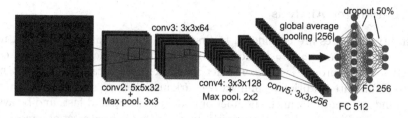

Fig. 2. The convolutional architecture proposed for complex network classification using DTE.

complexity $O(n^3 + mn \log n)$ for its complete solution in the worst-case. On the other hand, the clustering coefficient c of nodes in a non-complete network with average degree $\sqrt{n}$ can be computed with cost $O(n^2)$. We will not discuss in depth the complexity of each centrality measure here, as it is outside the scope of our work (the reader may refer to the references). Let us refer to the cost of computing a given centrality measure f as $O(f)$. The cost for computing the joint frequency is negligible compared to $O(f)$, regardless of b, as it only requires that each vertex is visited to check its measures ($O(n)$, or $O(1)$ if done together with the measure's calculation). Thus b has no impact on the overall computational cost and can be ignored. As the dimension of $\Phi_{b,z}$ increases with additional measures (increasing z), we can define the final complexity by $O(fz)$. If we consider that $z<<n$, we can simply consider the complexity as $O(f)$. In other words, the complexity is limited by the chosen measure with the highest cost, i.e., in our study, it would be the current flow betweenness CF_b with $O(n^3 + mn \log n)$. Nevertheless, it is important to stress that although b and z have minimal impacts on the cost of building the DTE, the size of the final embedding impacts directly the CNN training and predicting costs, so smaller values are preferable.

4 Experiments and Results

4.1 Datasets

To validate our approach, we considered the datasets proposed in [18] composed of complex network models with varying parameters. The 4-models (4 classes) dataset comprises complex networks generated according to the following models: 1) random, small-world, scale-free, and geographical. Network sizes (number of nodes) vary between $[500, 2000]$, and the average degree $<k> = 4, 6, 8, 10, 12, 14, 16$, with 400 samples for each configuration, totalling 11200 samples. 4-models + k is an extension of the previous dataset, where the goal is to classify both the network model and average degree; therefore, there are 28 classes (4 models and 7 degrees). The scale-free (5 classes) dataset consists of 5 different specific models of only scale-free networks, with both linear and nonlinear preferential attachment. All networks have 1000 nodes and $<k> = 8$, in a total of 500 samples (100 per class).

4.2 Parameter Analysis

Centrality measures are considered to first build a 1-dimensional complex network representation $|\varphi_f| = b$ (Eq. 5). For choosing specific measures, we considered a set of properties to construct network representations: the measure must discriminate traditional complex network models (e.g., scale-free and small-world) independently from the number of nodes, be computed fast, and be available in known libraries. We then empirically tested and chose a set of 5 measures that satisfy these premises. They are imported from the NetworkX 2.4 library[1] [12], which is one of the most complete and diffused code implementations for network analysis. In the following, we give specific details on the use of each measure:

- **Local clustering (c)**: Traditional clustering coefficient.
- **Eigenvector centrality (ev)**: This measure is calculated using a maximum of 100 iterations and an error tolerance of 10^{-6}.
- **Current flow betweenness (CF_b)**: We employ an approximation technique [5], using a limited number of source-target pairs of at most 10^4 choices and error tolerance of 0.6.
- **Current flow closeness (CF_c)**: The complete solution is considered.
- **Subgraph centrality (sc)**: Computed considering all closed walks of all lengths.

   Our first experiment seeks to highlight the impact of the bin size (b). To build feature vectors $\varphi_{b,f}$, we calculated the local clustering measure $f = c$ with bin sizes $b = [14, 28, 56, 121, 224]$. We then couple this approach to a fully-connected neural network (MLP). We use a 4-layers deep architecture, with 2 hidden layers of 128 and 64 neurons, Glorot Normal initialization, ReLU activation function, and 30% dropout. They are trained using SGD with a learning rate 10^{-2} and Nesterov momentum 0.9, optimizing a categorical cross-entropy loss function (output layer equals the number of classes). The model was trained for 150 epochs, using batches of size 128. The validation consists of 10 repetitions of a stratified 10-fold cross-validation approach (total of 100 iterations). We considered the 4-models + k dataset, divided into training, validation, and test independent sets with proportions of 80%, 10%, and 10%, respectively. We performed a z-score normalization on each of the three sets individually. After training, we selected the weights that produce the best validation accuracy to be applied on the test samples. We then measured the neural network accuracy average and standard deviation over the cross-validation iterations. Figure 3 shows the results throughout the training epochs for each different bin size. From the figure, we can see that $b = 112$ and $b = 224$ yielded the best results within each other's error margins. Therefore, we consider $b = 112$ as the best approach, as it needs half the precision of $b = 224$.

   The next experiment focuses on each measure (f), using the same experimental protocol as the previous experiment, aside from the fixed bin size $b = 112$.

---

[1] https://networkx.org/documentation/networkx-2.4/.

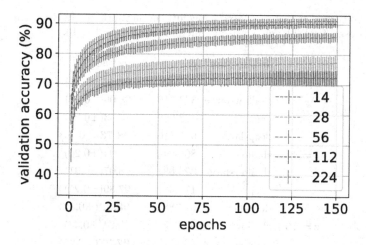

Fig. 3. MLP validation accuracy by epoch on complex network classification using different bin sizes b and $f = c$.

Table 1. MLP performance for different complex network topological measures using $b = 112$.

f	train acc.	test acc.
c	92.03($\pm$0.32)	90.08($\pm$0.19)
CF_c	78.15($\pm$0.43)	74.03($\pm$0.26)
ev	52.76($\pm$0.47)	47.95($\pm$0.46)
CF_b	48.43($\pm$0.50)	42.57($\pm$0.66)
sc	42.80($\pm$0.51)	35.13($\pm$0.42)

The results are shown in Table 1, where we can notice that the clustering coefficient yields the best results, while the worst is the subgraph centrality. The small difference between train and test accuracy indicates that the approach can learn topological patterns without overfitting. We then use these results for ranking the best measures for constructing our DTE ($\Phi_{b,z}$).

To analyze the proposed DTE ($\Phi_{b,z}$), we consider $b = 112$ and vary the parameter z, which determines the depth of the obtained features. In this context: $z = 1$ implies using the two best measures (c and CF_c, thus $m = 2$); $z = 3$ considers the top three measures ($m = 3$); and $z = 10$ all the five measures ($m = 5$). The CNN models are trained with SGD, learning rate 10^{-3}, Nesterov momentum 0.9, and 100 epochs with batch size 32. The remaining experimental protocol is the same as the previous experiment. The classification results are given in Table 2, along with the total number of parameters of each model. The highest results are achieved with the deep-large model using $\Phi_{112,z=1}$. Another insight here is each model's particularity; for instance, using $\Phi_{112,z=3}$, the shallow approach achieves 0.79% lower accuracy while compared to deep-large. Still, it uses only 13% of its number of parameters.

Table 2. Accuracy of each proposed convolutional network on the 4-models + k (28 classes) dataset, for DTEs $\Phi_{112,z}$ using different depths $z = 1, 3, 10$.

	architecture	parameters	test acc.
$z = 1$	shallow	85,740	97.36($\pm$1.14)
	shallow-large	323,516	98.06($\pm$0.47)
	deep	172,668	98.53($\pm$0.20)
	deep-large	676,316	**98.73($\pm$0.16)**
$z = 3$	shallow	86,524	97.94($\pm$0.26)
	shallow-large	325,084	98.07($\pm$0.31)
	deep	173,452	97.89($\pm$0.21)
	deep-large	677,884	**98.39($\pm$0.12)**
$z = 10$	shallow	89,268	97.24($\pm$0.46)
	shallow-large	330,572	**97.97($\pm$0.25)**
	deep	176,196	96.31($\pm$0.48)
	deep-large	683,372	97.40($\pm$0.28)

4.3 Literature Comparison

Finally, we compare the proposed deep-large ($\Phi_{112,1}$) and shallow ($\Phi_{112,3}$) models with the available literature results on all datasets. We considered the method Life-Like Network Automata Descriptor (LLNA) [18], LLNA-BP [22] and network descriptors composed of global centrality measures as a baseline approach (as in [22]). Table 3 shows the obtained results, where we can notice that the proposed methods overcome the compared approaches. The deep-large architecture achieves the highest accuracy in all datasets. The shallow architecture alone also achieves significant performance while using a smaller hyperparameter number.

Table 3. Comparison of methods classification performance on the studied complex network datasets.

dataset	proposed DTE + CNN		literature		
	deep-large	shallow	LLNA-BP	LLNA	centrality
4 models	100.0($\pm$0.00)	100.0($\pm$0.00)	100.0($\pm$0.00)	99.99($\pm$0.00)	100.0($\pm$0.00)
4 models + k	**98.73($\pm$0.16)**	97.94($\pm$0.26)	98.31($\pm$0.02)	90.76($\pm$0.07)	60.20($\pm$0.20)
scale-free	**100.0($\pm$0.00)**	99.96($\pm$0.12)	99.52($\pm$0.19)	98.30($\pm$0.20)	96.20($\pm$0.04)

5 Conclusion

We proposed a technique for classifying complex networks using CNNs. Our method uses network embedding called Deep Topological Embedding (DTE) that combines centrality measures and deep convolutional neural networks.

When compared to other classification methods, ours achieved high-classification accuracy and produced promising results when using DTE with both deeper or shallow CNNs. These results show that the proposed DTEs contain rich topological information suitable for complex network characterization, regardless of the employed neural architecture. This flexibility is a desirable feature as it allows for low computational costs when deploying the method to various applications.

For future works, we plan to test our method on different and deeper CNN architectures as well as analyze whether knowledge learned from synthetic data could be transferred to real-world networks.

Acknowledgments. L. Scabini and L. C. Ribas acknowledge support from FAPESP (grants #2019/07811-0, #2021/09163-6, and #2016/23763-8). O. M. Bruno acknowledges support from CNPq (Grant #307897/2018-4) and FAPESP (grants #2014/08026-1 and 2016/18809-9). The authors are also grateful to the NVIDIA GPU Grant Program.

References

1. Banerjee, A., Jost, J.: Spectral plot properties: towards a qualitative classification of networks. Netw. Heterogen. Media **3**(2), 395 (2008)
2. Barabási, A.L.: Network Science. Cambridge University Press, Cambridge (2016)
3. Barabási, A.L., Albert, R.: Emergence of scaling in random networks. Science **286**(5439), 509–512 (1999)
4. Bonacich, P.: Power and centrality: a family of measures. Am. J. Sociol. **92**(5), 1170–1182 (1987)
5. Brandes, U., Fleischer, D.: Centrality measures based on current flow. In: Diekert, V., Durand, B. (eds.) STACS 2005. LNCS, vol. 3404, pp. 533–544. Springer, Heidelberg (2005). https://doi.org/10.1007/978-3-540-31856-9_44
6. Bronstein, M.M., Bruna, J., LeCun, Y., Szlam, A., Vandergheynst, P.: Geometric deep learning: going beyond Euclidean data. IEEE Sig. Process. Mag. **34**(4), 18–42 (2017)
7. Costa, L.F., Rodrigues, F.A., Travieso, G., Villas Boas, P.R.: Characterization of complex networks: a survey of measurements. Adv. Phys. **56**(1), 167–242 (2007)
8. Dorogovtsev, S.N., Mendes, J.F.: Evolution of networks. Adv. Phys. **51**(4), 1079–1187 (2002)
9. Estrada, E., Rodriguez-Velazquez, J.A.: Subgraph centrality in complex networks. Phys. Rev. E **71**(5), 056103 (2005)
10. Glorot, X., Bengio, Y.: Understanding the difficulty of training deep feedforward neural networks. In: International Conference on Artificial Intelligence and Statistics, pp. 249–256 (2010)
11. Glorot, X., Bordes, A., Bengio, Y.: Deep sparse rectifier neural networks. In: International Conference on Artificial Intelligence and Statistics, pp. 315–323 (2011)
12. Hagberg, A., Swart, P., S Chult, D.: Exploring network structure, dynamics, and function using networkX. Technical report, Los Alamos National Lab. (LANL), Los Alamos, NM (United States) (2008)
13. Kipf, T.N., Welling, M.: Semi-supervised classification with graph convolutional networks. arXiv preprint arXiv:1609.02907 (2016)

14. Krizhevsky, A., Sutskever, I., Hinton, G.E.: ImageNet classification with deep convolutional neural networks. In: Advances in Neural Information Processing Systems, pp. 1097–1105 (2012)
15. Lin, M., Chen, Q., Yan, S.: Network in network. arXiv preprint arXiv:1312.4400 (2013)
16. Liu, C., Wu, X., Niu, R., Wu, X., Fan, R.: A new SAIR model on complex networks for analysing the 2019 novel coronavirus (COVID-19). Nonlinear Dyn. **101**(3), 1777–1787 (2020)
17. Machicao, J., Corrêa, E.A., Jr., Miranda, G.H., Amancio, D.R., Bruno, O.M.: Authorship attribution based on Life-Like Network Automata. PLoS ONE **13**(3), e0193703 (2018)
18. Miranda, G.H.B., Machicao, J., Bruno, O.M.: Exploring spatio-temporal dynamics of cellular automata for pattern recognition in networks. Sci. Rep. **6**, 37329 (2016)
19. Najafabadi, M.M., Villanustre, F., Khoshgoftaar, T.M., Seliya, N., Wald, R., Muharemagic, E.: Deep learning applications and challenges in big data analytics. J. Big Data **2**(1), 1–21 (2015). https://doi.org/10.1186/s40537-014-0007-7
20. Oliveira, M., Ribeiro, E., Bastos-Filho, C., Menezes, R.: Spatio-temporal variations in the urban rhythm: the travelling waves of crime. EPJ Data Sci. **7**(1), 29 (2018). https://doi.org/10.1140/epjds/s13688-018-0158-4
21. Perozzi, B., Al-Rfou, R., Skiena, S.: DeepWalk: online learning of social representations. In: Proceedings of the 20th ACM SIGKDD International Conference on Knowledge Discovery and Data Mining, pp. 701–710. ACM (2014)
22. Ribas, L.C., Machicao, J., Bruno, O.M.: Life-Like Network Automata descriptor based on binary patterns for network classification. Inf. Sci. **515**, 156–168 (2020)
23. Rubinov, M., Sporns, O.: Complex network measures of brain connectivity: uses and interpretations. Neuroimage **52**(3), 1059–1069 (2010)
24. Scabini, L.F., Condori, R.H., Gonçalves, W.N., Bruno, O.M.: Multilayer complex network descriptors for color-texture characterization. Inf. Sci. **491**, 30–47 (2019)
25. Scabini, L.F., Ribas, L.C., Neiva, M.B., Junior, A.G., Farfán, A.J., Bruno, O.M.: Social interaction layers in complex networks for the dynamical epidemic modeling of COVID-19 in Brazil. Phys. A Stat. Mech. Appl. **564**, 125498 (2020)
26. Scarselli, F., Gori, M., Tsoi, A.C., Hagenbuchner, M., Monfardini, G.: The graph neural network model. IEEE Trans. Neural Netw. **20**(1), 61–80 (2008)
27. Sutskever, I., Martens, J., Dahl, G., Hinton, G.: On the importance of initialization and momentum in deep learning. In: International Conference on Machine Learning, pp. 1139–1147 (2013)
28. Watts, D.J., Strogatz, S.H.: Collective dynamics of 'small-world' networks. Nature **393**(6684), 440–442 (1998)
29. Xin, R., Zhang, J., Shao, Y.: Complex network classification with convolutional neural network. Tsinghua Sci. Technol. **25**(4), 447–457 (2020)

Modularity-Based Backbone Extraction in Weighted Complex Networks

Stephany Rajeh[✉], Marinette Savonnet, Eric Leclercq, and Hocine Cherifi

Laboratoire d'Informatique de Bourgogne, University of Burgundy, Dijon, France
stephany.rajeh@u-bourgogne.fr

Abstract. The constantly growing size of real-world networks is a great challenge. Therefore, building a compact version of networks allowing their analyses is a must. Backbone extraction techniques are among the leading solutions to reduce network size while preserving its features. Coarse-graining merges similar nodes to reduce the network size, while filter-based methods remove nodes or edges according to a specific statistical property. Since community structure is ubiquitous in real-world networks, preserving it in the backbone extraction process is of prime interest. To this end, we propose a filter-based method. The so-called "modularity vitality backbone" removes nodes with the lower contribution to the network's modularity. Experimental results show that the proposed strategy outperforms the "overlapping nodes ego backbone" and the "overlapping nodes and hub backbone." These two backbone extraction processes recently introduced have proved their efficacy to preserve better the information of the original network than the popular disparity filter.

Keywords: Backbone · Modular structure · Modularity · Weighted networks

1 Introduction

Complex networks, such as communication, biological, transportation, and contact networks, are widely analyzed. The daily production of data results in tremendously large real-world networks. Consequently, the analysis of such networks containing millions of nodes and billions of edges is more and more challenging, if not impossible, due to memory and time constraints. Thus, suitable extraction of the pertinent nodes and edges that preserve the essential information while reducing the size of the network is fundamental. Network backbones offer a way to do so. Two main research paths tackle this problem: coarse-grain backbones or filter-based backbones. In the former, one clusters together nodes sharing similarities to reduce the network size [1,2]. In the latter, one removes nodes or edges from the network based on a given property [3,4]. The community structure is one of the significant properties in real-world networks. Indeed, it heavily determines their dynamics and their underlying functionalities [5]. It

© Springer Nature Switzerland AG 2022
P. Ribeiro et al. (Eds.): NetSci-X 2022, LNCS 13197, pp. 67–79, 2022.
https://doi.org/10.1007/978-3-030-97240-0_6

is generally illustrated by dense regions of connected nodes that barely connect from one region to another. Communities can be non-overlapping or overlapping [6], hierarchical [7], and attributed [8]. Community detection is one of the most prolific research areas in network science. It relies on numerous measures quantifying the quality of the community structure. Modularity is among the most popular[9]. It compares the density of connections of the uncovered community structure with a similar random network. The higher the modularity, the higher the confidence in the tight community structure of the network.

Recent works have shown that one can exploit the community structure efficiently to extract backbones [10,11]. Inspired by these works, we propose a filtering technique based on the preservation of the community structure of the network. It exploits the community structure using the concept of vitality. Vitality quantifies the contribution of a node to a given quality measure by removing this node and computing the variation of the quality measure. To assess its importance, we compute modularity as a quality measure, with and without the node in question. Then, one ranks the nodes from the lowest contribution on modularity to the highest. Subsequently, nodes with the lowest contribution are removed until one reaches the desired size of the network.

Comparative experimental evaluations are conducted on real-world weighted networks of different sizes and domains. The developed backbone extraction technique called "modularity vitality backbone" is compared with the recently introduced community-based method "overlapping nodes ego backbone" [10]. Results show that it is more effective in preserving the core information of the network and the community structure.

The main contributions of the paper summarize as follows:

- We propose a backbone filtering technique exploiting the community structure of networks.
- Experiments with weighted networks show that it outperforms another alternative measure.
- It can be easily adapted to any type of network (i.e., undirected, unweighted, and directed networks).

The remaining of the article is organized as follows. Section 2 discusses briefly the related works. Section 3 introduces the modularity vitality backbone. Sections 4 and 5 present respectively the datasets and the evaluation measures used in this study. Section 6 reports the results of the comparative evaluation. Section 7 discusses the results. Finally, Sect. 8 concludes the paper.

2   Related Works

Backbones offer an ideal solution to the trade-off between preserving essential information in the network and reducing the network size. Backbone extraction studies concerns mainly two types of networks: mono-mode networks [4,12,13] and bipartite networks [14–16]. In this work, we consider mono-mode networks.

Within this class of networks, there are two leading approaches for extracting backbones. The first is coarse-graining, and the second is filtering.

In coarse-graining methods, one group nodes with similar characteristics into a single node. For instance, authors in [17] merge the nodes based on random walks. In the work of [18], authors use the k-nearest neighbors algorithm (k-NN) to group similar nodes based on the nearest higher-density-neighbor.

In filter-based methods, the goal is to remove redundant information by pruning nodes or edges in the network. Redundancy is assessed based on a statistical property.

Most of the works reported in the literature concern edge-filtering techniques. Serrano et al. propose the disparity filter. It uses a null model of the edge weights to preserve statistically significant edges [19]. Authors in [20] compute the betweenness centrality of edges and remove the ones that don't exceed a specific threshold. Authors in [21] use a combination of local and global information to extract the backbone. More precisely, they use the link weights to build the h-strength graph and the betweenness centrality to build the h-bridge graph. Then one obtains the backbone by merging h-strength and h-bridge. Simas et al. [4] present the distance backbone based on the triangular organization of edges which preserves all shortest paths.

Node filtering techniques are less frequent. They rely on topological features to associate a score to the nodes. Nodes with the higher scores are then extracted [22,23]. In this line, in their recent work, Ghalmane et al. prune nodes based on the community structure characteristics of the network [10]. They propose two node-filtering techniques. The first one preserves the overlapping nodes and the hubs of the network. In contrast, the second conserves the overlapping nodes and their one-step neighbors to form the backbone. These two algorithms exhibit superior performances as compared to the popular disparity filter. These results illustrate the community structure's importance in preserving the core information in a network while reducing its size. Inspired by these findings, we propose the "modularity vitality backbone" algorithm. This node filtering technique also exploits the community structure of the network. It uses a measure of the node contribution to the modularity. Roughly speaking, nodes with the lowest contribution to the quality measure of the community structure are filtered. The remaining nodes form the backbone.

3   Modularity Vitality Backbone

This section presents the vitality concept. Then, we briefly discuss various mesoscopic quality measures. We explain why we choose Newman's modularity as a quality measure. Finally, the algorithm of the proposed backbone extractor is given.

Vitality Index. Let $G(V, E)$ be a simple and undirected graph where $V = \{v_1, v_2, ..., v_N\}$ is the set of nodes totaling $N = |V|$ and $E = \{(v_i, v_j)|v_i, v_j \in V\}$ is the set of edges. Denote $f(G)$ and $f(G \setminus \{u\})$ as two real-valued functions defined on the complete graph G and on graph $G \setminus \{u\}$ without node or edge u. Then, the vitality index is the difference between both functions, defined as $\nu(G, u) = f(G) - f(G \setminus \{u\})$. The resulting value is a signed value, indicating the positive or negative contribution of the node or edge u on graph G [24].

Mesoscopic Quality Measures. There are numerous quality measures to characterize communities [25–27]. Their goal is to answer how good is the community structure in a network. They use topological properties defined at the mesoscopic level. Let set $C = \{c_1, c_2, ..., c_l, ..., c_{n_c}\}$ represent $n_c = |C|$ communities of a graph G and $f(c_l)$ represents a quality function of community c_l. One can categorize the quality functions into three main groups:

1. Based on internal connectivity: such as internal density characterizing how densely connected the nodes are in a community compared to other communities.

2. Based on internal and external connectivity: such as Flake-ODF measuring the fraction of nodes in a community with fewer internal edges than external ones.

3. Based on a network model: such as Newman's modularity [9] which assesses the difference between the real connections in the community c_l and the random connections in the same community.

All of these quality functions characterize a single community. Hence, to quantify the quality of the overall community structure, one averages $f(c_l)$ over all the communities.

Newman's modularity is one of the most popular mesoscopic quality measures. Indeed, it is widely used in community detection algorithms as an optimization criterion [28–30]. This is the main reason why it is one of the well-accepted benchmarks for characterizing the community structure of the networks. Numerous extensions have also been proposed for modularity to account for networks with overlapping and hierarchical community structure [31]. In this work, we use Newman's modularity as a quality measure to assess the vitality of nodes due to the following reasons:

1. Modularity can naturally be extended to unweighted, undirected, and directed networks.

2. Modularity vitality ensures that nodes that are the main contributors to the community structure are retained, regardless of their type (i.e., hub- or bridge-like).

3. Previous works on modularity vitality centrality has proved to assign high scores to the most influential nodes [32].

Algorithm. The "modularity vitality backbone" is based on the vitality concept, where one can measure the contribution of a node or an edge using any quality measure computed on graphs. We use Newman's modularity as a quality measure. Nonetheless, one can opt for other quality measures to quantify the node and edge influence.

Newman's modularity enables us to differentiate between highly internally connected nodes (hubs) and nodes at the borders of the communities (bridges). Indeed, hubs increase the internal density of the communities. Therefore, they contribute positively to modularity. In contrast, bridges increase the connections between the communities. Consequently, they tend to decrease the modularity. As we choose to give equal importance to both types of nodes, we rank the nodes according to the absolute value of their modularity vitality score. It allows keeping nodes with the highest contribution to modularity, regardless of their role (i.e., hub nodes or bridge nodes). Then, one removes the nodes that barely contribute to modularity. The backbone extraction procedure is given in Algorithm 1.

Algorithm 1: Modularity Vitality Backbone Extraction

Input: Graph $G(V, E)$, Community set: $C = \{c_1, c_2, ..., c_{n_c}\}$, Size s
Output: Pruned graph $\hat{G}(\hat{V}, \hat{E})$

1 $Q(G) \leftarrow Modularity(G, C)$ // Computing modularity vitality of nodes
2 $D \leftarrow \varnothing$
3 **for** $v \in V$ **do**

4 $\qquad Q(G \setminus \{v\}) \leftarrow \sum_{c \in C} \left[\frac{|E_c^{in}| - |E_{v,c}^{in}|}{|E| - |E_v|} - \left(\frac{2(|E_c^{in}| - |E_{v,c}^{in}|) + (|E_c^{out}| - |E_{v,c}^{out}|)}{2(|E| - |E_v|)} \right)^2 \right]$

5 $\qquad \alpha(v) \leftarrow Q(G) - Q(G \setminus \{v\})$
6 $\qquad D[v] = |\alpha(v)|$

7 $D \leftarrow sort(D)$
8 **while** $|V| > s$ **do**
9 $\qquad \eta \leftarrow D.pop(v)$ // Extracting the backbone
10 $\qquad G \leftarrow G \setminus \eta$
11 $\qquad V \leftarrow V \setminus \eta$
12 $\qquad$ **if** G *is disconnected* **then**
13 $\qquad\qquad G \leftarrow LCC(G)$

Note that the vitality computation is not naively computed two times for each node. In such a case, the complexity can rapidly become prohibitive. Indeed, one computes instead the modularity variation reducing the computation's complexity to $O(|E| + Nn_c)$. It makes the vitality measure suitable for large-scale weighted networks. We also note that the symbol $|E|$ is extended to weighted networks.

4 Datasets

We use a set of seven real-world networks originating from various domains (social, collaborative, ecological, and technological) in the experiments. The nodes and edges range from hundreds to thousands. We choose to integrate small networks in the experiments in order to get a better understanding on the filtering process. Table 1 presents their basic topological characteristics. All the networks are freely available online[12]. As there is no ground truth available, we rely on the Louvain community detection algorithm to uncover their community structure [30].

1. Zachary's Karate Club: Nodes are members of a karate club and are connected if they are friends inside and outside the club. Edges are weighted by the relative interactions occurring between the members.

2. Wind Surfers: Nodes are windsurfers in southern California in the fall of 1986. They are connected if they're friends. Edges are weighted based on the social closeness of the surfers to one another.

3. Madrid Train Bombing: Nodes are terrorists in the train bombing of March 11, 2004, in Madrid. Edges represent contacts between the terrorists and are weighted based on the strength of their underlying relationship.

4. Les Misérables: Nodes are the characters in the novel "Les Misérables." Edges represent characters' co-appearances in the same chapter. They are weighted by the number of co-appearances.

5. Wiki Science: Nodes are either applied, formal, natural, or social sciences Wikipedia pages. They're weighted by the cosine similarity between them.

6. Unicode Languages: A bipartite network representing languages and countries. Weights represent the fraction of people in a given country having the literacy (reading and writing) of a specific language.

7. Scientific Collaboration: Nodes are authors of articles in the "Condensed Matter" category of arXiv. Edges represent co-authorship and are weighted by the number of joint papers among the authors.

Table 1. Basic topological properties of the real-world networks under study. N is the number of nodes. $|E|$ is the number of edges. $<k>$ is the average weighted degree. ω is the density. ζ is the transitivity. $k_{nn}(k)$ is the assortativity. ϵ is the efficiency. Q is the weighted modularity of the network.

Network	N	$|E|$	$<k>$	ω	ζ	$k_{nn}(k)$	ϵ	Q
Zachary's Karate Club	33	77	13.59	0.139	0.256	−0.476	0.492	0.444
Wind Surfers	43	336	56.09	0.372	0.564	−0.147	0.679	0.371
Madrid Train Bombing	62	243	8.81	0.121	0.561	0.029	0.448	0.435
Les Misérables	77	254	21.30	0.087	0.499	−0.165	0.435	0.565
Wiki Science	687	6,523	7.35	0.028	0.469	0.244	0.323	0.631
Unicode Languages	868	1,255	0.697	0.003	0.00	−0.171	0.255	0.772
Scientific Collaboration	16,726	47,594	9.23	0.0003	0.360	0.185	0.117	0.873

[1] Aaron Clauset, Ellen Tucker, and Matthias Sainz, "The Colorado Index of Complex Networks." https://icon.colorado.edu/ (2016).

[2] Tiago P. Peixoto, "The Netzschleuder network catalogue and repository," https://networks.skewed.de/ (2020).

5   Evaluation Measures

We compare the effectiveness of the proposed backbone extraction technique and the "overlapping nodes ego backbone" based on four different evaluation measures classically used.

1. Average weighted degree: The weighted degree of a node is the sum of the weights of all the edges connected to it. Hence, a higher average weighted degree backbone means that important nodes are kept in the graph, reflecting its connectedness. It is defined as follows:

$$<k> = \frac{1}{N} \sum_{i=1}^{N} k_i = \sum_{j \in \mathcal{N}(1)} w_{ij} \tag{1}$$

where $\mathcal{N}(1)$ is the first-order neighborhood of node i.

2. Average link weight: Links in the backbone preserve the information flow of the network. In other words, the higher the value of the links, the better the backbone in maintaining the core information of the graph. It is defined as follows:

$$<w> = \frac{1}{N} \sum_{i,j \in V} w_{ij} \tag{2}$$

3. Average betweenness: Nodes with higher betweenness can disseminate information quickly. Hence, a backbone with higher average betweenness indicates that the speed of information dissemination is barely altered. It is defined as follows:

$$<b> = \frac{1}{N} \sum_{i=1}^{N} b_i = \sum_{i \neq s \neq t} \frac{\sigma_{s,t}^{i}}{\sigma_{s,t}} \tag{3}$$

where $\sigma_{s,t}$ denotes the number of shortest paths between nodes s and t and $\sigma_{s,t}^{i}$ denotes the number of shortest paths between nodes s and t passing through node i.

4. Weighted modularity: Modularity assesses the quality of the community structure based on the difference between the actual and the expected fraction of edges in the communities. A backbone with higher modularity suggests that the community structure is less altered. It can be computed on unweighted and weighted networks [33]. It is defined as follows:

$$Q = \frac{1}{2|E|} \sum_{i,j} \left[A_{ij} - \frac{w_i w_j}{\sum_{i,j} w_{ij}} \right] \delta(c_i, c_j) \tag{4}$$

where A_{ij} is the weighted adjacency matrix of graph G and $\delta(c_i, c_j)$ equals 1 if nodes i and j belong to the same community, otherwise it equals 0.

6   Experimental Results

The effectiveness of "modularity vitality backbone" is compared with another community-aware backbone extraction technique recently introduced [10]. The authors propose two backbones in their work, namely "overlapping nodes ego backbone" and "overlapping nodes and hubs backbone." In their comparative evaluation, they show that both techniques perform favorably compared to the popular disparity filter.

Therefore, in this work, we restrict our comparison to the most effective: overlapping nodes ego backbone. Table 2 reports the experimental results for seven real-world networks under study. The backbones quality measures are the average weighted degree ($<k>$), the average link weight ($<w>$), the average betweenness ($<b>$), and the weighted modularity (Q). As in their paper, we fix the backbone size to 30% of the original network.

Let's first discuss the average weighted degree. The higher its value, the better the backbone is in keeping the salient nodes maintaining its connectedness. Table 2 reports that the modularity vitality backbone outperforms overlapping nodes ego backbone in all of the networks under study. Moreover, the difference ranges from very small magnitudes to orders of magnitude higher. For example, in Wiki Science, the average weighted degree in the modularity vitality backbone is eleven times higher than the "overlapping nodes ego backbone." On the contrary, in Scientific Collaboration, the difference is barely noticeable (0.02).

Let's turn to average link weight. The average link weight characterizes the relevance of the links kept in a backbone. Hence, the higher its value, the better the backbone is in preserving essential links. The results show that the modularity vitality backbone outperforms the overlapping nodes ego backbone in six out of the seven networks.

Now, we discuss the average betweenness. This measure indicates the amount of information flow that can pass through the nodes of a given backbone. The higher its value, the higher the efficiency of the backbone in information spreading. The modularity vitality backbone outperforms the overlapping nodes ego backbone in only one out of the seven networks. In Scientific Collaboration networks, their values are comparable. It indicates that the information spread within the modularity vitality backbone is not as efficient as overlapping nodes ego backbone. Note, however, that the differences between the two backbones are less pronounced.

Finally, we turn to weighted modularity. The higher the modularity of the backbone, the better the quality of its community structure. As reported in Table 2, the modularity vitality backbone outperforms the overlapping nodes ego backbone on all the networks under study. These results are not surprising. Indeed, the modularity vitality backbone prunes the nodes contributing less to the modularity of the network. Hence, it tends to preserve the modularity as pruning proceeds.

To summarize, the modularity vitality backbone exhibits a higher weighted modularity than the overlapping nodes ego backbone. It preserves essential nodes in the network (i.e., hubs and bridges), thus achieving a higher average weighted degree and average link weight. However, maintaining the community structure comes at a price of a lower average betweenness.

Table 2. The computed values for the average weighted degree ($<k>$), link weight ($<w>$), and betweenness ($<b>$) alongside the weighted modularity (Q) of the backbones with 30% of the initial size of the network. For brevity, MV stands for "modularity vitality backbone," and OE stands for "overlapping nodes ego backbone."

Network	$<k>$		$<w>$		$<b>$		Q	
	MV	OE	MV	OE	MV	OE	MV	OE
Zachary's Karate Club	**13.00**	8.40	**6.05**	4.07	0.12	**0.27**	**0.35**	0.32
Wind Surfers	**71.38**	35.08	**35.69**	17.54	0.11	**0.15**	**0.36**	0.32
Madrid Train Bombing	**8.53**	3.90	**4.26**	1.95	0.09	**0.14**	**0.38**	0.17
Les Misérables	**39.48**	19.08	**19.74**	9.54	0.08	**0.14**	**0.49**	0.48
Wiki Science	**10.16**	0.92	**5.08**	0.46	0.01	**0.08**	**0.73**	0.72
Unicode Languages	**1.46**	1.28	**0.73**	0.64	**0.03**	0.02	**0.79**	0.78
Scientific Collaboration	**17.22**	17.20	4.71	**8.60**	0.001	0.001	**0.81**	0.71

7 Discussion

The constant increase of real-world networks size has prompted researchers to design a smaller yet accurate representation of networks. This problem is tackled either with coarse-graining or filter-based methods. A recent work by Ghalmane et al. [10] has shown interest in exploiting the modular structure of the network to deal with this issue. Building on this finding, we propose a new backbone extractor, "modularity vitality backbone," that aims to preserve the quality of the community structure. Assigning a modularity vitality score to the nodes, it prunes those with a low contribution to the network's modularity.

We performed a comparative analysis with the recently introduced "overlapping nodes ego backbone. These investigations on a set of seven real-world networks from various domains are globally at the advantage of the proposed technique. After pruning 70% of the network, results show that the modularity vitality backbone maintains higher modularity than overlapping nodes ego backbone. This expected behavior comes with higher performance in terms of average node degree and average link weight. Nonetheless, information efficiency isn't guaranteed. Indeed, one can point out that in five out of seven networks, the modularity vitality backbone suffers from lower information efficiency.

It can be explained by how the modularity vitality backbone proceeds. Indeed, one removes nodes that barely affect modularity. Those nodes may have high betweenness, yet they do contribute much to the network's modular structure. If we consider the overlapping nodes ego backbone, it appears that nodes with high betweenness tend to be overlapping nodes or nodes near the overlaps. Consequently, they are preferred and kept in the backbone. Nonetheless, they may not contribute to the modularity of the network as other less influential nodes. Another distinction lies in the fact that the modularity vitality backbone doesn't remove edges with low weights. On average, it has a higher number of links compared to the overlapping nodes ego backbone. Thus, it is normal to have lower average betweenness values due to the existence of those edges that play a role in maintaining the network's modularity. In other words, they play a role in showing a clearly defined community structure.

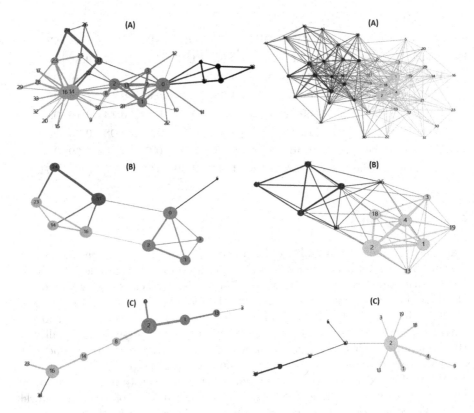

Fig. 1. The backbone extraction of two networks: Zachary Karate Club on the left and Wind Surfers on the right. (A) represents the original network. (B) represents the modularity vitality backbone. (C) represents the overlapping nodes ego backbone. The different colors of the nodes correspond to the various communities uncovered using the Louvain community detection algorithm. The size of the nodes is proportional to their weighted degree. The size of the edges is proportional to their edge weight.

To illustrate these differences, we refer to two small networks, namely Zachary Karate Club and Wind Surfers, given in Fig. 1. Let's discuss Zachary Karate Club first, represented on the left side of Fig. 1. One can point out that the modularity vitality backbone represented in (B) has a clique-like topology. In contrast, the overlapping nodes ego backbone reported in (C) exhibits a star-like structure. It is a good illustration of why the modularity vitality backbone has higher modularity while "overlapping nodes ego backbone" is characterized by higher information spreading efficiency. Moreover, one can note that the number of communities is the same as the original network using the proposed technique. In contrast, there are no more nodes from the green community in the overlapping nodes ego backbone. Diving deeper, the modularity vitality backbone keeps node 24 in the blue community and node 5 in the green community. They are discarded by overlapping nodes ego backbone and replaced by node 13 from the yellow community and node 8 from the red community. If we look at the modularity vitality and betweenness scores of these nodes, we find that nodes 24 and 5 have high modularity but low betweenness. In contrast, nodes 13 and 8 have high betweenness and low modularity vitality scores.

The Wind Surfers network exhibits similar behavior. Indeed, the modularity vitality backbone shows a clear clique-like structure while a star-like structure emerges in the "overlapping nodes ego backbone." Overall, the modularity vitality backbone integrates more peripherical nodes while the overlapping nodes ego backbone tends to retain more nodes at the core of the communities.

Note that the proposed backbone extraction process can also integrate a further step reducing the number of edges. One may consider several strategies to do so. For instance, one may remove the links based on their weights in each community, preserving its connectedness. Another approach is to use the disparity filter to prune these edges. Additionally, one may prune edges in proportion to the size of the edge set in each community of the original network. So doing allows better preservation of the original community structure. Additionally, preserving the nodes in the backbone according to the absolute value of the modularity vitality scores can be too brutal. One may integrate more information about the community structure, such as the community size, to better deal with the resolution limit issue [34].

8   Conclusion

Analyzing large-scale networks is essential to characterize their underlying topology and dynamics. However, the large size of networks hinders this process. Therefore, it is vital to remove redundant information from the network while keeping nodes and edges that preserve the relevant information. Backbones, whether coarse-grained or filter-based, tackle this problem.

Aware of the ubiquity of the modular structure of real-world networks, we propose a filter-based technique called "modularity vitality backbone." The proposed algorithm aims to preserve the network's modularity as nodes are removed. This enables researchers to conduct studies on networks with smaller sizes yet maintain their dense regions, which in turn represent the main building blocks of the network. The proposed method extracts the backbone of real-world weighted networks after quantifying the contribution of the nodes to the overall modularity of the network. Based on these scores, one prunes the nodes that barely contribute to the network's modularity until one reaches the desired size of the backbone.

Experiments show that the modularity vitality backbone compares favorably with its alternative in terms of weighted modularity, average weighted degree, and average link weight. However, it doesn't necessarily keep the nodes contributing to the efficiency of information spreading. Instead, it preserves the nodes and their edges that strategically contribute to the modularity of the network. These results pave the way to developing a filtering backbone extractor dedicated to optimizing several quality measures simultaneously using the vitality framework.

In the short term, we plan to extend this preliminary work in various directions. Since modularity has known drawbacks, we plan to evaluate alternative mesoscopic quality measures. Moreover, we will develop the analysis using multiple mesoscopic and macroscopic evaluation measures. Additionally, we aim to investigate the influence of community detection algorithms on the backbone extraction process.

References

1. Zeng, A., Lü, L.: Coarse graining for synchronization in directed networks. Phys. Rev. E **83**(5), 056123 (2011)
2. Zeng, L., Jia, Z., Wang, Y.: A new spectral coarse-graining algorithm based on k-means clustering in complex networks. Mod. Phys. Lett. B **33**(01), 1850421 (2019)
3. Coscia, M., Neffke, F.: Network backboning with noisy data. In: International Conference on Data Engineering (ICDE) (2017)
4. Simas, T., Correia, R.B., Rocha, L.M.: The distance backbone of complex networks. J. Complex Netw. **9**(6), cnab021 (2021)
5. Boccaletti, S., Latora, V., Moreno, Y., Chavez, M., Hwang, D.-U.: Complex networks: structure and dynamics. Phys. Rep. **424**(4–5), 175–308 (2006)
6. Jebabli, M., Cherifi, H., Cherifi, C., Hamouda, A.: Community detection algorithm evaluation with ground-truth data. Physica A Stat. Mech. Appl. **492**, 651–706 (2018)
7. Peel, L., Schaub, M.T.: Detectability of hierarchical communities in networks. arXiv preprint arXiv:2009.07525 (2020)
8. Atzmueller, M., Günnemann, S., Zimmermann, A.: Mining communities and their descriptions on attributed graphs: a survey. Data Min. Knowl. Disc. **35**(3), 661–687 (2021). https://doi.org/10.1007/s10618-021-00741-z
9. Newman, M.E.J.: Modularity and community structure in networks. Proc. Natl. Acad. Sci. **103**(23), 8577–8582 (2006)
10. Ghalmane, Z., Cherifi, C., Cherifi, H., El Hassouni, M.: Extracting backbones in weighted modular complex networks. Sci. Rep. **10**(1), 1–18 (2020)
11. Ghalmane, Z., Cherifi, C., Cherifi, H., El Hassouni, M.: Extracting modular-based backbones in weighted networks. Inf. Sci. **576**, 454–474 (2021)
12. Van Den Heuvel, M.P., Kahn, R.S., Goñi, J., Sporns, O.: High-cost, high-capacity backbone for global brain communication. Proc. Natl. Acad. Sci. **109**(28), 11372–11377 (2012)
13. Cao, J., Ding, C., Shi, B.: Motif-based functional backbone extraction of complex networks. Physica A Stat. Mech. Appl. **526**, 121123 (2019)
14. Katharina Anna Zweig and Michael Kaufmann: A systematic approach to the one-mode projection of bipartite graphs. Soc. Netw. Anal. Min. **1**(3), 187–218 (2011)
15. Neal, Z.: Identifying statistically significant edges in one-mode projections. Soc. Netw. Anal. Min. **3**(4), 915–924 (2013). https://doi.org/10.1007/s13278-013-0107-y
16. Neal, Z.: The backbone of bipartite projections: inferring relationships from co-authorship, co-sponsorship, co-attendance and other co-behaviors. Soc. Netw. **39**, 84–97 (2014)

17. Gfeller, D., De Los Rios, P.: Spectral coarse graining of complex networks. Phys. Rev. Lett. **99**(3), 038701 (2007)
18. Chen, M., Li, L., Wang, B., Cheng, J., Pan, L., Chen, X.: Effectively clustering by finding density backbone based-on KNN. Pattern Recogn. **60**, 486–498 (2016)
19. Serrano, M.Á., Boguná, M., Vespignani, A.: Extracting the multiscale backbone of complex weighted networks. Proc. Natl. Acad. Sci. **106**(16), 6483–6488 (2009)
20. Goh, K.-I., Salvi, G., Kahng, B., Kim, D.: Skeleton and fractal scaling in complex networks. Phys. Rev. Lett. **96**(1), 018701 (2006)
21. Zhang, R.J., Stanley, H.E., Fred, Y.Y.: Extracting h-backbone as a core structure in weighted networks. Sci. Rep. **8**(1), 1–7 (2018)
22. Dai, L., Derudder, B., Liu, X.: Transport network backbone extraction: a comparison of techniques. J. Transp. Geogr. **69**, 271–281 (2018)
23. Malang, K., Wang, S., Lv, Y., Phaphuangwittayakul, A.: Skeleton network extraction and analysis on bicycle sharing networks. Int. J. Data Warehouse. Min. (IJDWM) **16**(3), 146–167 (2020)
24. Koschützki, D., Lehmann, K.A., Peeters, L., Richter, S., Tenfelde-Podehl, D., Zlotowski, O.: Centrality indices. In: Brandes, U., Erlebach, T. (eds.) Network Analysis. LNCS, vol. 3418, pp. 16–61. Springer, Heidelberg (2005). https://doi.org/10. 1007/978-3-540-31955-9_3
25. Yang, J., Leskovec, J.: Defining and evaluating network communities based on ground-truth. Knowl. Inf. Syst. **42**(1), 181–213 (2013). https://doi.org/10.1007/ s10115-013-0693-z
26. Leskovec, J., Lang, K.J., Mahoney, M.: Empirical comparison of algorithms for network community detection. In: Proceedings of the 19th International Conference on World Wide Web, pp. 631–640 (2010)
27. Rajeh, S., Savonnet, M., Leclercq, E., Cherifi, H.: Characterizing the interactions between classical and community-aware centrality measures in complex networks. Sci. Rep. **11**(1), 1–15 (2021)
28. Clauset, A., Newman, M.E.J., Moore, C.: Finding community structure in very large networks. Phys. Rev. E **70**(6), 066111 (2004)
29. Brandes, U., et al.: On modularity clustering. IEEE Trans. Knowl. Data Eng. **20**(2), 172–188 (2007)
30. Blondel, V.D., Guillaume, J.-L., Lambiotte, R., Lefebvre, E.: Fast unfolding of communities in large networks. J. Stat. Mech. Theor. Exp. **2008**(10), P10008 (2008)
31. Chen, M., Szymanski, B.K.: Fuzzy overlapping community quality metrics. Soc. Netw. Anal. Min. **5**(1), 1–14 (2015). https://doi.org/10.1007/s13278-015-0279-8
32. Magelinski, T., Bartulovic, M., Carley, K.M.: Measuring node contribution to community structure with modularity vitality. IEEE Trans. Netw. Sci. Eng. **8**(1), 707–723 (2021)
33. Newman, M.E.J.: Analysis of weighted networks. Phys. Rev. E **70**(5), 056131 (2004)
34. Fortunato, S., Barthelemy, M.: Resolution limit in community detection. Proc. Nat. Acad. Sci. **104**(1), 36–41 (2007)

Vessel Destination Prediction Using a Graph-Based Machine Learning Model

Racha Gouareb[1], Francois Can[2], Sohrab Ferdowsi[1,3],
and Douglas Teodoro[1,3(✉)]

[1] University of Geneva, Geneva, Switzerland
{racha.gouareb,douglas.teodoro}@unige.ch
[2] Riverlake Shipping SA, Geneva, Switzerland
can@riverlake.ch
[3] HES-SO University of Applied Sciences and Arts of Western Switzerland,
Geneva, Switzerland
sohrab.ferdowsi@hesge.ch

Abstract. As the world's population continues to expand, maritime transport is critical to ensure economic growth. To improve security and safety of maritime transportation, the Automatic Identification System (AIS) collects real-time data about vessels and their positions. While a large portion of the AIS data is provided via an automatic tracking system, some key fields, such as destination and draught, are entered manually by the ship navigator and are thus prone to errors. To support decision making in maritime industries, in this paper we propose a data-driven vessel destination prediction algorithm based on heterogeneous graph and machine learning models. We design the task as a multi-class classification problem, where the destination port is the category to be predicted given the vessel and origin information. Then, we use a link prediction model in a weighted heterogeneous graph to predict the vessel destination. Experimental comparison against baseline methods, such as logistic regression and k-nearest neighbors, showed that our model provides a robust performance, outperforming the baseline algorithms by 9% and 33% in terms of accuracy and F1-score, respectively. Thus, heterogeneous graph models provide a powerful alternative to predict port destination, and could support enhancing AIS data quality and better decision making in maritime transportation industries.

Keywords: Destination prediction · Maritime transportation ·
Machine learning · Graph model · Link prediction · AIS ·
Heterogeneous graph

1 Introduction

Maritime shipping is one of the main pillars of freight transportation around the world. Due to its economic and environmental advantages, 90% of commodity shipment travels by the sea. With the expected world's population increase of 3.3 billion people by the end of the century [35], maritime traffic will continue

© Springer Nature Switzerland AG 2022
P. Ribeiro et al. (Eds.): NetSci-X 2022, LNCS 13197, pp. 80–93, 2022.
https://doi.org/10.1007/978-3-030-97240-0_7

to expand due to strong commodity needs. In turn, this expansion will lead to high transportation demand and increased traffic congestion, collisions, and accidents [18]. Thus, it is important to enhance available maritime data quality and explore different solutions for decision-making in the maritime industry.

The Automatic Identification System (AIS) is an automatic tracking system used by vessel traffic services and boats [19]. AIS uses a transceiver placed on ships to transmit their data. As of December 2004, installing AIS aboard vessels of a specific size and tonnage has become mandatory [20]. This regulation facilitated in the past two decades the collection of vessel information, including static data, such as vessel size, in addition to voyage information, such as position and destination. Since 2008, satellites equipped with receivers are able to receive AIS signals sent by the transceivers and easily collect AIS data [45]. By automatically sharing this information between ships and coastal authorities, the safety of ship management can be improved [4]. AIS information can be divided into three subcategories [1]. First, static data contain vessel-related information that defines the vessel's identity, such as MMSI and IMO, and are specified when the AIS system is installed on the ship. Second, navigational data, such as position coordinates, are transmitted automatically to track vessel movements every two to ten seconds, depending on the type and speed of the vessel. Finally, voyage data give general information about the voyage, including destination port, estimated time of arrival, and draught, and are entered manually before each journey.

The quality of AIS data can vary depending on the class of AIS equipment, that is, class A or class B. The choice of equipment is based on the type and size of vessels and the type of voyages a ship makes [43]. Despite its tabular format, AIS data is complex, requiring significant processing before it can be useful. For example, voyages' start and end flags are not readily available from the data. Moreover, due to technical failures, such as instability of the signal transmission rate, data transmission congestion [7], or environmental and human factors, it is estimated that as much as 80% of AIS messages contain errors [2,49], resulting in incorrect vessel name, Maritime Mobile Service Identity (MMSI) number, International Maritime Organization (IMO) number, position, and speed over ground [16], among others. Yang et al. [44] estimated that 40% of the data are wrongly entered on purpose or involuntarily, while Wu et al. [42] estimated that 62% of AIS destinations are mistaken and not always updated. For some ports, some studies showed that the accuracy of the reported destination information can be as low as 4% [27].

To improve the quality of AIS data and support maritime shipping decision-making, in this paper, we propose a link prediction algorithm in a heterogeneous graph model to address the problem of predicting voyage destinations using historical AIS data. Historical AIS data, such as latitude, longitude, and speed over ground (SOG), are used to construct the voyages. The resulting segments are used to create the navigation network, which is modeled as a heterogeneous graph and used to train and validate the prediction models. We defined the problem as a multi-label classification task. The algorithm's goal is to predict one of the destination ports from a pre-defined list extracted from the navigation network. Then, using the graph model, a link prediction algorithm is used to predict the next port for a vessel.

The remainder of the paper is divided into the following sections. Section 2 summarizes previous and most recent research work related to AIS data, including destination and trajectory predictions. Section 3 illustrates the data pre-processing and voyages creation process and describes the data and the proposed prediction models. Section 4 shows the results of prediction algorithms, followed by Sect. 5 that illustrates limitations and potential extensions of this work and concludes the study.

2   Related Work

Due to the high demand for shipping services [22], the development of maritime industries, and the increase in maritime traffic, accidents, and collisions [23], AIS data-driven solutions have received considerable attention from researchers. Thus, several studies were conducted to investigate research questions in the field of maritime traffic using historical AIS data. Examples of these studies include the detection of abnormal ship behavior [48], prediction of vessel trajectory [32, 47], data analysis, such as outlier detection [5] and collision risk analysis [29], and the application of machine learning algorithms [46] to improve the quality of AIS data and enhance the performance of handling maritime processes.

AIS data were used to develop various destination prediction models using both classic and deep learning-based machine learning approaches. Zhang et al. [46] used a random forest-based model supported by historical AIS data to create a destination prediction model based on similarities between trajectories. The data were labeled using a data clustering algorithm, the density-based spatial clustering of applications with noise method [14]. Their results showed better model accuracy when predicting cities rather than ports. Wang et al. [39] also used a random forest-based model combined with a port frequency-based decision strategy for destination prediction problems for ships. The authors highlighted different approaches used to pre-process and construct ship trajectories from raw AIS data and noise filtering methods, such as the average and Kalman filters and heuristic-based outlier detection methods. Lin et al. [24] used deep learning models for destination and arrival time prediction for different ship types. They proposed an incremental majority filter, which captures the most frequently predicted port instead of the last predicted one.

Artificial neural networks was applied to trajectory prediction using AIS data [25,33,37,38]. Chen et al. [7] highlighted the noise issue affecting the quality of AIS data and proposed a method to predict trajectories using neural networks. They followed a three-step pre-processing approach: i) organised the data, ii) removed outliers and iii) normalised the data into data samples using cubic spline interpolation and a moving average model. Their study is limited in the number of trajectories and vessels used to validate the results (only two). Zhang et al. [34] proposed an ensemble learning model for AIS trajectory prediction using a 200-segments sample from AIS data. They trained models on clusters of patterns to improve the prediction accuracy, where each cluster represents a boat trajectory. Similarly, Suo *et al.* [33] presented a real-time ship track prediction model using different recurrent neural network (RNN) architectures [13], focusing on the port of Zhangzhou in China. The authors showed that the vanilla RNN had similar accuracy to that of long short-term memory (LSTM) architecture [17], while the gated recurrent unit (GRU) [9] model outperformed the LSTM in terms of computational time. Wang *et al.* proposed a trajectory prediction model for multiple vessels simultaneously sharing the same area. The authors used a generative adversarial network with attention and interaction module [15]. They improved the accuracy compared to sequence to sequence, plain GAN, and the Kalman models by a minimum of 20%.

More recently, graph-based models have been proposed to improve predictive outcomes by representing data as a graph, such as the work in [26]. Carlini *et al.* [6] presented a network analysis using an AIS dataset to build a set of voyage graphs and capture the evolution of networks based on several topological features. Another example of a graph-based method is the work proposed by Magnusen *et al.* [26]. The authors represented the sea traffic in a graph, where vertices represent sea areas that can be a turning or staying point, and links are created by splitting a trajectory into several sub-trajectories. A port-to-port trajectory is described in this work by a sequence of vertices used to train a recurrent neural network model to predict destinations for oil tankers on both port and regional levels. The proposed model achieved 41% accuracy when predicting destination ports versus 87% predicting regions.

To the best of our knowledge, little attention has been given to heterogeneous graph methods for voyage destination prediction, despite being a powerful framework for modelling maritime navigation networks and capturing relations between heterogeneous entities, such as ports and vessels. Furthermore, the graph modelling approach allows the destination prediction task to be designed as a link prediction algorithm, which is also new and little explored.

3   Methods

This section describes the AIS data pre-processing, voyage creation algorithms, the voyage destination prediction model, and the evaluation approach. We modeled the destination prediction problem as a multi-classification problem to predict the destination port. Given a vessel, a departure port, and the list of destination ports available in the network, the algorithm predicts the most likely destination for the ship. We will first describe the cleaning, filtering, and organizing methods applied to AIS data. This process is critical, particularly as we cannot use the destination information found in AIS messages as a validation gold-standard [27,42]. Therefore, we propose a heuristic algorithm to create different voyages per vessel, and positional-based validated moored ports.

3.1 AIS Dataset

In our experiments, voyage segments were created using the publicly available historical AIS data from the Danish maritime authority website (www.dma.dk). This dataset covers the region around Danish waters. Nevertheless, destination ports can cover ports outside of the specified area. We have processed a snapshot from January 2014 until March 2021 containing around 10TB. However, for computational reasons, we are using a randomly generated sample containing 2757 tanker vessels, 58690 voyage samples, and 620 ports (see Table 1). We have focused on ships of type tankers due to their high rate of data completion and availability for most attributes.

Table 1. Statistics for the training and test sets.

	Training	Test
Number of vessels	2399	1713
Number of unique source ports	539	413
Number of unique destination ports	499	391
Number of segments	35214	11738
Median segments per vessel	3	2
Minimum segments per vessel	1	1
Maximum segments per vessel	5614	1897

3.2 AIS Pre-processing Approach

In this work, we define a vessel voyage segment as a voyage from a source port A to a destination port B and describe every voyage by a unique id, departure date and port, and arrival date and port. We used the attributes of AIS messages, such as coordinates, speed, and navigational status (under way using engine, at anchor, moored, etc.) to generate the voyages. Speed is used since ships will slow down when approaching a port and then stop at the voyage destination.

AIS historical data offer numerous dynamic attributes related to voyages, such as draught, estimated arrival time, and destination. However, as such data are entered manually, human errors often occur. We defined vessel stops using different AIS attributes such as speed and position to determine the actual moored ports to overcome this issue. Additionally, we used the World Port Index (WPI) 2019 database [40] to link vessel positions to the closest ports.

Draught is the only AIS data that provides information about the activity of a ship in a port. If it increases, the boat is heavier and therefore loaded commodities in the port. If it decreases, the boat unloaded in the last port. While we cannot trust the value of the draught at every signal as it is entered manually, every ship must have the correct value of draught when entering a port. Thus, at every stop, we get the valid value of the draught related to the previous voyage and correct the draught value if it is different.

3.3 Voyage Creation

To generate port stops and construct voyages for every vessel, we calculated the distance between every vessel stop position and ports listed in the WPI using the Haversine Formula [8]. The port with the minimum distance to the vessel position is defined as the closest (moored) port. Then, using the nearest defined ports, we create the voyage following Algorithm 1. For each ship, we traverse its positions. Based on the speed of the vessel at every position, we predefined *VesselMoving*. If the boat has stopped (*VesselMoving* = 0), we define the current timestamp as the date and time of arrival and the nearest port as the arrival port of the current voyage. Once the vessel starts moving away from the current port (*VesselMoving* = 1), we define it as the departure port of the next voyage and set the departure date as the current timestamp.

To avoid ill-defined segments, e.g., as a result of ships travelling outside the coverage area, an empirical 12 min no-signal threshold is defined (that is, twice the maximum time span of shared static data). A voyage is then suppressed if the time interval between two consecutive signals exceeds the defined threshold.

Algorithm 1. Voyage creation

For Each Vessel
  $VesselDeparted = 0$
  $InPort = 0$
  For Each VesselPosition
    If VesselMoving == 0
      If (VesselDeparted == 0) **and** (InPort == 0)
        Assign $DepartPort{\leftarrow}ClosestPort$
        $InPort = 1$
      Else If VesselDeparted == 1
        Assign $ArrivalPort{\leftarrow}ClosestPort$
        Assign $ArrivalDate{\leftarrow}TimeStamp$
        $VesselDeparted = 0$
    Else If InPort == 1
      Assign $DepartDate{\leftarrow}TimeStamp$
      $VesselDeparted = 1$
      $InPort = 0$
  EndFor
EndFor

3.4 Proposed Graph-Based Machine Learning Model

The heterogeneous graph abstraction proposed to model the maritime transportation network is described in Fig. 1. A heterogeneous graph is denoted by $\mathcal{G} = (\mathcal{V}, \mathcal{E}, \mathcal{A}, \mathcal{R})$ where $\mathcal{V}$ and $\mathcal{E}$ denote the node and link sets, respectively. Each node $v, p \in \mathcal{V}$ and each link $e \in \mathcal{E}$ is associated with a mapping function, where $\phi(v) : \mathcal{V} \leftarrow \mathcal{A}$ and $\rho(e) : \mathcal{E} \leftarrow \mathcal{R}$ represent the node mapping function and edge mapping function, respectively. A graph is defined as heterogeneous if it contains more than one node type and/or more than one edge type. Therefore, $\mathcal{A}$ and $\mathcal{R}$ denote the sets of node and edge types satisfying $|\mathcal{A}| + |\mathcal{R}| > 2$.

Figure 1a shows that nodes represent vessels (blue) and ports (yellow), while edges w_i define links between the vessel node v_i and a destination port node p_j for a specific voyage. Vessel nodes are described by three features - length, width, and MMSI - while port nodes' features include port name, country, and region id information. On the other hand, link features describe specific vessel voyage information, including the departure port, month, draught, and cargo type. The departure time is added as weights to the link to represent voyages of the same vessel with the same source-destination occurring at different dates.

Figure 1b shows a real example of seven voyages related to three vessels and three ports. The vessel with MMSI *255806151* is traveling in *March* (03) from *Kalundborg* to *Malmo* with a cargo type of *Category Y* and a draught of value *6.1*. Each node type is defined by different features. Port node *Malmo* is described by the country *SE*, which represents Sweden and a region id *23860*. Vessel node *564517000* is described by its length (*183* m) and width (*28* m). The weight of each link is defined by the departure date of a voyage. For example, w1 is the weight of the link representing a voyage of the boat with MMSI *255806151* traveling on the *2020-10-02* to the *Kiel* port.

Following the methodology described in [12,28], we use word2vec [30] to perform link prediction task. To create a low dimensional representation of a node, that is, a node embedding, random walks are computed using the heterogeneous graph model. The node embedding shall ensure that the distance between nodes is preserved in the embedding space. If two nodes are close to each other in the graph, their closeness shall be maintained in the embedding space. The resulting list of paths created by the random walk for a node is then provided to a word2vec model to generate the node embedding for the respective nodes. Then, using the vessel and destination node embeddings, link embedding is computed for the voyage segments. Negative voyage segments are randomly generated using possible vessel-port connections available in the network to provide negative examples to the learning algorithms. Link embeddings are similarly created for the negative samples. Finally, link embedding is used to train the predictive model. The entire destination prediction pipeline is shown in Fig. 2.

3.5   Experiments

We divided the data into training, dev, and validation sets (60% training, 20% dev, and 20% validation), as shown in Table 1, where the test set statistics include both dev and validation samples. Scikit-learn and Stellargraph were used to build the machine learning models. We use the Stellar graph library [11] to create the heterogeneous graph, and node and link embeddings. A k-nearest neighbors (kNN) algorithm was used as the machine learning model for our graph-based methodology (after an empirical comparison with other classic machine learning models). The graph-based model was compared to different traditional machine learning approaches (logistic regression, kNN, random forest, and Catboost [3, 10,31,41]) using only the vessel-, port- and voyage-related features, without the

link embeddings. The experiments were conducted on a server with 40 Intel®
Xeon® CPU E5-2690 v2 @ 3.00 GHz cores and 756 GB RAM.

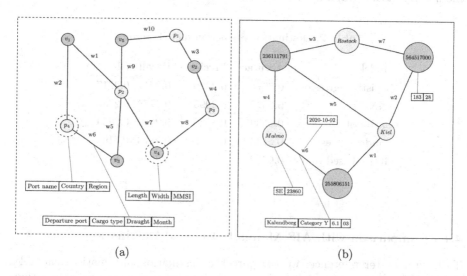

(a)   (b)

Fig. 1. A heterogeneous graph with blue and yellow nodes referring to vessels and
ports respectively, and edges between vessels and destination ports. (a) Feature types
related to vessels, ports and voyages are shown for nodes p4 and v4, and for edge w6,
respectively. (b) A real example of seven voyages for three vessels and three ports.
(Color figure online)

4 Results

Macro-averaged results for the destination prediction models are presented in
Table 2. As we can notice, the graph-based machine learning model outperforms
all the classic models that do use graph-based features. It outperforms the best
baseline algorithm - random forest - with an increase in accuracy of approximately 3%, the precision almost doubled, going from 34% to 69%, and recall
and F1-score improved by 7% and 23% respectively. While our best model is
able to predict the correct destination port nearly 70% correct, it is only able
to do so for around 1/3 of the ports in the network. If we only compare among
the baseline models, the random forest algorithm performs the best, with an
accuracy of 61%, precision of 34%, recall of 29%, and F1-score of 31%, followed
closely by Catboost. Surprisingly, the logistic regression, despite being a strong
classification method, performs the worst.

Lastly, we can verify the power that the graph-based features bring to the
model by comparing the performance of the kNN model (without graph-based
features) and our model, that is, a kNN enhanced with graph-based features.
As we can see from Table 2, there is a significant increase in precision, more

than doubling with a subsequent impact on the F1-score (which is also almost double). We believe that the addition of the topological features derived from the heterogeneous graph are thus able to better characterise a voyage segment.

Table 2. Destination prediction models results

Model	Accuracy	Precision	Recall	F1-score
Logistic regression	0.5574	0.2225	0.2211	0.2217
kNN	0.5822	0.2995	0.2774	0.2880
Catboost	0.6036	0.3136	0.2620	0.2854
Random forest	0.6133	0.3369	0.2873	0.3101
Graph-based (ours)	0.6472	0.6877	0.3604	0.5426

4.1   Comparison with AIS Manually Entered Destinations

To have a better reference, we compare the destination information available in the AIS message with the destination derived by our voyage reconstruction algorithm, which uses automatic AIS position and speed data, and an external port database (WPI). Before comparing the datasets, we cleaned AIS destinations by removing samples with meaningless or random destination values, such as *HERE WE GO AGAIN, HOME*, etc. We also created various rules to link AIS destination codes with WPI port names. We can cite examples of ports in AIS data with values *SEGOT* and *SE GBG* destinations, both equivalent to *GOTEBORG* in the generated voyage dataset.

The resulting comparison shows that we covered around 48% of AIS destination ports, which means that we generated the same AIS destination for almost half of our data. As a comparison, the graph-based model is accurate in 65% of its predictions. If we relax the matching process between AIS and the port names of WPI, using a fuzzy search with a minimum similarity percentage of 90%, still only 55% of AIS destinations matches, which is a similar accuracy to the worst baseline model. These can be explained by the high risk of errors within manually entered AIS data.

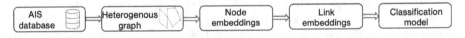

Fig. 2. Overview of the proposed graph-based voyage destination prediction model.

4.2   Error Analysis

We present a summary of prediction results for our graph-based model in the confusion matrix of Fig. 3. Due to the high number of ports available in the test set, we show the results only for the 10 top destination ports. We added "Other ports" to represent any port that is not in the list of ports displayed in the confusion matrix. As we can notice, most of the confusions of the top ports are with ports lower-destination ports ("Other ports"), e.g., *Nysted, Rostock*, etc. Among the top ports, *Karsto* is confused often with *Nykobing (MOR)* (20%), and *Skudeneshavn* with *Karsto* (22%) and *Nykobing (MOR)* (22%). We believe this might be due to the fact that *Skudeneshavn* and *Karsto* are very close geographically and also visited by the same boat *257144700* in Fig. 4.

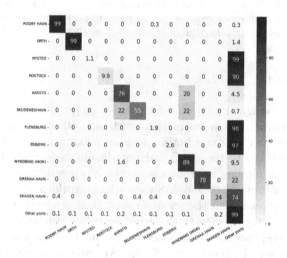

Fig. 3. Link prediction confusion matrix for the top destination ports. "Other ports" represent the remainder predictions.

Figure 4a shows an overview of the distribution of data related to the top 10 destination ports with the highest number of voyages in test set. We notice that vessel with MMSI 219000737, during 2000 voyages, has been visiting *Rodby Havn* port 50% of the time and *Orth* port the rest of the voyages. This means that the probability of predicting the right port is 0.5. The dominant ports have little diversity in terms of visiting boats. Only three of the five ports have been visited by one to three boats. This explains why ports, such as *Rodby Havn* and *Orth*, have such good performance as shown in Fig. 3. Figure 4b shows the distribution of data in the test set related to the top destinations that a maximum number of vessels has visited. We can see that for ports such as *Skagen Haven*, a much higher confusion is found (see Fig. 3), indicating that the algorithm is biased towards the majority classes, having significantly better performance for ships that always go to the same destination than for ships that make voyages to different destinations.

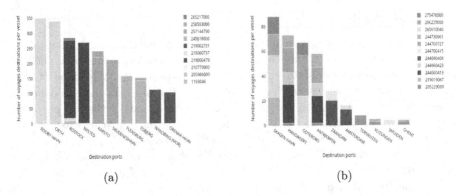

Fig. 4. Test set. (a) Number of port destinations per vessel for the top 10 destinations with the maximum number of voyages. (b) Number of port destinations per MMSI for top destinations shared by a maximum number of vessels.

5   Discussion

In this paper, we designed a novel method based on graph-based machine learning models to predict voyage destination. Such methods can be used to improve AIS data quality and promote better decision making in the maritime transportation. In addition to the usual tasks of cleaning and removing conflicting data, and filling in missing information wherever is possible, we created voyage segments by combining historical AIS data with a world port database (WPI). In our experiments, we cover the region around Danish waters, nevertheless, the methodology is readily applied to the world maritime transportation network.

In the proposed model, we organized AIS data by vessels and created voyages based on a set of rules using different AIS attributes combined with the WPI dataset. Then, voyages are abstracted using a heterogeneous undirected graph, which is used to train a machine learning model that solves the voyage destination port prediction problem as a multi-class classification based on a link prediction algorithm. The graph-enriched model was compared to baseline models that do not exploit the network properties, achieving significant performance improvement upon them. While more complex graph-based models exist, such as those based on graph neural networks, e.g., graph convolution neural network [21] and graph attention network [36], the objective here is to demonstrate that the topological features can contribute positively to the performance of the predictive models. Their investigation is left for a future work.

To represent the time factor in the proposed model, we conducted two experiments. First, the one presented in this paper, where time is added as a link property, that is, new travels have a higher weight. Second, we evaluated a recurrent model, where previous voyage features (time - n), e.g., previous voyage departure and destination ports, are added to the current set of features. However, adding recurrent information did not make any significant change to the performance of the models, only improved their complexity. Therefore, these results were not presented in this paper, but they could still be relevant in a wider coverage database.

Our work has some limitations. The AIS used only covers a region around the Danish waters. The destination mentioned can be outside the covered region. Therefore, we do not capture the position information of the ship at the final destination. Using data covering the whole world and considering other types of ships will increase the diversity of the data and improve the analysis of the ships' behaviours. Moreover, enhanced learning models, such as graph neural networks, as aforementioned, could be also analysed. Finally, some features, such as ships' id, while might help to enhance the learning of ships' behaviours, they open the risk of overfitting. Therefore, more robust evaluation methods, such as a cross-validation, could be employed.

To conclude, by approaching the voyage destination prediction problem as a multi-class link prediction task, we have explored the possibility of using the network features, such as link embeddings, in a graph-based model to improve the predictive power of learning algorithms. Despite the significant performance enhancement, voyage destination prediction remains as a challenge. Nevertheless, our results show that the performance of the graph-based predictive model outperforms the manually entered AIS destination data. Therefore, they could be used to augment AIS data quality and support data-driven maritime support systems.

References

1. AISM: IALA guidelines on the universal automatic identification system (2002). https://ucakikazlambasi.com.tr/wp-content/uploads/2017/04/iala-guidelines.pdf. Accessed 8 Jan 2022
2. Bailey, N.J.: Training, technology and AIS: looking beyond the box. In: SIRC Symposium 2005, Seafarers International Research Centre (SIRC), pp. 108–128 (2005)
3. Breiman, L.: Random forests. Mach. Learn. **45**(1), 5–32 (2001)
4. Bye, R., Almklov, P.G.: Normalization of maritime accident data using AIS. Marine Policy (2019)
5. Cai, M., Zhang, J., Zhang, D., Yuan, X., Soares, C.G.: Collision risk analysis on ferry ships in Jiangsu section of the Yangtze river based on AIS data. Reliab. Eng. Syst. Safety **215**, 107901 (2021)
6. Carlini, E., de Lira, V.M., Júnior, A.S., Etemad, M., Machado, B.B., Matwin, S.: Uncovering vessel movement patterns from AIS data with graph evolution analysis. In: EDBT/ICDT Workshops (2020)
7. Chen, X., et al.: Ship trajectory reconstruction from AIS sensory data via data quality control and prediction. Math. Probl. Eng. **2020** (2020)
8. Chopde, N.R., Nichat, M.: Landmark based shortest path detection by using a* and haversine formula. Int. J. Innov. Res. Comput. Commun. Eng. **1**(2), 298–302 (2013)

9. Chung, J., Gulcehre, C., Cho, K., Bengio, Y.: Empirical evaluation of gated recurrent neural networks on sequence modeling. arXiv preprint arXiv:1412.3555 (2014)
10. Cunningham, P., Delany, S.J.: k-nearest neighbour classifiers: (with python examples). arXiv preprint arXiv:2004.04523 (2020)
11. Data61, C.: Stellargraph machine learning library. Publication Title: GitHub Repository. GitHub (2018)
12. Dong, Y., Chawla, N.V., Swami, A.: metapath2vec: scalable representation learning for heterogeneous networks. In: Proceedings of the 23rd ACM SIGKDD International Conference on Knowledge Discovery and Data Mining, pp. 135–144 (2017)
13. Elman, J.L.: Finding structure in time. Cogn. Sci. **14**(2), 179–211 (1990)
14. Ester, M., Kriegel, H.P., Sander, J., Xu, X., et al.: A density-based algorithm for discovering clusters in large spatial databases with noise. In: KDD (1996)
15. Goodfellow, I., et al.: Generative adversarial nets. Adv. Neural Inf. Process. Syst. **27** (2014)
16. Harati-Mokhtari, A., Wall, A., Brooks, P., Wang, J.: Automatic identification system (AIS): data reliability and human error implications. J. Navig. **60**(3), 373–389 (2007)
17. Hochreiter, S., Schmidhuber, J.: Long short-term memory. Neural Comput. **9**(8), 1735–1780 (1997)
18. Hu, Y., Park, G.K.: Collision risk assessment based on the vulnerability of marine accidents using fuzzy logic. Int. J. Naval Archit. Ocean Eng. **12**, 541–551 (2020)
19. Ifrim, C., Wallace, M., Poulopoulos, V., Mourti, A.: Methods and techniques for automatic identification system data reduction. In: Pop, F., Neagu, G. (eds.) Big Data Platforms and Applications. CCN, pp. 253–269. Springer, Cham (2021). https://doi.org/10.1007/978-3-030-38836-2_12
20. IMO: AIS transponder (2020). https://www.imo.org/en/OurWork/Safety/Pages/AIS.aspx. Accessed 11 Dec 2021
21. Kipf, T.N., Welling, M.: Semi-supervised classification with graph convolutional networks. arXiv preprint arXiv:1609.02907 (2016)
22. Kisialiou, Y., Gribkovskaia, I., Laporte, G.: Robust supply vessel routing and scheduling. Transp. Res. Part C: Emerg. Technol. **90**, 366–378 (2018)
23. Li, B., Lu, J., Lu, H., Li, J.: Predicting maritime accident consequence scenarios for emergency response decisions using optimization-based decision tree approach. Marit. Policy Manage. 1–23 (2021)
24. Lin, C.X., Huang, T.W., Guo, G., Wong, M.D.: MtDetector: a high-performance marine traffic detector at stream scale. In: Proceedings of the 12th ACM International Conference on Distributed and Event-Based Systems (2018)
25. Ma, S., Liu, S., Meng, X.: Optimized BP neural network algorithm for predicting ship trajectory. In: 2020 IEEE 4th Information Technology, Networking, Electronic and Automation Control Conference (ITNEC), vol. 1, pp. 525–532. IEEE (2020)
26. Magnussen, B.B., Bläser, N., Jensen, R.M., Ylänen, K.: Destination prediction of oil tankers using graph abstractions and recurrent neural networks. In: Mes, M., Lalla-Ruiz, E., Voß, S. (eds.) ICCL 2021. LNCS, vol. 13004, pp. 51–65. Springer, Cham (2021). https://doi.org/10.1007/978-3-030-87672-2_4
27. Mestl, T., Dausendschön, K.: Port eta prediction based on AIS data. In: 15th International Conference on Computer and IT Applications in the Maritime Industries, Lecce, pp. 9–11 (2016)
28. Metapath2Vec: Link prediction with metapath2vec (2019). https://stellargraph.readthedocs.io/en/stable/demos/link-prediction/metapath2vec-link-prediction.html. Accessed 10 Jan 2022

29. Mieczyńska, M., Czarnowski, I.: K-means clustering for SAT-AIS data analysis. WMU J. Marit. Aff. **20**(3), 377–400 (2021)
30. Mikolov, T., Chen, K., Corrado, G., Dean, J.: Efficient estimation of word representations in vector space. arXiv preprint arXiv:1301.3781 (2013)
31. Prokhorenkova, L., Gusev, G., Vorobev, A., Dorogush, A.V., Gulin, A.: CatBoost: unbiased boosting with categorical features. arXiv:1706.09516 (2017)
32. Stogiannos, M., Papadimitrakis, M., Sarimveis, H., Alexandridis, A.: Vessel trajectory prediction using radial basis function neural networks. In: IEEE EUROCON 2021–19th International Conference on Smart Technologies. IEEE (2021)
33. Suo, Y., Chen, W., Claramunt, C., Yang, S.: A ship trajectory prediction framework based on a recurrent neural network. Sensors **20**(18), 5133 (2020)
34. Tu, E., Zhang, G., Mao, S., Rachmawati, L., Huang, G.: Modeling historical AIS data for vessel path prediction: a comprehensive treatment. CoRR abs/2001.01592 (2020). http://arxiv.org/abs/2001.01592
35. UN: Global issues (2019). https://www.un.org/en/global-issues/population
36. Veličković, P., Cucurull, G., Casanova, A., Romero, A., Lio, P., Bengio, Y.: Graph attention networks. arXiv preprint arXiv:1710.10903 (2017)
37. Wang, C., Fu, Y.: Ship trajectory prediction based on attention in bidirectional recurrent neural networks. In: 2020 5th International Conference on Information Science, Computer Technology and Transportation (ISCTT). IEEE (2020)
38. Wang, S., He, Z.: A prediction model of vessel trajectory based on generative adversarial network. J. Navig. **74**, 1–11 (2021)
39. Wang, W., Zhang, C., Guillaume, F., Halldearn, R., Kristensen, T.S., Liu, Z.: From AIS data to vessel destination through prediction with machine learning techniques. Artif. Intell. Models, Algor. Appl. 1 (2021)
40. WPI: (2019). https://msi.nga.mil/Publications/WPI. Accessed 13 Nov 2021
41. Wright, R.E.: Logistic regression. In: Reading and Understanding Multivariate Statistics, pp. 217–244. American Psychological Association (1995)
42. Wu, L., Xu, Y., Wang, F.: Identifying port calls of ships by uncertain reasoning with trajectory data. ISPRS Int. J. Geo-Inf. **9**, 756 (2020)
43. Xiao, F., Ligteringen, H., Van Gulijk, C., Ale, B.: Comparison study on AIS data of ship traffic behavior. Ocean Eng. **95**, 84–93 (2015)
44. Yang, D., Wu, L., Wang, S.: Can we trust the AIS destination port information for bulk ships?-Implications for shipping policy and practice. Transp. Res. Part E: Logistics Transp. Rev. **149**, 102308 (2021)
45. Yang, D., Wu, L., Wang, S., Jia, H., Li, K.X.: How big data enriches maritime research-a critical review of automatic identification system (AIS) data applications. Transp. Rev. **39**(6), 755–773 (2019)
46. Zhang, C., et al.: AIS data driven general vessel destination prediction: a random forest based approach. Transp. Res. Part C: Emerg. Technol. **118**, 102729 (2020)
47. Zhang, T., Liu, C., Wen, B.: Abnormal ship behavior detection after the closure of AIS based on radar data (2021). https://doi.org/10.21203/rs.3.rs-551597/v1
48. Zhang, Z., Suo, Y., Yang, S., Zhao, Z.: Detection of complex abnormal ship behavior based on event stream. In: 2020 Chinese Automation Congress (CAC), pp. 5730–5735 (2020). https://doi.org/10.1109/CAC51589.2020.9327793
49. Zhao, L., Shi, G., Yang, J.: Ship trajectories pre-processing based on AIS data. J. Navig. **71**(5), 1210–1230 (2018)

Hunting for Dual-Target Set on a Class of Hierarchical Networks

Moein Khajehnejad[1]([⊠])(iD) and Forough Habibollahi[2](iD)

[1] Department of Data Science and AI, Faculty of IT, Monash University,
Melbourne, Australia
`moein.khajehnejad@monash.edu`
[2] Department of Biomedical Engineering, The University of Melbourne,
Parkville, Australia
`fhabibollahi@student.unimelb.edu.au`

Abstract. In the past decades, complex networks have proved to be an exceedingly powerful and efficacious tool for describing a wide range of systems in nature and society. Thereafter, random search processes, as an effective and informative way of exploring these networks, have attracted considerable attention towards them. In this work, we study the problem of partial cover time in a dual-target search when performing a random walk on a (1,2)-flower network. For the first time, we derive an exact expression for the partial cover time of a random searcher on such a network to hunt both target nodes of interest. The introduced formula for calculating this quantity outranks previous work in the sense that it can be conveniently applied to general types of networks. Utilizing this expression can introduce a pivotal change for efficiently solving the problem of partial cover time in its wide range of applicable fields.

Keywords: Partial Cover Time · Dual-target Search · Pseudofractal Scale-free Web · Mean First Passage Time · Probability Generating Function

1 Introduction

Random search processes have become vastly popular and investigated due to their applications in various domains over the past decades. The theoretical developments in this field have affected wide mathematics areas especially probability theory, computer science, statistical physics, operations research, and more. Random walks have also been applied in areas such as locomotion and foraging of animals [1,2], disease and information spreading [3], decision making in the brain [4,5], gene transcription [6], and also descriptions of financial markets [7,8], ranking systems [9], and dimension reduction and feature extraction from high-dimensional data [10] and network embedding [11–13] as well as socially responsible network science studies [14,15]. On the other hand, there has been a large trend towards modeling many real-world phenomena with complex

© Springer Nature Switzerland AG 2022
P. Ribeiro et al. (Eds.): NetSci-X 2022, LNCS 13197, pp. 94–111, 2022.
https://doi.org/10.1007/978-3-030-97240-0_8

networks [16]. Coupled biological and chemical systems, neural networks, social interacting species, the Internet and the World Wide Web are just a few examples of real systems which are characterized by complex networks. Also covering problems are being widely studied specifically in fields like discrete optimization [17, 18]. To mention a classical problem in this framework, we can name the general set cover problem [19].

The wide and common requirements for the simultaneous search for multiple targets in many fields of chemistry, biology, and social interactions motivates us to study a dual-target search. Figure 1 presents a general overview of the dual-target search problem on a typical network where a random walker (starting from node S) explores the network until meeting both targets of interest (T_1 and T_2). To be able to characterize this type of search on a network, we use the partial cover time that can quantify the required time for a random walker to hit several different targets in the network. The specific designation of this concept has been a persistent problem in the realm of random walk theory since its birth [20, 21]. Despite the long-lasting trend to solve this problem, the studies in this field are still in the early stages and not much effort has been made for finding a precise solution for it. Most recent studies in mathematics or physics literature focus on the boundary of cover time on regular graphs [22] or provide numerical results of the cover time [23]. It is worth mentioning that in one of the valuable contributions to this field [24], a global expression for the full distribution of the cover time in a graph is proposed. Though, all these past studies were concentrated on simply the cover time and not specifically partial cover time until a recent study [25] where for the first time, an iterative approach has been proposed to analytically determine the partial cover time of complex networks.

Here, despite most recent efforts which study random walks and covering problems on complex networks and mainly focus on a single-target case [6, 26–28], we are trying to study multi-target search on complex systems. We specifically focus on the problem of hunting a target set containing two members on (1,2)-flowers (pseudofractal scale-free web) as an example of hierarchical networks. Several key characteristics of complex networks can be modeled using these recursive, finitely articulated models. At the same time, these models can be precisely analyzed, giving us important insights into the nature of complex networks in everyday life. Our proposed method can easily be applied to more general topologies of hierarchical lattices like (u,v)-nets and also the structures exhibiting a self-similar construction as well. In this paper, we attempt to derive an exact expression for computation of the partial cover time on (1,2)-flowers when our target domain consists of two members. We have successfully achieved an explicit expression for this quantity in terms of mean first passage time (MFPT) for a single absorbing domain which can be exactly calculated utilizing the concept of probability generating functions. Our achievements in this work can be exploited as a pivotal method to solve the problem of partial cover time in general networks and also establish the groundwork for future investigation in problems with a target set which includes an arbitrary number of nodes.

This paper is organized as follows. Section 2 provides brief properties and construction methods of (1,2)-flowers. The comprehensive analysis of the dual-target search and its presentation in terms of MFPT are explained in Sect. 3. Section 4 illustrates the general method to analytically compute the MFPT employing the probability generating function and then introduces the exact expression of partial cover time for dual-target set in (1,2)-flowers. Finally, we present our conclusions in Sect. 5.

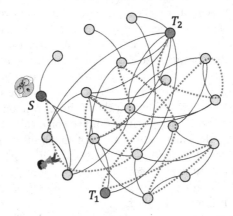

Fig. 1. An extensive visualization for the problem of dual-target hunt by a random searcher on a general network. The searcher (starting from node S) is hunting for two target nodes (T_1 and T_2) by performing a random walk on the network.

2   Properties and Construction of (1,2)-Flowers

In this section, we introduce the utilized model which is called (1,2)-flower (also denoted as pseudofractal scale-free web, PSFW) in the family of (u,v)-flowers [29], that is a large class of scale-free hierarchical networks. These networks are built using an iterative method. We convey our investigations on (1,2)-flower model because of its decisive structure which has attracted a surge of interest in the past decade and allows one to study the diffusion processes on it [30–32]. Let us denote the (1,2)-flower after t ($t \geq 0$) number of iterations by $G(t)$. This number of iterations is also called the generation of the network. The construction initially starts from $t = 0$ ($G(0)$) where we have a triangle of three nodes. For $t \geq 1$, $G(t)$ is obtained from $G(t-1)$ by performing the following operation on each edge: Attaching a new node to both ends of the edge. Figure 2.a illustrates the evolution process of a (1,2)-flower showing the first several generations. According to the mentioned algorithm for building PSFW, at each step t_i, the number of newly added nodes is $\bar{V}(t_i) = 3^{t_i}$. Therefore, we can easily know that the total number of nodes in $G(t)$ is equal to $V(t) = \sum_{t_i=0}^{t} \bar{V}(t_i) = (3^{t+1}+3)/2$. From this perspective, the nodes of G(t) can be classified into different levels.

The nodes existing at iteration $t = 0$ belong to level 0 while nodes present at the k_{th} generation are considered to be of level k. As a consecution, the nodes of level 0 are just the three main hubs of $G(t)$, and any node of $G(t)$ belongs to level t.

This class of networks exhibits some intriguing characteristics of real-life networks existing in nature. The degrees of nodes obeys the power law distribution $P(k) \sim k^{-\gamma}$ with the exponent $\gamma = 1 + ln(3)/ln(2) \approx 2.585$ [29]. Also, the average clustering coefficient tends to 0.8 when the network order is large enough and the average path length increases logarithmically with the size of the network [33]. Hence, we can conclude that the (1,2)-flower expresses small-world behavior [34].

It is worth mentioning that the PSFW can also be constructed using another method (see Fig. 2.b for details of this construction method). Given the generation $t - 1$, $G(t)$ will be obtained by joining three sub-units, which are replicas of $G(t - 1)$, denoted as G_1, G_2, and G_3 respectively, at their hubs (nodes with the highest degree) denoted by A, B, C. Also, each of G_1, G_2, and G_3 is in turn composed of three replicas of $G(t - 2)$ and the algorithm continues similarly. These sub-units can be classified into different levels; Recursively, for any $k \geq 0$, L_k is supposed to be a copy of $G(t - k)$ and hence, it is clear that 3^k sub-units of L_k exist in $G(t)$. To discern the sub-units of the same level, we label L_k $(1 \leq k \leq t)$ by a sequence $\{i_1, i_2, \ldots, i_k\}$, where each $i_j \in \{1, 2, 3\}$ $(1 \leq j \leq k)$ based on its location in the parent sub-unit L_{k-1} [31,35]. Figures 3.a and 3.b illustrate this labeling process. For convenience, we show the three hubs of all sub-units L_k as A_k, B_k, C_k in Fig. 3.b.

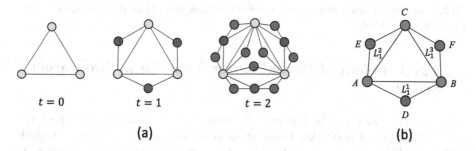

Fig. 2. (a) An illustration of the hierarchical building process of a typical (1-2)-flower for the first three generations. (b) An alternative method of construction for a typical (1-2)-flower using three replicas of each generation. The network of generation t, denoted by $G(t)$, is composed of three copies of $G(t - 1)$ labeled as L_1^1, L_1^2, and L_1^3. Each copy encompasses three main hubs (say, A, B, and D in L_1^1). These hubs in each of L_1^1, L_1^2, and L_1^3 are topologically equivalent due to the intrinsic symmetry of the model. For the generation of $G(t)$, two out of three main hubs are selected (say, A and B in L_1^1) and merged pairwise with the other selected hubs from the other copies. The resulting structure displays A, B, and C as main hubs of generation t, while nodes labeled as D, E, and F, are the second most connected nodes.

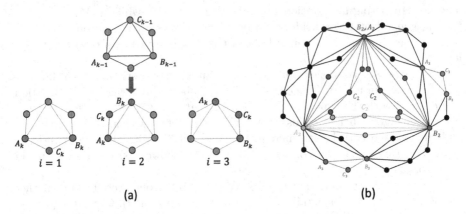

Fig. 3. (a) An illustration of the labeling process for distinguishing sub-units in each level of the network. The relation between the value of i and the location of sub-unit L_k (colored in red, bottom row) in L_{k-1} (upper row). Sub-unit represented by solid red triangle is the sub-unit L_k corresponding to value of i below. The hubs labeled as A_{k-1} and B_{k-1} in L_{k-1} are also the hubs of L_k labeled as A_k and B_k while $i = 1$; the hubs labeled as A_{k-1} and C_{k-1} in L_{k-1} are also the hubs of L_k labeled as A_k and B_k while $i = 2$; and finally the hubs labeled as B_{k-1} and C_{k-1} in L_{k-1} are also the hubs of L_k labeled as B_k and A_k while $i = 3$. **(b)** A bigger picture of a more developed (1-2)-flower with sub-units from different levels being labeled with different colors. The three hubs of each sub-unit L_k are shown as A_k, B_k, C_k. In this network, the blue sub-unit corresponds to level 2 and is labeled by the sequence $\{2, 1\}$; The yellow sub-unit is also from level 2 and represented by $\{1, 1\}$; Whereas the red one from the same level is shown with $\{3, 1\}$. Moreover, the purple structure from level 3 is labeled with $\{1, 2, 3\}$ and the green sub-unit in the same level has $\{3, 3, 2\}$ as its labeling sequence (Color figure online).

3   The Problem of Partial Cover Time for a Two Target Search

In this section, we try to find an exact solution for a dual-target search problem in general types of networks. We start from an undirected connected network with V nodes ($i = 1, \ldots, V$), described by a symmetric adjacency matrix A, whose element $a_{ij} = 1(0)$ if there is (not) a link between nodes i and j. Consider a random searcher (walker) on this network who jumps from the current node i to one of its k_i neighbors (e.g., node j) at each time step with transition probability which is defined as $p_{ij} = 1/k_i$. Without loss of generality, we assume that the two targets are located at distinct nodes 1 and 2. Here, it is appealing for us to compute the partial cover time $T_{i,\{1,2\}}$ which alternatively means how long it takes for the searcher to reach both target nodes for the first time starting from node i. This is precisely the expected time to thoroughly cover the nodes $\{1, 2\}$. In this case, if the first step of the walk is to node 1 (or 2), the required partial cover time is $1 + T_{12}$ (or $1 + T_{21}$), where T_{12} (or T_{21}) is the mean first passage time (MFPT) from node 1 (or 2) to node 2 (or 1). However, if the first step is to another node j, the required partial cover time will be equal to $1 + T_{j,\{1,2\}}$. Thus, for $i \neq 1, 2$, we obtain the following equation:

$$T_{i,\{1,2\}} = p_{i1}(1 + T_{12}) + p_{i2}(1 + T_{21}) + \sum_{j \neq 1,2} p_{ij}(1 + T_{j,\{1,2\}}) \tag{1}$$

It is obvious that $T_{12} = T_{1,\{1,2\}}$ and $T_{21} = T_{2,\{1,2\}}$. So, the previous equation can be deduced to:

$$T_{i,\{1,2\}} = 1 + \sum_{j} p_{ij} T_{j,\{1,2\}} \tag{2}$$

Analogously, let $r_{1,\{1,2\}}$ denote the expected number of steps needed to revisit nodes 1 and 2 starting from node 1. It can be expressed as:

$$r_{1,\{1,2\}} = \sum_{j} p_{1j}(1 + T_{j,\{1,2\}}) \tag{3}$$

Now, merging Eq. (2) and Eq. (3), we obtain the following matrix relation:

$$(I - P)T = C - R \tag{4}$$

where I denotes the identity matrix and T, C, and R are respectively determined as the following:

$$T = \begin{pmatrix} T_{1,\{1,2\}} & \cdots & T_{1,\{1,V\}} & T_{1,\{2,3\}} & \cdots & T_{1,\{V-1,V\}} \\ T_{2,\{1,2\}} & \cdots & T_{2,\{1,V\}} & T_{2,\{2,3\}} & \cdots & T_{1,\{V-1,V\}} \\ \vdots & \vdots & \vdots & \vdots & \vdots & \vdots \\ T_{V,\{1,2\}} & \cdots & T_{V,\{1,V\}} & T_{V,\{2,3\}} & \cdots & T_{V,\{V-1,V\}} \end{pmatrix}_{V \times \binom{V}{2}} \quad ; C = \begin{pmatrix} 1 & 1 & \cdots & 1 \\ 1 & 1 & \cdots & 1 \\ \vdots & \vdots & \vdots & \vdots \\ 1 & 1 & \cdots & 1 \end{pmatrix}_{V \times \binom{V}{2}} \quad ;$$

$$R = \begin{pmatrix} r_{1,\{1,2\}} - T_{12} & r_{1,\{1,3\}} - T_{13} \cdots & & 0 \\ r_{2,\{1,2\}} - T_{21} & 0 & \cdots & 0 \\ \vdots & \vdots & \vdots & \vdots \\ 0 & 0 & \cdots r_{V,\{V-1,V\}} - T_{VV-1} \end{pmatrix}_{V \times \binom{V}{2}}$$

Multiplying both sides of Eq. (4) by the matrix W, in which each row is the stationary distribution of the random walk and which is, in fact, an ergodic Markov chain, gives:

$$W(I - P) = \mathbf{0} \longrightarrow WC - WR = \mathbf{0} \tag{5}$$

and

$$w_1(r_{1,\{1,2\}} - T_{12}) + w_2(r_{2,\{1,2\}} - T_{21}) = 1 \tag{6}$$

where w_i is the ith component of the stationary distribution.

It is well known that for generic types of random walks, the MFPT or T_{ij} can be represented exactly in terms of the elements z_{ij} of the fundamental matrix Z for the corresponding Markov process [36,37]. This is defined by:

$$Z = (I - P + W)^{-1} \tag{7}$$

Now, multiplying both sides of Eq. (4) by Z we obtain:

$$T = C - ZR + WT \tag{8}$$

which gives us:

$$T_{i,\{1,2\}} = 1 - z_{i1}(r_{1,\{1,2\}} - T_{12}) - z_{i2}(r_{2,\{1,2\}} - T_{21}) + \sum_j w_j T_{j,\{1,2\}} \tag{9}$$

Achieving $T_{1,\{1,2\}}$ and $T_{2,\{1,2\}}$ from above equation and merging them with Eq. (6), it gives:

$$r_{1,\{1,2\}} = T_{12} + \frac{T_{21}}{w_1(T_{12} + T_{21})}; \quad r_{2,\{1,2\}} = T_{21} + \frac{T_{12}}{w_2(T_{12} + T_{21})} \tag{10}$$

Eventually, inserting the above equation in Eq. (9), we gain the following exact expression for partial cover time:

$$T_{i,\{1,2\}} = \frac{T_{12}T_{21} + T_{i1}T_{21} + T_{i2}T_{12}}{T_{12} + T_{21}} \tag{11}$$

So we have now derived an analytical representation for the problem of dual-target search and computed it in terms of mean first passage times in any arbitrary undirected network.

4   General Method Based on Probability Generating Function

In this section, by employing a method based on the probability generating function (PGF) [38], we try to derive an exact expression for the partial cover time for a two target search in a (1,2)-flower. This technique can be applied to other self-similar structures in the same fashion and solve the problem of hunting dual-target set on such networks.

Firstly, we bring a brief description of the properties of probability generating functions and thereafter, by utilizing these features, we attack on our main goal of this work. Now let X be a discrete random variable which takes only non-negative integers $\{0, 1, \dots\}$. By definition the probability generating function of X is:

$$\Psi_X(z) = \mathbb{E}(z^X) = \sum_{x=0}^{\infty} p(x)z^x \tag{12}$$

where p is the probability mass function of X. Given $\Psi_X(z)$, $p(x)$ can be recovered as the coefficient of z^x in the Taylor's series expansion of $\Psi_X(z)$ around $z = 0$ as the following:

$$p(x) = \frac{\frac{\partial^x \Psi_X(z)}{\partial z^x}\big|_{z=0}}{x!} \tag{13}$$

Also, the expectation of X can be written as:

$$\mathbb{E}(X) = \frac{\partial \Psi_X(z)}{\partial z}\big|_{z=1} \tag{14}$$

And eventually, it must be mentioned that the probability generating function has a peculiar property in dealing with the summation of independent random variables which is beneficial in this work. To clarify this property, let N be a random variable with PGF $\Psi_N(z)$, and $X_1, X_2, \ldots, X_N$ be a sequence of independent and identically distributed random variables with PGF $\Psi_X(z)$, and $S_N = \sum_{i=1}^{N} X_i$. The PGF of S_N is given by

$$\Psi_{S_N}(z) = \Psi_N(\Psi_X(z)) \tag{15}$$

Following this preface, we will introduce a precise presentation for the generating function of the first passage probability. Corresponding to different choices for an absorbing domain, here we particularly focus on nodes of level 1 (nodes with the largest and the second largest degree) and without loss of generality, we suppose that nodes A and F constitute the dual-target set in the (1,2)-flower. In the following section, we drive an explicit expression of the first passage probability and mean first passage time for A and F separately and then utilizing Eq. (11), we obtain the exact value of partial cover time.

4.1   First Passage Properties to Node A

In order to compute the probability generating function from an arbitrary source node to node A, we first consider the case where the starting and the absorbing nodes are from the main hubs (i.e., A, B, and C). This assumption provides us with a useful framework to calculate the PGF of starting nodes from different levels recursively. Due to the existing structural symmetry in a (1,2)-flower, we assume node C is the starting node and $\mathcal{D} = \{A, B\}$ is the absorbing domain. We want to find the probability generating function from node C to any of the other two hubs A and B.

Let $X_C(t)$ indicate the first passage time from node C to $\mathcal{D}$ and $\mathcal{P}_C(t, n)$ denote the first passage probability that $X(t) = n$, where t is the generation of the (1,2)-flower. So, the PGF of $X(t)$ can be expressed as the following:

$$\theta(t, z) = \sum_{n=0}^{\infty} \mathcal{P}_C(t, n) z^n \tag{16}$$

Now, one can show any path from hub C to the absorbing domain $\mathcal{D}$ as:

$$\Omega = (v_{\tau_0} = C,\ v_{\tau_1}, \ldots,\ v_{\tau_N} = A(\text{or } B)) \tag{17}$$

where $\tau_0 = 0,\ v_{\tau_1}, v_{\tau_2}, \ldots,\ v_{\tau_N - 1} \in \Gamma = \{C, D, E, F \mid nodes\ of\ level\ 1\ except\{A, B\}\}$, and $N - 1$ indicates the number of times that the random searcher has visited any node in Γ until attaining node A or B for the first time. Therefore, Ω contains only the nodes of level 1 where the time interval between each two steps is stochastic and N is the first passage time from node C to any of nodes A and B from generation 1. Thus, the PGF of N is $\theta(1, z)$. Let us define the random variable $\eta_i = \tau_i - \tau_{i-1}$ as the time needed for the walker to relocate from $v_{\tau_{i-1}}$ to v_{τ_i}. It is noticeable that η_i s $(i = 1, \ldots, N)$ are independent and identically distributed random variables. Each of these variables is the first passage time from node C to any of the other two hubs of generation $t - 1$ since nodes of level 1 are the hubs of G_1, G_2, and G_3 which are replicas of $G(t - 1)$. Hence, the PGF of each η_i is $\theta(t - 1, z)$. Now, whereas $X(t) = \sum_{i=1}^{N} \eta_i$ and according to Eq. (15), we have:

$$\theta(t, z) = \theta(1, \theta(t - 1, z)) \tag{18}$$

To compute the above equation, it is sufficient to find $\theta(1, z)$ and then, $\theta(t, z)$ can be achieved in a straightforward manner. Let $\boldsymbol{P}$ denote the transition probability matrix of the generation 1 on the (1,2)-flower such that the absorbing domain is $\mathcal{D} = \{A, B\}$. So all elements of the first and second row of $\boldsymbol{P}$ are equal to 0:

$$\boldsymbol{P} = \begin{pmatrix} 0 & 0 & 0 & 0 & 0 & 0 \\ 0 & 0 & 0 & 0 & 0 & 0 \\ 1/4 & 1/4 & 0 & 0 & 1/4 & 1/4 \\ 1/2 & 1/2 & 0 & 0 & 0 & 0 \\ 1/2 & 0 & 1/2 & 0 & 0 & 0 \\ 0 & 1/2 & 1/2 & 0 & 0 & 0 \end{pmatrix}_{6 \times 6} \tag{19}$$

The probability generating function matrix $[\Psi_{ij}(z)]_{6 \times 6}$ of matrix $\boldsymbol{P}$ can be calculated as:

$$[\Psi_{ij}(z)]_{6 \times 6} = \sum_{n=0}^{\infty} (z\boldsymbol{P})^n = (I - z\boldsymbol{P})^{-1} \tag{20}$$

where $\Psi_{ij}(z)$ is the PGF of passage time from node i to j. Substituting Eq. (19) into Eq. (20), the probability generating function of the first passage time from node C to any of the other two hubs A or B will be equal to:

$$\theta(1, z) = \Psi_{31}(z) + \Psi_{32}(z) = \frac{z}{2 - z} \tag{21}$$

Now, combining Eq. (21) and Eq. (18), we get:

$$\theta(t, z) = \frac{z}{2^t - z(2^t - 1)} \tag{22}$$

At this point, we return to our main goal, namely computing the probability generating function $\Psi_v(t,z) = \sum_{n=0}^{\infty} P_v(t,n) z^n$ from an arbitrary source node v to target node A. In other words, the absorbing domain in this case is $\mathcal{D} = \{A\}$ and the aforementioned achievements are now useful for our aim.

For any sub-unit L_k, it can be easily deduced that:

$$\Psi_{C_k}(t,z) = \frac{1}{2}\, \theta(t-k,z)\, [\Psi_{A_k}(t,z) + \Psi_{B_k}(t,z)] \tag{23}$$

Inserting $\Psi_A(t,z)$, $\Psi_B(t,z)$, and $\Psi_C(t,z)$ as the initial conditions of the above equation, it can be calculated recursively. It is clear that $\Psi_A(t,z) = 1$ and based on the existing similarity $\Psi_B(t,z) = \Psi_C(t,z)$ and also analogous to what we had in Eq. (16) and Eq. (18), we get:

$$\Psi_C(t,z) = \Psi_C(1, \theta(t-1,z)) \tag{24}$$

It is sufficient to find $\Psi_C(1,z)$ and use Eq. (22) to compute the above equation. In this case the transition probability matrix P is:

$$P = \begin{pmatrix} 0 & 0 & 0 & 0 & 0 & 0 \\ 1/4 & 0 & 1/4 & 1/4 & 0 & 1/4 \\ 1/4 & 1/4 & 0 & 0 & 1/4 & 1/4 \\ 1/2 & 1/2 & 0 & 0 & 0 & 0 \\ 1/2 & 0 & 1/2 & 0 & 0 & 0 \\ 0 & 1/2 & 1/2 & 0 & 0 & 0 \end{pmatrix}_{6\times 6} \tag{25}$$

Calculating $[\Psi_{ij}(z)]_{6\times 6}$ by inserting the above P into Eq. (20), we obtain:

$$\Psi_C(1,z) = \Psi_{31}(z) = \frac{z}{4 - 3z} \tag{26}$$

Now, combining Eq. (22) and Eq. (24), we have:

$$\Psi_C(t,z) = \frac{z}{2^{t+1} - z(2^{t+1} - 1)} \tag{27}$$

As it is forenamed previously in Eq. (14), the mean first passage time from node C to node A can be derived as:

$$T_{CA} = \mathbb{E}(X_C(t)) = \frac{\partial \Psi_{X_C}(t,z)}{\partial z}\Big|_{z=1} = 2^{t+1} \tag{28}$$

Now, exploiting Eq. (23) in addition to the achieved results regarding the main hubs (i.e., A, B, and C), we can also calculate the PGF and MFPT from an arbitrary node of level k ($0 < k \le t$) to the target node A. As an example, suppose three sub-units L_k^1, L_k^2, and L_k^3 which are labeled by sequences $\{1, \underbrace{1, \ldots, 1}_{k-1}\}$, $\{2, \underbrace{1, \ldots, 1}_{k-1}\}$, and $\{3, \underbrace{1, \ldots, 1}_{k-1}\}$ respectively. We compute $\Psi_{C_k}(t,z)$ and $T_{C_k A}$ for each sub-unit as follows:

Case 1:

$$L_k^1 : \begin{cases} A_k = A_{k-1} = \cdots = A_1 = A \\ B_k = B_{k-1} = \cdots = B_1 = B \end{cases}$$

Inserting the value of $\theta(t-k,z)$ from Eq. (22) into Eq. (23), we obtain:

$$\Psi_{C_k}(t,z) = \frac{\frac{1}{2}z}{2^{t-k} - z(2^{t-k} - 1)} + \frac{\frac{1}{2}z^2}{[2^{t-k} - z(2^{t-k} - 1)][2^{t+1} - z(2^{t+1} - 1)]} \tag{29}$$

Also, the mean first passage time from node C_k to main hub A is:

$$T_{C_k A} = \mathbb{E}(X_{C_k}(t)) = \frac{\partial \Psi_{X_{C_k}}(t,z)}{\partial z} \Big|_{z=1} = 2^t(2^{-k} + 1) \tag{30}$$

As a consequence, the MFPT vector of the three hubs A_k, B_k, and C_k of L_k^1, can be represented as:

$$T^{(k)} \equiv \begin{pmatrix} T_{A_k A} \\ T_{B_k A} \\ T_{C_k A} \end{pmatrix}_{3 \times 1} = \begin{pmatrix} 0 \\ 2^{t+1} \\ 2^t(2^{-k} + 1) \end{pmatrix}_{3 \times 1} \tag{31}$$

Similarly, for the other two cases L_k^2 and L_k^3, we have:
Case 2:

$$L_k^2 : \begin{cases} A_k = A_{k-1} = \cdots = A_1 = A \\ B_k = B_{k-1} = \cdots = B_1 = C \end{cases}$$

$$\Psi_{C_k}(t,z) = \frac{\frac{1}{2}z}{2^{t-k} - z(2^{t-k} - 1)} + \frac{\frac{1}{2}z^2}{[2^{t-k} - z(2^{t-k} - 1)][2^{t+1} - z(2^{t+1} - 1)]} \tag{32}$$

$$T_{C_k A} = \mathbb{E}(X_{C_k}(t)) = \frac{\partial \Psi_{X_{C_k}}(t,z)}{\partial z} \Big|_{z=1} = 2^t(2^{-k} + 1) \tag{33}$$

$$T^{(k)} \equiv \begin{pmatrix} T_{A_k A} \\ T_{B_k A} \\ T_{C_k A} \end{pmatrix}_{3 \times 1} = \begin{pmatrix} 0 \\ 2^{t+1} \\ 2^t(2^{-k} + 1) \end{pmatrix}_{3 \times 1} \tag{34}$$

Case 3:

$$L_k^3 : \begin{cases} A_k = A_{k-1} = \cdots = A_1 = C \\ B_k = B_{k-1} = \cdots = B_1 = B \end{cases}$$

$$\Psi_{C_k}(t,z) = \frac{z^2}{[2^{t-k} - z(2^{t-k} - 1)][2^{t+1} - z(2^{t+1} - 1)]} \tag{35}$$

$$T_{C_k A} = \mathbb{E}(X_{C_k}(t)) = \frac{\partial \Psi_{X_{C_k}}(t,z)}{\partial z} \Big|_{z=1} = 2^t(2^{-k} + 2) \tag{36}$$

$$T^{(k)} \equiv \begin{pmatrix} T_{A_k A} \\ T_{B_k A} \\ T_{C_k A} \end{pmatrix}_{3\times1} = \begin{pmatrix} 2^{t+1} \\ 2^{t+1} \\ 2^t(2^{-k}+2) \end{pmatrix}_{3\times1} \tag{37}$$

At this stage, it is also important to compute the average MFPT over all possible starting nodes of level k. To reach this goal, one can first calculate the following statement over all possible sub-units:

$$\Sigma_k^A = \sum_{\{i_1,\dots,i_k\}} \left(\bigoplus T^{(k)} \right) \tag{38}$$

where $\bigoplus T^{(k)}$ adds all elements of vector $T^{(k)}$. Then, to obtain the summation of mean first passage time for all nodes in level k, the repetition of each node in Σ_k^A should be subtracted. In other words, since each arbitrary starting node v of level i emerges 2^{k-i} times in Σ_k^A and just once in $\Sigma_k^A - \sum_{i=0}^{k-1} \Sigma_i^A$, the sum of MFPT for all nodes in level k will be $\Sigma_k^A - \sum_{i=0}^{k-1} \Sigma_i^A$.

To calculate the Σ_k, we pursue the same manner as [35,39] in the following. For any $k \in \{1,\dots,t\}$, it is straightforward to acknowledge that:

$$T^{(k)} = \mathcal{M}_{i_k} T^{(k-1)} + \mathcal{V}^{(k)}; \quad i_k = 1,2,3 \tag{39}$$

where

$$\mathcal{M}_1 = \begin{pmatrix} 1 & 0 & 0 \\ 0 & 1 & 0 \\ \frac{1}{2} & \frac{1}{2} & 0 \end{pmatrix}_{3\times3} , \mathcal{M}_2 = \begin{pmatrix} 1 & 0 & 0 \\ 0 & 0 & 1 \\ \frac{1}{2} & 0 & \frac{1}{2} \end{pmatrix}_{3\times3} , \mathcal{M}_3 = \begin{pmatrix} 0 & 0 & 1 \\ 0 & 1 & 0 \\ 0 & \frac{1}{2} & \frac{1}{2} \end{pmatrix}_{3\times3} , \mathcal{V}^{(k)} = \begin{pmatrix} 0 \\ 0 \\ 2^{t-k} \end{pmatrix}_{3\times1}$$

In the recursive procedure of Eq. (39), we obtain:

$$\sum_{\{i_1,\dots,i_k\}} T^{(k)} = \mathcal{M}_{tot}^k T^{(0)} + \sum_{l=1}^{k} 3^l \mathcal{M}_{tot}^{k-l} \mathcal{V}^{(l)} \tag{40}$$

where

$$T^{(0)} \equiv \begin{pmatrix} T_{AA} \\ T_{BA} \\ T_{CA} \end{pmatrix}_{3\times1} = \begin{pmatrix} 0 \\ 2^{t+1} \\ 2^{t+1} \end{pmatrix}_{3\times1} ; \quad \mathcal{M}_{tot} = \mathcal{M}_1 + \mathcal{M}_2 + \mathcal{M}_3 = \begin{pmatrix} 2 & 0 & 1 \\ 0 & 2 & 1 \\ 1 & 1 & 1 \end{pmatrix}_{3\times3}$$

Hence, by using orthogonal decomposition of matrix $\mathcal{M}_{tot}$ we get:

$$\mathcal{M}_{tot} T^{(0)} = 2^{t+1} \begin{pmatrix} 2^k + 2 \times 3^{k-1} \\ -2^k + 2 \times 3^{k-1} \\ 2 \times 3^{k-1} \end{pmatrix}_{3\times1} ; \quad \sum_{l=1}^{k} 3^l \mathcal{M}_{tot}^{k-l} \mathcal{V}^{(l)} = (2^t - 3^{t-k})3^{k-1} \begin{pmatrix} 1 \\ 1 \\ 1 \end{pmatrix}_{3\times1} \tag{41}$$

Substituting from Eq. (41) into Eq. (40) and calculating $\bigoplus T^{(k)}$, we gain:

$$\Sigma_k^A = 3^k(2^{t+2} + 2^t - 2^{t-k}) \tag{42}$$

Eventually, the average MFPT over all the staring nodes of level k, can be captured as:

$$\langle T_A^{(k)} \rangle = \frac{\Sigma_k^A - \sum_{i=0}^{k-1} \Sigma_i^A}{V(k)-1} = 2^t \left[\frac{3^k \times 5 + (\frac{3}{2})^k \times 2 + 1}{3^{k+1}+1} \right] \tag{43}$$

By replacing $k = t$ in the above equation, we find the global MFPT to node A as $\langle T_A^{(t)} \rangle = \frac{5 \times 6^t + 2 \times 3^t + 2^t}{3^{t+1}+1}$, which is in agreement with the results in [30].

4.2 First Passage Properties to Node F

In this section, the followed procedure resembles the previous part. Here, the absorbing domain is $\mathcal{D} = \{F\}$ and once more, we find the first passage properties from the main hubs $(A, B, \text{and } C)$ to the target node F. Then, utilizing Eq. (23), PGF and MFPT values from any arbitrary source node can be computed. It is obvious that by symmetry, $\Psi_B(t,z) = \Psi_C(t,z)$. So, it is adequate to derive $\Psi_A(t,z)$ and $\Psi_C(t,z)$. In this case, the transition probability matrix $\mathbf{P}$ of the generation 1 on the (1,2)-flower is:

$$\mathbf{P} = \begin{pmatrix} 0 & 1/4 & 1/4 & 1/4 & 1/4 & 0 \\ 1/4 & 0 & 1/4 & 1/4 & 0 & 1/4 \\ 1/4 & 1/4 & 0 & 0 & 1/4 & 1/4 \\ 1/2 & 1/2 & 0 & 0 & 0 & 0 \\ 1/2 & 0 & 1/2 & 0 & 0 & 0 \\ 0 & 0 & 0 & 0 & 0 & 0 \end{pmatrix}_{6\times6} \tag{44}$$

Inserting $\mathbf{P}$ from the above equation in Eq. (20), gives:

$$\Psi_A(1,z) = \Psi_{16} = \frac{-z^2}{z^2+6z-8}; \quad \Psi_C(1,z) = \Psi_{36} = \frac{z(z-2)}{z^2+6z-8} \tag{45}$$

Now, using above relations and combining Eq. (22) and Eq. (24), we obtain:

$$\Psi_A(t,z) = \frac{-z^2}{-z^2[2^{2t+1}-5(2^t)+1]+z[2^{2t+2}-5(2^t)]-2^{2t+1}} \tag{46}$$

$$\Psi_C(t,z) = \frac{z^2(2^t-1)-z(2^t)}{-z^2[2^{2t+1}-5(2^t)+1]+z[2^{2t+2}-5(2^t)]-2^{2t+1}} \tag{47}$$

And, the mean first passage time from nodes A, B, and C to node F can be derived as:

$$T_{AF} = \frac{\partial \Psi_{X_A}(t,z)}{\partial z}\Big|_{z=1} = 5 \times 2^t; \quad T_{BF} = T_{CF} = \frac{\partial \Psi_{X_C}(t,z)}{\partial z}\Big|_{z=1} = 4 \times 2^t \tag{48}$$

By substituting Eq. (46) and Eq. (47) in Eq. (23), the probability generating function of any arbitrary node from level k can be captured recursively. Similar to Eqs. (29–37) and as an example, we derive the first passage properties of C_k to the absorbing domain $\mathcal{D} = \{F\}$ in L_k^1, L_k^2, and L_k^3.

Case 1:

$$L_k^1: \begin{cases} A_k = A_{k-1} = \cdots = A_1 = A \\ B_k = B_{k-1} = \cdots = B_1 = B \end{cases}$$

Inserting the value of $\theta(t - k, z)$ from Eq. (22) into Eq. (23), we obtain:

$$\Psi_{C_k}(t, z) = \frac{-z^3(2^{t-1} - 1) + z^2(2^{t-1})}{[2^{t-k} - z(2^{t-k} - 1)][z^2[2^{2t+1} - 5(2^t) + 1] - z[2^{2t+2} - 5(2^t)] + 2^{2t+1}]} \quad (49)$$

Hence,

$$T_{C_k F} = \frac{\partial \Psi_{X_{C_k}}(t, z)}{\partial z}\Big|_{z=1} = 2^t(2^{-k} + \frac{9}{2}) \quad (50)$$

and again, the MFPT vector of the three hubs A_k, B_k, and C_k equals:

$$\mathbf{T}^{(k)} \equiv \begin{pmatrix} T_{A_k A} \\ T_{B_k A} \\ T_{C_k A} \end{pmatrix}_{3\times 1} = \begin{pmatrix} 5 \times 2^t \\ 4 \times 2^t \\ 2^t(2^{-k} + \frac{9}{2}) \end{pmatrix}_{3\times 1} \quad (51)$$

Case 2:

$$L_k^2: \begin{cases} A_k = A_{k-1} = \cdots = A_1 = A \\ B_k = B_{k-1} = \cdots = B_1 = C \end{cases}$$

$$\Psi_{C_k}(t, z) = \frac{-z^3(2^{t-1} - 1) + z^2(2^{t-1})}{[2^{t-k} - z(2^{t-k} - 1)][z^2[2^{2t+1} - 5(2^t) + 1] - z[2^{2t+2} - 5(2^t)] + 2^{2t+1}]} \quad (52)$$

$$T_{C_k F} = \frac{\partial \Psi_{X_{C_k}}(t, z)}{\partial z}\Big|_{z=1} = 2^t(2^{-k} + \frac{9}{2}) \quad (53)$$

$$\mathbf{T}^{(k)} \equiv \begin{pmatrix} T_{A_k A} \\ T_{B_k A} \\ T_{C_k A} \end{pmatrix}_{3\times 1} = \begin{pmatrix} 5 \times 2^t \\ 4 \times 2^t \\ 2^t(2^{-k} + \frac{9}{2}) \end{pmatrix}_{3\times 1} \quad (54)$$

Case 3:

$$L_k^3: \begin{cases} A_k = A_{k-1} = \cdots = A_1 = C \\ B_k = B_{k-1} = \cdots = B_1 = B \end{cases}$$

$$\Psi_{C_k}(t,z) = \frac{-z^3(2^t - 1) + z^2(2^t)}{\left[2^{t-k} - z(2^{t-k} - 1)\right]\left[z^2[2^{2t+1} - 5(2^t) + 1] - z[2^{2t+2} - 5(2^t)] + 2^{2t+1}\right]} \quad (55)$$

$$T_{C_kF} = \frac{\partial \Psi_{X_{C_k}}(t,z)}{\partial z}\bigg|_{z=1} = 2^t(2^{-k} + 4) \quad (56)$$

$$\boldsymbol{T}^{(k)} \equiv \begin{pmatrix} T_{A_kA} \\ T_{B_kA} \\ T_{C_kA} \end{pmatrix}_{3\times1} = \begin{pmatrix} 4 \times 2^t \\ 4 \times 2^t \\ 2^t(2^{-k} + 4) \end{pmatrix}_{3\times1} \quad (57)$$

Calculating the average MFPT for all starting nodes of level k is analogous to the case where the absorbing domain is $\mathcal{D} = \{A\}$. Here, since we know all the values of $T_{AF} = 5 \times 2^t$, $T_{BF} = 4 \times 2^t$, $T_{CF} = 4 \times 2^t$, $T_{DF} = 5 \times 2^t$, $T_{EF} = 5 \times 2^t$, and $T_{FF} = 0$, $\boldsymbol{T}^{(1)}$ can be provided for all cases of $i_1 = \{1, 2, 3\}$. Similar to Eq. (40), we can derive the following relation:

$$\sum_{\{i_1,\dots,i_k\}} \boldsymbol{T}^{(k)} = \mathcal{M}_{tot}^{k-1} \sum_{i_1=1}^{3} \boldsymbol{T}^{(0)} + \sum_{l=2}^{k} 3^l \mathcal{M}_{tot}^{k-l} \mathcal{V}^{(l)} \quad (58)$$

Again, by orthogonal decomposition of matrix $\mathcal{M}_{tot}$ and calculating $\bigoplus \boldsymbol{T}^{(k)}$, we reach:

$$\Sigma_k^F = 3^k(2^{t+2} + 13 \times 2^t - 9 \times 2^{t-1} - 2^{t-k}) \quad (59)$$

Also note that $\Sigma_0 = T_{AF} + T_{BF} + T_{CF} = 13 \times 2^t$. Consequently, the average MFPT over all the staring nodes of level k to node F is:

$$\langle T_F^{(k)} \rangle = \frac{\Sigma_k^F - \sum_{i=0}^{k-1} \Sigma_i^F}{V(k) - 1} = 2^{t+2}\left[\frac{3^k(\frac{25}{8} - 2^{-k-1}) + (\frac{3}{2})^k + \frac{11}{8}}{3^{t+1} + 1}\right] \quad (60)$$

4.3   Partial Cover Time for Two Targets A and F

Now, it is time to reach our ultimate goal in this paper by following the previously proposed steps. The partial cover time from any arbitrary source node i to the target set of $\{A, F\}$ can be derived by substituting the associated values of mean first passage time to nodes A and F into Eq. (11). For example, suppose the node C_k of sub-unit L_k^1 as the starting node. From Eq. (30), Eq. (48), and Eq. (50), we know that $T_{C_kA} = 2^t(2^{-k} + 1)$, $T_{AF} = 5 \times 2^t$, and $T_{C_kF} = 2^t(2^{-k} + \frac{9}{2})$. Also, it can be simply acquired that $T_{FA} = 5 \times 2^t$. Therefore, we obtain:

$$T_{C_k,\{A,F\}} = \frac{T_{AF} T_{FA} + T_{C_kA} T_{FA} + T_{C_kF} T_{AF}}{T_{AF} + T_{FA}} = 2^t(2^{-k} + \frac{21}{4}) \quad (61)$$

In the last step, we try to calculate the global partial cover time which is the averaged value over all starting nodes from all possible values of $k \in \{1, 2, \dots, t\}$.

One can obtain the accumulated quantity of mean first passage times from all source nodes to node A (similarly to node F) by $\Sigma_t^A - \sum_{i=0}^{t-1} \Sigma_i^A$ as:

$$\left(\Sigma_t^A - \sum_{i=0}^{t-1} \Sigma_i^A\right) = \frac{5}{2} \times 6^t + 3^t + \frac{1}{2} \times 2^t; \quad \left(\Sigma_t^F - \sum_{i=0}^{t-1} \Sigma_i^F\right) = \frac{25}{4} \times 6^t + 3^t + \frac{11}{4} \times 2^t$$

Ultimately, the global partial cover time can be expressed precisely in the following form:

$$\langle T_{\{A,F\}}^{(t)} \rangle = \frac{V(t) \cdot (T_{AF} \, T_{FA}) + T_{FA}(\Sigma_t^A - \sum_{i=0}^{t-1} \Sigma_i^A) + T_{AF}(\Sigma_t^F - \sum_{i=0}^{t-1} \Sigma_i^F)}{V(t) \cdot (T_{AF} + T_{FA})}$$
$$= 2^t \left[\frac{3^t \times \frac{65}{4} + (\frac{3}{2})^t \times 2 + \frac{43}{4}}{3^{t+1} + 3} \right] \qquad (62)$$

We have now delivered the exact solution for the problem of partial cover time in a dual-target search on a $(1,2)$-flower as it was the final goal of this study.

5 Conclusions

In this work, we investigate the problem of global partial cover time in a dual-target search as the averaged cover time value over all possible starting nodes to visit two target nodes. We utilize a $(1,2)$-flower as the network of interest. These scale-free networks have recently attracted much interest due to being prevalent in scientific research and real-life applications. These recursively constructed networks exhibit rich behaviors such as the small-world phenomenon and pseudofractal properties. For the first time, we capture an expression to explicitly compute the partial cover time of the random walker until reaching both target nodes. This is in contrary to most previous efforts which only focus on cover time calculation or more straightforward single-target search problems. Random search processes have long been recognized as an important branch of network science based on their broad applications including disease spreading, animal foraging, and biochemical reactions. Nevertheless, much remains unknown about the search time for finding more than one target at a time. The derived formula in this work is extremely efficacious and has the capacity to be simply generalized to other types of generic networks. This study can make a valuable contribution to the field of multi-target search and also prompt future work towards formulating an expression for partial cover time in case of having an arbitrary number of target nodes.

References

1. Codling, E.A., Plank, M.J., Benhamou, S.: Random walk models in biology. J. R. Soc. Interface **5**(25), 813–834 (2008)
2. Humphries, N.E., et al.: Environmental context explains Lévy and Brownian movement patterns of marine predators. Nature **465**(7301), 1066–1069 (2010)
3. Lloyd, A.L., May, R.M.: How viruses spread among computers and people. Science **292**(5520), 1316–1317 (2001)
4. Usher, M., McClelland, J.L.: The time course of perceptual choice: the leaky, competing accumulator model. Psychol. Rev. **108**(3), 550 (2001)
5. Gold, J.I., Shadlen, M.N.: The neural basis of decision making. Annu. Rev. Neurosci. **30**, 535–574 (2007)
6. Bénichou, O., Voituriez, R.: From first-passage times of random walks in confinement to geometry-controlled kinetics. Phys. Rep. **539**(4), 225–284 (2014)
7. Campbell, J.Y., et al.: The econometrics of financial markets. Macroecon. Dyn. **2**(04), 559–562 (1998)
8. Mantegna, R.N., Stanley, H.E.: Introduction to Econophysics: Correlations and Complexity in Finance. Cambridge University Press (1999)
9. Porter, M.A., Bianconi, G.: Network analysis and modelling: special issue of European Journal of Applied Mathematics. Eur. J. Appl. Math. **27**, 807–811 (2016)
10. Coifman, R.R., Lafon, S.: Diffusion maps. Appl. Comput. Harmon. Anal. **21**(1), 5–30 (2006)
11. Perozzi, B., Al-Rfou, R., Skiena, S.: DeepWalk: online learning of social representations. In: Proceedings of the 20th ACM SIGKDD International Conference on Knowledge Discovery and Data Mining (2014)
12. Grover, A., Leskovec, J.: node2vec: scalable feature learning for networks. In: Proceedings of the 22nd ACM SIGKDD International Conference on Knowledge Discovery and Data Mining (2016)
13. Khajehnejad, M.: SimNet: similarity-based network embeddings with mean commute time. PLoS ONE **14**(8), e0221172 (2019)
14. Khajehnejad, M., et al.: Adversarial graph embeddings for fair influence maximization over social networks. arXiv preprint arXiv:2005.04074 (2020)
15. Khajehnejad, A., et al.: CrossWalk: fairness-enhanced node representation learning. arXiv preprint arXiv:2105.02725 (2021)
16. Boccaletti, S., et al.: Complex networks: structure and dynamics. Phys. Rep. **424**(4), 175–308 (2006)
17. Ehrgott, M., Gandibleux, X.: A survey and annotated bibliography of multiobjective combinatorial optimization. OR-Spektrum **22**(4), 425–460 (2000)
18. Ehrgott, M.: Multicriteria Optimization, vol. 491. Springer, Heidelberg (2005). https://doi.org/10.1007/3-540-27659-9
19. Johnson, D.S.: Approximation algorithms for combinatorial problems. J. Comput. Syst. Sci. **9**(3), 256–278 (1974)
20. Aldous, D.: An introduction to covering problems for random walks on graphs. J. Theor. Probab. **2**(1), 87–89 (1989)
21. Dembo, A., et al.: Cover times for Brownian motion and random walks in two dimensions. Ann. Math. **160**, 433–464 (2004)
22. Nemirovsky, A.M., Mártin, H.O., Coutinho-Filho, M.D.: Universality in the lattice-covering time problem. Phys. Rev. A **41**(2), 761 (1990)
23. Mendonça, J.R.G.: Numerical evidence against a conjecture on the cover time of planar graphs. Phys. Rev. E **84**(2), 022103 (2011)

24. Chupeau, M., Bénichou, O., Voituriez, R.: Cover times of random searches. Nat. Phys. **11**(10), 844–847 (2015)
25. Weng, T., et al.: Multitarget search on complex networks: a logarithmic growth of global mean random cover time. Chaos Interdisc. J. Nonlin. Sci. **27**(9), 093103 (2017)
26. Condamin, S., et al.: First-passage times in complex scale-invariant media. Nature **450**(7166), 77–80 (2007)
27. Khajehnejad, M.: Efficiency of long-range navigation on Treelike fractals. Chaos, Solitons Fractals **122**, 102–110 (2019)
28. Weng, T., et al.: Navigation by anomalous random walks on complex networks. Sci. Rep. **6**(1), 1–9 (2016)
29. Rozenfeld, H.D., Havlin, S., Ben-Avraham, D.: Fractal and transfractal recursive scale-free nets. New J. Phys. **9**(6), 175 (2007)
30. Zhang, Z., et al.: Exact solution for mean first-passage time on a pseudofractal scale-free web. Phys. Rev. E **79**(2), 021127 (2009)
31. Peng, J., Agliari, E., Zhang, Z.: Exact calculations of first-passage properties on the pseudofractal scale-free web. Chaos Interdisc. J. Nonlinear Sci. **25**(7), 073118 (2015)
32. Bollt, E.M., ben Avraham, D.: What is special about diffusion on scale-free nets? New J. Phys. **7**(1), 26 (2005)
33. Zhang, Z., Zhou, S., Chen, L.: Evolving pseudofractal networks. Eur. Phys. J. B **58**(3), 337–344 (2007)
34. Watts, D.J., Strogatz, S.H.: Collective dynamics of 'small-world' networks. Nature **393**(6684), 440 (1998)
35. Meyer, B., et al.: Exact calculations of first-passage quantities on recursive networks. Phys. Rev. E **85**(2), 026113 (2012)
36. Zhang, Z., et al.: Mean first-passage time for random walks on undirected networks. Eur. Phys. J. B **84**(4), 691–697 (2011)
37. Weng, T., et al.: Navigation by anomalous random walks on complex networks. Sci. Rep. **6**, 37547 (2016)
38. Rudnick, J., Gaspari, G.: Elements of the Random Walk: An Introduction for Advanced Students and Researchers. Cambridge University Press (2004)
39. Peng, J., Guoai, X.: Efficiency analysis of diffusion on T-fractals in the sense of random walks. J. Chem. Phys. **140**(13), 134102 (2014)

Generalized Linear Models Network Autoregression

Mirko Amillotta$^{(\boxtimes)}$, Konstantinos Fokianos, and Ioannis Krikidis

University of Cyprus, PO BOX 20537, Nicosia, Cyprus
{armillotta.mirko,fokianos,krikidis}@ucy.ac.cy

Abstract. We discuss a unified framework for the statistical analysis of streaming data obtained by networks with a known neighborhood structure. In particular, we deal with autoregressive models that make explicit the dependence of current observations to their past values and the values of their respective neighborhoods. We consider the case of both continuous and count responses measured over time for each node of a known network. We discuss least squares and quasi maximum likelihood inference. Both methods provide estimators with good properties. In particular, we show that consistent and asymptotically normal estimators of the model parameters, under this high-dimensional data generating process, are obtained after optimizing a criterion function. The methodology is illustrated by applying it to wind speed observed over different weather stations of England and Wales.

Keywords: Adjacency matrix · autocorrelation · least squares estimation · link function · multivariate time series · network analysis · quasi-likelihood estimation

1 Introduction

Measuring the impact of a network structure to a multivariate time series process has attracted considerable attention over the last years, mainly due to the growing availability of streaming network data (social networks, GPS data, epidemics, air pollution monitoring systems and more generally environmental wireless sensor networks, among many other applications). The methodology outlined in this work has potential application in several network science fields. In general, any stream of data for a sample of units whose relations can be modeled as an adjacency matrix (neighborhood structure) the statistical techniques reviewed in this work are directly applicable. Indeed, a wide variety of available spatial streaming data related to physical phenomena can fit this framework. As an illustrative example, we analyze wind speed data observed over different weather stations

This work has been co-financed by the European Regional Development Fund and the Republic of Cyprus through the Research and Innovation Foundation, under the project INFRASTRUCTURES/1216/0017 (IRIDA).

© Springer Nature Switzerland AG 2022
P. Ribeiro et al. (Eds.): NetSci-X 2022, LNCS 13197, pp. 112–125, 2022.
https://doi.org/10.1007/978-3-030-97240-0_9

of England and Wales. Network autoregressions allows meaningful analysis of the actual wind speed, for each node, based on the effect of past speeds and the velocity measured on its neighbor stations; see Sect. 4. This methodology is potentially useful to model sensor networks for environmental monitoring. See [6,8,22,25], among others, who discuss application of wireless sensor network for environmental, agricultural and intelligent home automation systems. See also [41] for an application to social network analysis. We discuss a statistical framework which encompasses the case of both continuous and count responses measured over time for each node of a known network.

1.1   The Case of Continuous Responses

When a response random variable, say $Y_{i,t}$, is measured for each node i of a known network, with N nodes, at time t, a $N \times 1$-dimensional random vector is obtained, say $\mathbf{Y}_t \in \mathbb{R}^N = (Y_{1,t} \ldots Y_{i,t} \ldots Y_{N,t})'$, for each measured time $t = 1, \ldots, T$. The Vector Autoregressive (VAR) model, is a standard tool for continuous time series analysis and it has been widely applied to model multivariate processes. However, if the size of the network is N, then the number of unknown parameters to be estimated is of the order $\mathcal{O}(N^2)$ which is much larger than the temporal sample size T. The VAR model cannot then be applied for modeling such data.

Other modelling strategies have been proposed to describe the dynamics of such processes. One method is based on sparsity, see for example [21], among other. Accordingly, the parameters of the model which have less impact to the response are automatically set to zero, allowing to estimate the remaining ones. Alternatively, a dimension reduction method which accounts for network impact has been recently developed by [41], who introduced the Network vector Autoregressive model (NAR). In this methodology, for each node $i = 1, \ldots, N$ the current response, $Y_{i,t}$, for the node i, at time t, is assumed to depend only on the lagged value of the response itself, say $Y_{i,t-1}$, and the mean of the past responses computed only over the nodes connected to the node i; this can be broadly thought as a factor which accounts for the impact of the network structure to node i. The NAR representation allows considerable simplification for the final model fitted to the data as it depends only on a few parameters. In addition, such representation still includes all essential information, i.e. the impact of the past values of the response and the influence of the network neighbors on each node.

NAR models are tailored to continuous response data. The parameters of the model are estimated via ordinary least squares (OLS), under two asymptotic regimes (a) with increasing time sample size $T \to \infty$ and fixed network dimension N (which is standard assumption for multivariate time series analysis) and (b) with both N, T increasing, i.e. $\min\{N, T\} \to \infty$. The latter is important in network science, since the asymptotic behavior of the network when its dimension grows ($N \to \infty$) is a crucial interest in network analysis. In practice, when only a sample of the network is available, the results obtained under (b) guarantee that the estimates of unknown parameters of the model have good statistical properties, even if N is big and, ultimately, bigger than T.

More recently, an extension to network quantile autoregressive models has been studied by [42]. Further works in this line of research includes the grouped least squares estimation, [40], and a Network GARCH model, see [39] under the standard asymptotic regime (a). Related work was developed by [23] who specified a Generalized Network Autoregressive model (GNAR) for continuous random variables, by taking into account different layers of relationships within neighbors of the network. All network time series models discussed so far are defined in terms of Independent Identically Distributed (IID) error random innovations; such an assumption is crucial for most of theoretical analysis.

1.2   The Case of Discrete Responses

Increasing availability of discrete-valued data, from diverse applications, has advanced the growth of a rich literature on modelling and inference for count time series processes. In this contribution, we consider the generalized linear model (GLM) framework, see [27], which includes both continuous-valued time series and integer-valued processes. Likelihood inference and testing can be developed in the GLM framework. Some examples of GLM models for count processes include the works by [9,15] and [14], among others. In [17] and [19], stability conditions and inference for linear and log-linear count time series models are developed. Further related contributions can be found in [5] for inference of negative binomial time series, [1,7,10,11] and [12], among others, for further generalizations. Even though a vast literature on the univariate case is available, results on multivariate count time series models for network data are still missing; see [26,30–32] for some exceptions. Recently [18], introduced multivariate linear and log-linear Poisson autoregression models. These authors described the joint distribution of the counts by means of a copula construction. Copulas are useful because of Sklar's theorem which shows that marginal distributions are combined to give a joint distribution when applying a copula, i.e. a N-dimensional distribution function all of whose marginals are standard uniforms. Further details are also available in the review of [16]. Recent work by [2] studied linear and log-linear multivariate count-valued extensions of the NAR model, called Poisson Network Autoregression (PNAR). These authors developed associated theory for the two types of asymptotic inference (a)–(b) discussed earlier, under the α-mixing property of the innovation term, see [13,33]. Intuitively, this assumption requires only *asymptotic independence* over time. The marginal distribution of the resulting count process is Poisson (but other marginals are possible including the Negative Binomial distribution) whereas the dependence among them is captured by the copula construction described in [18]. Inference relies on the Quasi Maximum Likelihood Estimation (QMLE), see [20], among others.

1.3 Outline

This paper summarizes some of the work by [41] and [2] and provides a unified framework for both continuous and integer-valued data. In addition it reviews the recent developments in this research area and illustrates the potential usefulness of this methodology. The paper is divided into three parts: Sect. 2 discusses the linear and log-linear NAR and PNAR model specifications. In Sect. 3, the quasi likelihood inference is described, for the two types of asymptotics (a)–(b). Finally, Sect. 4 reports the results of an application on a wind speed network in England and Wales, and gives a model selection procedure for the lag order of the NAR model.

Notation

For a $q \times p$-dimensional matrix $\mathbf{A}$ whose elements are a_{ij}, for $i = 1, \ldots, q$, $j = 1, \ldots, p$, denotes generalized matrix norm, defined as $\|\|\mathbf{A}\|\|_r = \max_{|\mathbf{x}|_r=1} |\mathbf{A}\mathbf{x}|_r$. If $r = 1$, $\|\|\mathbf{A}\|\|_1 = \max_{1 \leq j \leq p} \sum_{i=1}^{q} |a_{ij}|$. $\|\|\mathbf{A}\|\|_2 = \rho^{1/2}(\mathbf{A}'\mathbf{A})$, where $\rho(\cdot)$ is the spectral radius, if $r = 2$. $\|\|\mathbf{A}\|\|_\infty = \max_{1 \leq i \leq q} \sum_{j=1}^{p} |a_{ij}|$, if $r = \infty$. If $q = p$, then these norms are matrix norms.

2 Models

We study a network of size N (number of nodes), indexed by $i = 1, \ldots N$, and adjacency matrix $\mathbf{A} = (a_{ij}) \in \mathbb{R}^{N \times N}$ where $a_{ij} = 1$, if there is a directed edge from i to j, $i \rightarrow j$ (e.g. user i follows user j on Twitter), and $a_{ij} = 0$ otherwise. Undirected graphs are also allowed ($i \leftrightarrow j$). The neighborhood structure is assumed to be known but self-relationships are not allowed, i.e. $a_{ii} = 0$ for any $i = 1, \ldots, N$ (this is reasonable because e.g. user i cannot follow himself). For more on networks see [24, 36]. Define a variable $Y_{i,t} \in \mathbb{R}$ for the node i at time t. The interest in on assessing the effect of the network structure on the stochastic process $\{\mathbf{Y}_t = (Y_{i,t}, i = 1, 2 \ldots N, t = 0, 1, 2 \ldots, T)\}$, with the corresponding N-dimensional conditional mean process defined in the following way $\{\boldsymbol{\lambda}_t = (\lambda_{i,t}, i = 1, 2 \ldots N, t = 1, 2 \ldots, T)\}$, where $\boldsymbol{\lambda}_t = \mathrm{E}(\mathbf{Y}_t|\mathcal{F}_{t-1})$ and $\mathcal{F}_{t-1} = \sigma(\mathbf{Y}_s : s \leq t - 1)$ is the σ-algebra generated by the past of the process.

2.1 NAR Model

For $i = 1, \ldots, N$, the Network Autoregressive model of order 1, NAR(1), is given by

$$\lambda_{i,t} = \beta_0 + \beta_1 n_i^{-1} \sum_{j=1}^{N} a_{ij} Y_{j,t-1} + \beta_2 Y_{i,t-1}, \qquad (1)$$

where $n_i = \sum_{j \neq i} a_{ij}$ is the out-degree, i.e. the total number of nodes which i has an edge with. The NAR(1) model implies that, for every single node i, the conditional mean of the process is regressed on the past of the variable itself for node i and the weighted average over the other nodes $j \neq i$ which have a connection with i. Hence only the nodes which are directly followed by the focal node i (neighborhoods) may have an impact on the mean process of the focal node i. It is a reasonable assumption in many applications; for example, in a social network the activity of node k, which satisfies $a_{ik} = 0$, does not affect node i. However, extensions to several layers of neighborhoods are also possible, see [23] and [2, Rem. 2]. The parameter β_1 is called network effect and it measures the average impact of node i's connections $n_i^{-1} \sum_{j=1}^{N} a_{ij} Y_{j,t-1}$. The coefficient β_2 is called autoregressive (or lagged) effect because it provides a weight for the impact of past process $Y_{i,t-1}$.

For a continuous-valued time series Y_t, [41] defined $Y_{i,t} = \lambda_{i,t} + \xi_{i,t}$, where $\lambda_{i,t}$ is specified in (1) and $\xi_{i,t} \sim IID(0, \sigma^2)$ across both $1 \leq i \leq N$ and $0 \leq t \leq T$ and with finite fourth moment. Then first two moments of the process $\mathbf{Y}_t$ modelled by (1) are given by [41, Prop. 1]

$$\mathrm{E}(\mathbf{Y}_t) = \beta_0 (1 - \beta_1 - \beta_2)^{-1} \mathbf{1}_N,$$
$$\mathrm{vec}[\mathrm{Var}(\mathbf{Y}_t)] = \sigma^2 (\mathbf{I}_{N^2} - \mathbf{G} \otimes \mathbf{G})^{-1} \mathrm{vec}(\mathbf{I}_N),$$

where $\mathbf{1}_N = (1, 1, \ldots, 1)' \in \mathbb{R}^N$ and $\mathbf{I}_N$ is the identity matrix $N \times N$ and $\mathbf{G} = \beta_1 \mathbf{W} + \beta_2 \mathbf{I}_N$, with $\mathbf{W} = \mathrm{diag}\{n_1^{-1}, \ldots, n_N^{-1}\} \mathbf{A}$ being the row-normalized adjacency matrix. Note that the matrix $\mathbf{W}$ is a stochastic matrix, as $\|\|\mathbf{W}\|\|_\infty = 1$, [34, Def. 9.16].

More generally, the NAR(p) model is defined by

$$\lambda_{i,t} = \beta_0 + \sum_{h=1}^{p} \beta_{1h} \left(n_i^{-1} \sum_{j=1}^{N} a_{ij} Y_{j,t-h} \right) + \sum_{h=1}^{p} \beta_{2h} Y_{i,t-h}, \tag{2}$$

allowing dependence on the last p values of the response node. Obviously, when $p = 1$, $\beta_{11} = \beta_1$, $\beta_{22} = \beta_2$ and we obtain (1). Without loss of generality, coefficients can be set equal to zero if the parameter order is different for the summands of (2).

2.2   PNAR Model

Consider the process $Y_{i,t}$, for $i = 1, \ldots, N$, is integer-valued (that is $\mathbf{Y}_t \in \mathbb{N}^N$) and it is assumed to be marginally Poisson, such as $Y_{i,t}|\mathcal{F}_{t-1} \sim Poisson(\lambda_{i,t})$. Other models can be developed, including the Negative Binomial distribution, but the marginal mean has to parameterized as in (1). The univariate conditional mean of the count process is still specified as (1), more generally (2), above. The interpretation of all coefficients is identical to the case of continuous-valued case. The innovation term is given by $\boldsymbol{\xi}_t = \mathbf{Y}_t - \boldsymbol{\lambda}_t$ and forms a martingale difference sequence by construction but, in general, it is not an IID sequence. This adds a level of complexity in the model because a joint count distribution is required for modelling and inference. Several alternatives of multivariate Poisson-type probability mass function (p.m.f) have been proposed in the literature, see the review in [16, Sect. 2]. However, they usually have a complicated closed form, the associated inference is theoretically cumbersome, and numerically difficult; moreover, the resulting model is largely constrained. Then, a copula approach has been preferred as in [2], where the joint distribution of the vector $\{\mathbf{Y}_t\}$ is constructed imposing a copula structure on waiting times of a Poisson process, see [18, p. 474]. More precisely, consider a set of values $(\beta_0, \beta_1, \beta_2)'$ and a starting vector $\boldsymbol{\lambda}_0 = (\lambda_{1,0}, \ldots, \lambda_{N,0})'$,

1. Let $\mathbf{U}_l = (U_{1,l}, \ldots, U_{N,l})$, for $l = 1, \ldots, L$ a sample from a N-dimensional copula $C(u_1, \ldots, u_N)$, where $U_{i,l}$ follows a Uniform$(0,1)$ distribution, for $i = 1, \ldots, N$.
2. The transformation $X_{i,l} = -\log U_{i,l}/\lambda_{i,0}$ is exponential with parameter $\lambda_{i,0}$, for $i = 1, \ldots, N$.
3. If $X_{i,1} > 1$, then $Y_{i,0} = 0$, otherwise $Y_{i,0} = \max\left\{k \in [1, K] : \sum_{l=1}^{k} X_{i,l} \leq 1\right\}$, by taking K large enough. Then, $Y_{i,0} \sim Poisson(\lambda_{i,0})$, for $i = 1, \ldots, N$. So, $\mathbf{Y}_0 = (Y_{1,0}, \ldots, Y_{N,0})$ is a set of marginal Poisson processes with mean $\boldsymbol{\lambda}_0$.
4. By using the model (1), $\boldsymbol{\lambda}_1$ is obtained.
5. Return back to step 1 to obtain $\mathbf{Y}_1$, and so on.

This constitutes an innovative data generating process with desired Poisson marginal distributions and flexible correlation. With the distribution structure presented above, the resulting model for the count process $\mathbf{Y}_t$, with conditional mean specified as in (1) for all i, has been introduced by [2], called linear Poisson Network Autoregression of order 1, PNAR(1), written in matrix notation:

$$\mathbf{Y}_t = \mathbf{N}_t(\boldsymbol{\lambda}_t), \quad \boldsymbol{\lambda}_t = \boldsymbol{\beta}_0 + \mathbf{G}\mathbf{Y}_{t-1}, \tag{3}$$

where $\{\mathbf{N}_t\}$ is a sequence of independent N-variate copula-Poisson process (see above), which counts the number of events in the time intervals $[0, \lambda_{1,t}] \times \cdots \times [0, \lambda_{N,t}]$. Moreover, $\boldsymbol{\beta}_0 = \beta_0 \mathbf{1}_N \in \mathbb{R}^N$. By considering the conditional mean specified as in (2) for all i, it is immediate to define the PNAR(p) model:

$$\mathbf{Y}_t = \mathbf{N}_t(\boldsymbol{\lambda}_t), \quad \boldsymbol{\lambda}_t = \boldsymbol{\beta}_0 + \sum_{h=1}^{p} \mathbf{G}_h \mathbf{Y}_{t-h}, \tag{4}$$

where $\mathbf{G}_h = \beta_{1h}\mathbf{W} + \beta_{2h}\mathbf{I}_N$ for $h = 1, \ldots, p$. Clearly, $\lambda_{i,t} > 0$ so $\beta_0, \beta_{1h}, \beta_{2h} \geq 0$ for all $h = 1 \ldots, p$. Although the network effect β_1 of model (1) is typically expected to be positive, see [4], in order to allow a connection to the wider GLM theory, [27], and allow coefficients which take values on the entire real line the following log-linear version of the PNAR(p) is proposed in [2]:

$$\nu_{i,t} = \beta_0 + \sum_{h=1}^{p} \beta_{1h}\left(n_i^{-1} \sum_{j=1}^{N} a_{ij} \log(1 + Y_{j,t-h})\right) + \sum_{h=1}^{p} \beta_{2h} \log(1 + Y_{i,t-h}), \tag{5}$$

where $\nu_{i,t} = \log(\lambda_{i,t})$ for every $i = 1, \ldots, N$. The model (5) do not require any constraints on the parameters, since $\nu_{i,t} \in \mathbb{R}$. The interpretation of coefficients and the summands of (5) is similar to that of linear model but in the log scale.

The condition $\sum_{h=1}^{p}(|\beta_{1h}| + |\beta_{2h}|) < 1$ is sufficient to obtain the process $\{\mathbf{Y}_t,\ t \in \mathbb{Z}\}$ to be stationary and ergodic for every Network Autoregressive model of order p. See [41, Thm. 4] and [2, Thm. 1–2]. For model (3), such stationary distribution has the first two moments

$$E(\mathbf{Y}_t) = (\mathbf{I}_N - \mathbf{G})^{-1}\boldsymbol{\beta}_0 = \beta_0(1 - \beta_1 - \beta_2)^{-1}\mathbf{1}_N\,,$$
$$\mathrm{vec}[\mathrm{Var}(\mathbf{Y}_t)] = (\mathbf{I}_{N^2} - \mathbf{G} \otimes \mathbf{G})^{-1}\mathrm{vec}[E(\boldsymbol{\Sigma}_t)]\,,$$

where $\boldsymbol{\Sigma}_t = E(\boldsymbol{\xi}_t\boldsymbol{\xi}_t'|\mathcal{F}_{t-1})$ denotes the *true* conditional covariance matrix of the vector $\mathbf{Y}_t$.

3   Inference

We approach the estimation problem by using the theory of estimating functions; see [3,37] and [20], among others. Consider the vector of unknown parameters $\boldsymbol{\theta} = (\beta_0, \beta_{11}, \ldots, \beta_{1p}, \beta_{21}, \ldots, \beta_{2p})' \in \mathbb{R}^m$, satisfying the stationarity condition, where $m = 2p + 1$. Define the quasi-log-likelihood function for $\boldsymbol{\theta}$ as $l_{NT}(\boldsymbol{\theta}) = \sum_{t=1}^{T}\sum_{i=1}^{N} l_{i,t}(\boldsymbol{\theta})$, which is not constrained to be the *true* log-likelihood of the process. The quasi maximum likelihood estimator (QMLE) is the vector of parameters $\hat{\boldsymbol{\theta}}$ which maximize the quasi-log-likelihood $l_{NT}(\boldsymbol{\theta})$. Such maximization is performed by solving the system of equations $S_{NT}(\boldsymbol{\theta}) = \mathbf{0}_m$, with respect to $\boldsymbol{\theta}$, where $\mathbf{S}_{NT}(\boldsymbol{\theta}) = \partial l_{NT}(\boldsymbol{\theta})/\partial\boldsymbol{\theta} = \sum_{t=1}^{T}\mathbf{s}_{Nt}(\boldsymbol{\theta})$ is the quasi-score function, and $\mathbf{0}_m$ is a $m \times 1$-dimensional vector of 0's. Moreover define the matrices

$$\mathbf{H}_{NT}(\boldsymbol{\theta}) = -\frac{\partial^2 l_{NT}(\boldsymbol{\theta})}{\partial\boldsymbol{\theta}\partial\boldsymbol{\theta}'}, \quad B_{NT}(\boldsymbol{\theta}) = E\left(\sum_{t=1}^{T}\mathbf{s}_{Nt}(\boldsymbol{\theta})\mathbf{s}_{Nt}(\boldsymbol{\theta})'\,\bigg|\,\mathcal{F}_{t-1}\right), \quad (6)$$

as the sample Hessian matrix and the sample conditional information matrix, respectively. We drop the dependence on $\boldsymbol{\theta}$ when a quantity is evaluated at the true value $\boldsymbol{\theta}_0$.

Define $X_{i,t} = n_i^{-1}\sum_{j=1}^{N} a_{ij}Y_{j,t-1}$ and $\mathbf{Z}_{i,t-1} = (1, X_{i,t-1}, Y_{i,t-1})'$. For continuous variables, the QMLE estimator for the NAR(1) model defined in (1) maximizes the quasi-log-likelihood

$$l_{NT}(\boldsymbol{\theta}) = -\sum_{t=1}^{T}(\mathbf{Y}_t - \mathbf{Z}_{t-1}\boldsymbol{\theta})'(\mathbf{Y}_t - \mathbf{Z}_{t-1}\boldsymbol{\theta})\,, \quad (7)$$

where $\mathbf{Z}_{t-1} = (\mathbf{Z}_{1,t-1}, \ldots, \mathbf{Z}_{N,t-1})' \in \mathbb{R}^{N \times m}$, with associated score function

$$\mathbf{S}_{NT}(\boldsymbol{\theta}) = \sum_{t=1}^{T}\mathbf{Z}_{t-1}'(\mathbf{Y}_t - \mathbf{Z}_{t-1}\boldsymbol{\theta})\,. \quad (8)$$

The maximization problem (8) has a closed form solution,

$$\hat{\boldsymbol{\theta}} = \left(\sum_{t=1}^{T}\mathbf{Z}_{t-1}'\mathbf{Z}_{t-1}\right)^{-1}\sum_{t=1}^{T}\mathbf{Z}_{t-1}'\mathbf{Y}_t \quad (9)$$

which is equivalent to perform an OLS estimation of the model $\mathbf{Y}_t = \mathbf{Z}_{t-1}\boldsymbol{\theta} + \boldsymbol{\xi}_t$. The extension to the NAR(p) model is straightforward, by defining $\mathbf{Z}_{i,t-1} = (1, X_{i,t-1}, \ldots, X_{i,t-p}, Y_{i,t-1}, \ldots, Y_{i,t-p})' \in \mathbb{R}^m$, see [41, Eq. 2.13]. Under regularity assumptions on the matrix $\mathbf{W}$ and $\xi_{i,t} \sim IID(0, \sigma^2)$, the OLS estimator (9) is consistent and $\sqrt{NT}(\hat{\boldsymbol{\theta}} - \boldsymbol{\theta}_0) \xrightarrow{d} N(\mathbf{0}_m, \sigma^2 \boldsymbol{\Sigma})$, as $\min\{N, T\} \to \infty$, where $\boldsymbol{\Sigma}$ is defined in [41, Eq. 2.10]. For details see [41, Thm. 3, 5]. The limiting covariance matrix $\boldsymbol{\Sigma}$ is consistently estimated by the Hessian matrix in (6), which takes the form $(NT)^{-1}\mathbf{H}_{NT} = (NT)^{-1}\sum_{t=1}^{T}\mathbf{Z}_{t-1}'\mathbf{Z}_{t-1}$. The error variance σ^2 is substituted by the sample variance $\hat{\sigma}^2 = (NT)^{-1}\sum_{i,t}(Y_{i,t} - \mathbf{Z}_{i,t-1}'\hat{\boldsymbol{\theta}})$.

For count variables, the QMLE defined in [2] maximizes the following quasi-log-likelihood

$$l_{NT}(\boldsymbol{\theta}) = \sum_{t=1}^{T}\sum_{i=1}^{N}\left(Y_{i,t}\log\lambda_{i,t}(\boldsymbol{\theta}) - \lambda_{i,t}(\boldsymbol{\theta})\right), \tag{10}$$

which is the independence log-likelihood, such as the likelihood obtained if processes $Y_{i,t}$ defined in (4), for $i = 1, \ldots, N$ were independent. This simplifies computations but guarantees consistency and asymptotic normality of the estimator. Note that, although for this choice the joint copula structure $C(\ldots)$ does not appear in the maximization of the "working" log-likelihood (10), this does not imply that inference is carried out under the assumption of independence of the observed process; dependence is taken into account because of the dependence of the likelihood function on the past values of the process through the regression coefficients.

With the same notation, the score function is

$$\mathbf{S}_{NT}(\boldsymbol{\theta}) = \sum_{i=1}^{T}\frac{\partial\boldsymbol{\lambda}_t'(\boldsymbol{\theta})}{\partial\boldsymbol{\theta}}\mathbf{D}_t^{-1}(\boldsymbol{\theta})\left(\mathbf{Y}_t - \boldsymbol{\lambda}_t(\boldsymbol{\theta})\right), \tag{11}$$

where

$$\frac{\partial\boldsymbol{\lambda}_t(\boldsymbol{\theta})}{\partial\boldsymbol{\theta}'} = (\mathbf{1}_N, \mathbf{W}\mathbf{Y}_{t-1}, \ldots, \mathbf{W}\mathbf{Y}_{t-p}, \mathbf{Y}_{t-1}, \ldots, \mathbf{Y}_{t-p})$$

is a $N \times m$ matrix and $\mathbf{D}_t(\boldsymbol{\theta})$ is the $N \times N$ diagonal matrix with diagonal elements equal to $\lambda_{i,t}(\boldsymbol{\theta})$ for $i = 1, \ldots, N$. It should be noted that (11) equals the score (8), up to a scaling matrix $\mathbf{D}_t^{-1}(\boldsymbol{\theta})$, as $\mathbf{Z}_{t-1} = \partial\boldsymbol{\lambda}_t(\boldsymbol{\theta})/\partial\boldsymbol{\theta}'$ and $\boldsymbol{\lambda}_t(\boldsymbol{\theta}) = \mathbf{Z}_{t-1}\boldsymbol{\theta}$. The Hessian matrix has the form

$$\mathbf{H}_{NT}(\boldsymbol{\theta}) = \sum_{t=1}^{T}\frac{\partial\boldsymbol{\lambda}_t'(\boldsymbol{\theta})}{\partial\boldsymbol{\theta}}\mathbf{C}_t(\boldsymbol{\theta})\frac{\partial\boldsymbol{\lambda}_t(\boldsymbol{\theta})}{\partial\boldsymbol{\theta}'}, \tag{12}$$

with $\mathbf{C}_t(\boldsymbol{\theta}) = \text{diag}\{Y_{1,t}/\lambda_{1,t}^2(\boldsymbol{\theta}) \ldots Y_{N,t}/\lambda_{N,t}^2(\boldsymbol{\theta})\}$ and the conditional information matrix is

$$\mathbf{B}_{NT}(\boldsymbol{\theta}) = \sum_{t=1}^{T}\frac{\partial\boldsymbol{\lambda}_t'(\boldsymbol{\theta})}{\partial\boldsymbol{\theta}}\mathbf{D}_t^{-1}(\boldsymbol{\theta})\boldsymbol{\Sigma}_t(\boldsymbol{\theta})\mathbf{D}_t^{-1}(\boldsymbol{\theta})\frac{\partial\boldsymbol{\lambda}_t(\boldsymbol{\theta})}{\partial\boldsymbol{\theta}'}, \tag{13}$$

where $\boldsymbol{\Sigma}_t(\boldsymbol{\theta}) = \boldsymbol{\xi}_t(\boldsymbol{\theta})\boldsymbol{\xi}_t'(\boldsymbol{\theta})$ and $\boldsymbol{\xi}_t(\boldsymbol{\theta}) = \mathbf{Y}_t - \boldsymbol{\lambda}_t(\boldsymbol{\theta})$. Consider the linear PNAR(p) model (4). By [2, Thm. 3–4], under regularity assumptions on the matrix $\mathbf{W}$ and the α-mixing property of the errors $\{\xi_{i,t}, t \in \mathbb{Z}, i \in \mathbb{N}\}$, the system of equations $\mathbf{S}_{NT}(\boldsymbol{\theta}) = \mathbf{0}_m$ has a unique solution, say $\hat{\boldsymbol{\theta}}$ (QMLE), which is consistent and $\sqrt{NT}(\hat{\boldsymbol{\theta}} - \boldsymbol{\theta}_0) \xrightarrow{d} N(\mathbf{0}_m, \mathbf{H}^{-1}\mathbf{B}\mathbf{H}^{-1})$, as $\min\{N, T\} \to \infty$, where

$$\mathbf{H} = \lim_{N \to \infty} N^{-1}\mathrm{E}\left[\frac{\partial \boldsymbol{\lambda}_t'(\boldsymbol{\theta}_0)}{\partial \boldsymbol{\theta}_0} \mathbf{D}_t^{-1}(\boldsymbol{\theta}_0)\frac{\partial \boldsymbol{\lambda}_t(\boldsymbol{\theta}_0)}{\partial \boldsymbol{\theta}_0'}\right],$$

$$\mathbf{B} = \lim_{N \to \infty} N^{-1}\mathrm{E}\left[\frac{\partial \boldsymbol{\lambda}_t'(\boldsymbol{\theta}_0)}{\partial \boldsymbol{\theta}_0} \mathbf{D}_t^{-1}(\boldsymbol{\theta}_0)\boldsymbol{\Sigma}_t(\boldsymbol{\theta}_0)\mathbf{D}_t^{-1}(\boldsymbol{\theta}_0)\frac{\partial \boldsymbol{\lambda}_t(\boldsymbol{\theta}_0)}{\partial \boldsymbol{\theta}'}\right].$$

Both $\mathbf{H}$ and $\mathbf{B}$ are consistently estimated by (12)–(13), respectively after divided by NT and evaluated at $\hat{\boldsymbol{\theta}}$ [2, Thm. 6]. Similar results are developed for the log-linear PNAR(p) model [2, Thm. 5].

All the results of this section work immediately for the classical time series inference, with N fixed and $T \to \infty$, as a particular case.

4   Applications

4.1   Simulated Example

In this section a limited simulation example regarding the estimation of the linear PNAR model is provided. First, a network structure is generated following one of the most popular network model, the stochastic block model (SBM), [28, 35] and [38] which assigns a block label $k = 1, \ldots, K$ for each node with equal probability and K is the total number of blocks. Define $\mathrm{P}(a_{ij} = 1) = \alpha N^{-0.3}$ the probability of an edge between nodes i and j, if they belong to the same block, and $\mathrm{P}(a_{ij} = 1) = \alpha N^{-1}$ otherwise. In this way, the model implicitly assumes that nodes within the same block are more likely to be connected with respect to nodes from different blocks. Here we set $K = 5$, $\alpha = 1$ and $N = 30$. This allow to obtain the weighted adjacency matrix $\mathbf{W}$. Now a vector of count variables $\mathbf{Y}_t$ is simulated according to the data generating mechanism (DGM) described in Sect. 2.2, for $t = 1, \ldots, T$, with $T = 400$ and starting value $\boldsymbol{\lambda}_0 = \mathbf{1}_N$. The PNAR(1) model is employed in the simulation with $(\beta_0, \beta_1, \beta_2) = (1, 0.3, 0.4)$. The Gaussian copula is selected in the DGM, with copula parameter $\rho = 0.5$, that is $C(u_1, \ldots, u_N) = \Phi_R\left(\Phi^{-1}(u_1), \ldots, \Phi^{-1}(u_N)\right)$, where Φ^{-1} is the inverse cumulative distribution function of a standard normal and Φ_R is the joint cumulative distribution function of a multivariate normal distribution with mean vector zero and covariance matrix equal to the correlation matrix $R = \rho^{N \times N}$, i.e. an $N \times N$ matrix whose all elements are equal to ρ. Results are based on 100 simulations.

Then, a PNAR model with one and two lags is estimated for the generated data by optimizing the quasi log-likelihood (10) with the `nloptr` R package. Results of the estimation are presented in Table 1. The standard errors (SE) are estimated as the square root from the main diagonal of the sandwich estimator matrix $\mathbf{H}_{NT}^{-1}(\hat{\boldsymbol{\theta}})\mathbf{B}_{NT}(\hat{\boldsymbol{\theta}})\mathbf{H}_{NT}^{-1}(\hat{\boldsymbol{\theta}})$, coming from (12) and (13). The t-statistic column is given by the ratio $Estimate/SE$. The first-order estimated coefficients are significant and close to the real values while the others are not significantly different from zero, as expected.

Table 1. QML estimation results for different PNAR models.

	PNAR(1)		
	Estimate	*SE*	*t-statistic*
β_0	1.0456	0.0732	14.29
β_1	0.2999	0.0161	18.64
β_2	0.3763	0.0135	27.87
	PNAR(2)		
β_0	1.0356	0.0810	12.79
β_{11}	0.2954	0.0209	14.16
β_{12}	0.0082	0.0203	0.40
β_{21}	0.3741	0.0157	23.80
β_{22}	0.0019	0.0133	0.14

4.2   Data Example

Here an application of the network autoregressive models on real data is provided, regarding 721 wind speeds taken at each of 102 weather stations in England and Wales. By considering weather stations as nodes of the potential network, if two weather stations share a border, an edge between them will be drawn. Then, an undirected network of such stations is drawn on geographic proximity. See Fig. 1. The dataset is available in the GNAR R package [23] incorporating the time series data vswindts and the associated network vswindnet. Moreover, a character vector of the weather station location names, vswindnames, and coordinates of the stations in two column matrix, vswindcoords, are reported. Full details can be found in the help file of the GNAR package.

As the wind speed is continuous-valued, the NAR(p) model is estimated with $p = 1, 2, 3$ by OLS (9). The results are summarised in Table 2. Standard errors are computed as the elements on the main diagonal of the matrix $\sqrt{\hat{\sigma}^2 \sum_{t=1}^{T} \mathbf{Z}_{t-1}'\mathbf{Z}_{t-1}}$. The estimated error variance is about $\hat{\sigma}^2 \approx 0.15$ for NAR models of every order analysed. All the coefficients are significant at 5% level.

The intercept and the coefficients of the lagged effect (β_{2h}, $h = 1, 2, 3$) are always positive. In particular, the lagged effect seems to have a predominant magnitude, especially at the first lag. Some network effects are also detected but their impact tends to become small after the first lag.

The OLS estimators is the maximizer of the quasi log-likelihood (7). This allows to compare the goodness of fit performances of competing models through information criteria. We compute usual Akaike information criterion (AIC) and the Bayesian information criterion (BIC) together with the Quasi information criterion (QIC) introduced by [29]. Such information criterion is a version of the AIC which takes into account the fact that a QMLE is performed instead of the standard MLE. In fact the QIC coincides with the AIC when the quasi likelihood equals the true likelihood of the model. In Table 3, all the information criteria select the NAR(1) as the best. This means that the expected wind speed for a weather station is mainly determined by its past speed and the past wind speeds detected on close stations, which gives a reasonable interpretation in practice.

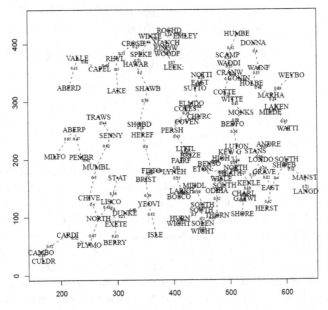

Fig. 1. Plot of the wind speed network. Geographic coordinates on the axis; numbers are relative distances between sites; labels are the site name. See [23].

Table 2. QML estimation results for wind speed data after fitting NAR(p) models for $p = 1, 2, 3$

	Estimate	SE($\times 10^2$)	t-statistic
NAR(1)			
β_0	0.1540	0.4616	33.37
β_1	0.1568	0.2717	57.48
β_2	0.7682	0.2429	316.26
NAR(2)			
β_0	0.1202	0.4553	26.40
β_{11}	0.1409	0.4811	29.28
β_{12}	−0.0263	0.4806	−5.48
β_{21}	0.5828	0.3620	160.99
β_{22}	0.2442	0.3618	67.52
NAR(3)			
β_0	0.1161	0.5297	21.91
β_{11}	0.1457	0.4927	29.56
β_{12}	−0.0116	0.5799	−2.00
β_{13}	−0.0222	0.4855	−4.56
β_{21}	0.5815	0.3623	160.53
β_{22}	0.2467	0.3637	67.84
β_{23}	0.0046	0.1763	2.63

Table 3. Information criteria for wind speed data model assessment

Model	AIC ($\times 10^{-3}$)	BIC ($\times 10^{-3}$)	QIC ($\times 10^{-3}$)
NAR(1)	−22.91	−22.89	−22.91
NAR(2)	−21.49	−21.47	−21.50
NAR(3)	−21.44	−21.41	−21.45

References

1. Ahmad, A., Francq, C.: Poisson QMLE of count time series models. J. Time Ser. Anal. **37**, 291–314 (2016)
2. Armillotta, M., Fokianos, K.: Poisson network autoregression. arXiv preprint arXiv:2104.06296 (2021)
3. Basawa, I.V., Prakasa Rao, B.L.S.: Statistical Inference for Stochastic Processes. Academic Press Inc, London (1980)
4. Chen, X., Chen, Y., Xiao, P.: The impact of sampling and network topology on the estimation of social intercorrelations. J. Mark. Res. **50**, 95–110 (2013)
5. Christou, V., Fokianos, K.: Quasi-likelihood inference for negative binomial time series models. J. Time Ser. Anal. **35**, 55–78 (2014)

6. Corke, P., Wark, T., Jurdak, R., Hu, W., Valencia, P., Moore, D.: Environmental wireless sensor networks. Proc. IEEE **98**(11), 1903–1917 (2010)
7. Cui, Y., Zheng, Q.: Conditional maximum likelihood estimation for a class of observation-driven time series models for count data. Stat. Probab. Lett. **123**, 193–201 (2017)
8. Dardari, D., Conti, A., Buratti, C., Verdone, R.: Mathematical evaluation of environmental monitoring estimation error through energy-efficient wireless sensor networks. IEEE Trans. Mob. Comput. **6**(7), 790–802 (2007)
9. Davis, R.A., Dunsmuir, W.T.M., Streett, S.B.: Observation-driven models for Poisson counts. Biometrika **90**, 777–790 (2003)
10. Davis, R.A., Liu, H.: Theory and inference for a class of nonlinear models with application to time series of counts. Stat. Sin. **26**, 1673–1707 (2016)
11. Douc, R., Doukhan, P., Moulines, E.: Ergodicity of observation-driven time series models and consistency of the maximum likelihood estimator. Stochast. Process. Appl. **123**, 2620–2647 (2013)
12. Douc, R., Fokianos, K., Moulines, E.: Asymptotic properties of quasi-maximum likelihood estimators in observation-driven time series models. Electron. J. Stat. **11**, 2707–2740 (2017)
13. Doukhan, P.: Mixing: Properties and Examples. Lecture Notes in Statistics, vol. 85. Springer, New York (1994). https://doi.org/10.1007/978-1-4612-2642-0
14. Ferland, R., Latour, A., Oraichi, D.: Integer-valued GARCH process. J. Time Ser. Anal. **27**, 923–942 (2006)
15. Fokianos, K., Kedem, B.: Partial likelihood inference for time series following generalized linear models. J. Time Ser. Anal. **25**, 173–197 (2004)
16. Fokianos, K.: Multivariate count time series modelling. arXiv preprint arXiv:2103.08028 (2021)
17. Fokianos, K., Rahbek, A., Tjøstheim, D.: Poisson auto regression. J. Am. Stat. Assoc. **104**, 1430–1439 (2009)
18. Fokianos, K., Støve, B., Tjøstheim, D., Doukhan, P.: Multivariate count autoregression. Bernoulli **26**, 471–499 (2020)
19. Fokianos, K., Tjøstheim, D.: Log-linear Poisson autoregression. J. Multivar. Anal. **102**, 563–578 (2011)
20. Heyde, C.C.: Quasi-Likelihood and its Application. A General Approach to Optimal Parameter Estimation. Springer Series in Statistics. Springer, New York (1997). https://doi.org/10.1007/b98823
21. Hsu, N.J., Hung, H.L., Chang, Y.M.: Subset selection for vector autoregressive processes using Lasso. Comput. Stat. Data Anal. **52**, 3645–3657 (2008)
22. Kelly, S.D.T., Suryadevara, N.K., Mukhopadhyay, S.C.: Towards the implementation of IoT for environmental condition monitoring in homes. IEEE Sens. J. **13**(10), 3846–3853 (2013)
23. Knight, M., Leeming, K., Nason, G., Nunes, M.: Generalized network autoregressive processes and the GNAR package. J. Stat. Softw. **96**, 1–36 (2020)
24. Kolaczyk, E.D., Csárdi, G.: Statistical Analysis of Network Data with R, vol. 65. Springer, Cham (2014). https://doi.org/10.1007/978-1-4939-0983-4
25. Kularatna, N., Sudantha, B.: An environmental air pollution monitoring system based on the IEEE 1451 standard for low cost requirements. IEEE Sens. J. **8**(4), 415–422 (2008)
26. Latour, A.: The multivariate GINAR(p) process. Adv. Appl. Probab. **29**, 228–248 (1997)
27. McCullagh, P., Nelder, J.A.: Generalized Linear Models, 2nd edn. Chapman & Hall, London (1989)

28. Nowicki, K., Snijders, T.A.B.: Estimation and prediction for stochastic blockstructures. J. Am. Stat. Assoc. **96**, 1077–1087 (2001)
29. Pan, W.: Akaike's information criterion in generalized estimating equations. Biometrics **57**, 120–125 (2001)
30. Pedeli, X., Karlis, D.: A bivariate INAR(1) process with application. Stat. Model. **11**, 325–349 (2011)
31. Pedeli, X., Karlis, D.: On composite likelihood estimation of a multivariate INAR(1) model. J. Time Ser. Anal. **34**, 206–220 (2013)
32. Pedeli, X., Karlis, D.: Some properties of multivariate INAR(1) processes. Comput. Stat. Data Anal. **67**, 213–225 (2013)
33. Rosenblatt, M.: A central limit theorem and a strong mixing condition. Proc. Natl. Acad. Sci. U.S.A. **42**, 43–47 (1956)
34. Seber, G.A.F.: A Matrix Handbook for Statisticians. Wiley Series in Probability and Statistics, Wiley-Interscience. Wiley, Hoboken (2008)
35. Wang, Y.J., Wong, G.Y.: Stochastic blockmodels for directed graphs. J. Am. Stat. Assoc. **82**, 8–19 (1987)
36. Wasserman, S., Faust, K., et al.: Social Network Analysis: Methods and Applications, vol. 8. Cambridge University Press, Cambridge (1994)
37. Zeger, S.L., Liang, K.Y.: Longitudinal data analysis for discrete and continuous outcomes. Biometrics **42**, 121–130 (1986)
38. Zhao, Y., Levina, E., Zhu, J., et al.: Consistency of community detection in networks under degree-corrected stochastic block models. Ann. Stat. **40**(4), 2266–2292 (2012)
39. Zhou, J., Li, D., Pan, R., Wang, H.: Network GARCH model. Stat. Sin. **30**, 1–18 (2020)
40. Zhu, X., Pan, R.: Grouped network vector autoregression. Stat. Sin. **30**, 1437–1462 (2020)
41. Zhu, X., Pan, R., Li, G., Liu, Y., Wang, H.: Network vector autoregression. Ann. Stat. **45**, 1096–1123 (2017)
42. Zhu, X., Wang, W., Wang, H., Härdle, W.K.: Network quantile autoregression. J. Econometrics **212**, 345–358 (2019)

Constructing Provably Robust Scale-Free Networks

Rouzbeh Hasheminezhad[(✉)] and Ulrik Brandes

Social Networks Lab, ETH Zürich, Zürich, Switzerland
{shashemi,ubrandes}@ethz.ch

Abstract. Scale-free networks have been described as robust to random failures but vulnerable to targeted attacks. We show that their degree sequences admit realizations that are, in fact, provably robust against any vertex removal strategy. We propose an algorithm that constructs such realizations almost surely, requiring only linear time and space. Our experiments confirm the robustness of the networks generated by this algorithm against adaptive and non-adaptive vertex removal strategies.

Keywords: graph generators · robustness · degree sequences

1 Introduction

The construction of simple graphs with prescribed degrees is known as the graph realization problem [29]. Constrained versions of the graph realization problem have also been addressed [26]. For example, the realized graph can be required to be Hamiltonian [8], to be connected [4,19], or to contain a specified type of subgraph (e.g., a k-factor) [10,21,23].

The constraint of interest in this paper is the robustness of the realized graph. Robustness is measured by the invariance of the structural properties of the network (e.g., connectivity) when its elements (e.g., vertices) are removed [20]. While robustness criteria are commonly applied in network design problems, we are not aware of any results with theoretical guarantees for the constrained graph realization problem where robustness against arbitrary (e.g., adaptive and adversary) vertex removal strategies is required. We present the first results for this problem, focusing mainly on scaling (power-law) sequences because they have been claimed to be empirically prevalent [5] and have found wide interest.

Our main contribution is an algorithm that almost surely requires only linear time and space to construct robust realizations for the class of extremely scaling integer sequences, where each integer sequence has a near-perfect power-law fit. When provable robustness is desired instead of almost sure robustness, and efficiency is not the primary concern, we show how the proposed algorithm can be modified to become fully deterministic and produce provably robust realizations in polynomial time.

Our results confirm the existence of scale-free networks, which are provably robust against any vertex removal strategy. One of the main implications is that

© Springer Nature Switzerland AG 2022
P. Ribeiro et al. (Eds.): NetSci-X 2022, LNCS 13197, pp. 126–139, 2022.
https://doi.org/10.1007/978-3-030-97240-0_10

there is no inherent trade-off between robustness against one vertex removal strategy (e.g., targeted attack) and another (e.g., random failure) for the class of scale-free networks. Therefore, previous claims that these networks have a "robust-yet-fragile" nature [9] should be considered stylized rather than absolute facts.

In Sect. 2 we introduce the basic terminology, background, and notation. In particular, in this section, we introduce and define extremely scaling integer sequences. In Sect. 3, we introduce our proposed method and its analysis. In Sect. 4, we present our experimental results. Finally, in Sect. 5, we conclude the paper. The appendix contains the proofs omitted in the main text.

2 Preliminaries

2.1 Basic Notation

We use $\mathbb{N}$ to denote the set of positive integers, namely $\{1, 2, \dots\}$. We use $\lfloor x \rceil$ to denote the integer closest to x, breaking ties in favor of higher values. More precisely, $\lfloor x \rceil = \lceil x \rceil$ if $x - \lfloor x \rfloor \geq 0.5$ and $\lfloor x \rceil = \lfloor x \rfloor$ otherwise. We say that a sequence of events (or properties) $\mathcal{A}_n$ almost surely occurs (or holds) if $\lim_{n \to \infty} \Pr[\mathcal{A}_n] = 1$ [12].

2.2 Graphs and Degree Sequences

In this paper, we use with a slight abuse of notation the terms network and graph interchangeably. We consider only simple undirected graphs $G = (V, E)$, where V is the set of vertices and $E \subseteq \binom{V}{2}$ is the set of edges.

The vertices $u \in V$ and $w \in V$ are adjacent if they are endpoints of the same edge, i.e., if $\{u, w\} \in E$. A vertex is incident to an edge if the vertex is one of the endpoints of that edge.

The neighbors of $v \in V$ are $N_G(v) = \{w \in V : \{v, w\} \in E\}$. The degree of $v \in V$ is $\deg_G(v) = |N_G(v)|$, i.e., the number of its neighbors. We say G is k-regular if all its vertex degrees are equal to k. A 3-regular graph is called cubic.

The graph $G' = (V', E')$ is a subgraph of $G = (V, E)$ if $V' \subseteq V, E' \subseteq E$ are such that $\{u, w\} \in E'$ implies $u, w \in V'$. The subgraph G' is spanning if $|V'| = |V|$. The subgraph G' is induced by V' if $E' = \{\{u, w\} \in E | u, w \in V'\}$. The subgraph of G induced by V' is denoted by $G[V']$.

The degree-preserving edge swap operation removes a pair of disjoint edges $\{u, w\}, \{u', w'\}$ and adds a pair of previously absent edges $\{u, u'\}, \{w, w'\}$.

The integer sequence $D = (d_1, d_2, \dots, d_n)$ is graphical if there exists a graph G with vertices $\{v_1, v_2, \dots, v_n\}$ such that $\deg_G(v_i) = d_i$, in which case we say G realizes D. There are efficient implementations of the greedy algorithm proposed by Havel [17] and Hakimi [15] that require only $O(\sum_{i=1}^{n} d_i)$ time and space to construct a realization of $D = (d_1, d_2, \dots, d_n)$ if one exists.[1]

---

[1] For an example of such an implementation, see Algorithm 1.2.1 in [22].

The reachability relation is the reflexive and transitive closure of adjacency. The subgraphs of a graph induced by equivalence classes of the reachability relation define the connected components of the graph. The size of a connected component is the number of its vertices. The largest connected component of $G = (V, E)$ is denoted by $\mathrm{LCC}(G)$ and G is called connected if $|\mathrm{LCC}(G)| = |V|$.

2.3   Network Robustness

The robustness of a network can be defined as the quantified invariance of one of its structural properties when its components are removed [20]. The domain we study in our paper is restricted to the removal of vertices, and the structural property we are interested in is the number of vertices in the largest connected component.

In a graph $G = (V, E)$, let $B = (b_1, \ldots, b_T)$ be the sequence of vertices in order of removal based on a vertex removal strategy, where $|B| = T$ denotes the number of removed vertices. We then quantify the robustness of G by

$$R_G(B) = \frac{1}{T} \sum_{t=1}^{T} \frac{|\mathrm{LCC}\left(G[V \setminus \{b_1, \ldots, b_t\}]\right)|}{|\mathrm{LCC}\left(G\right)|},$$

as proposed in [16]. This robustness score captures the normalized size of the largest connected component and the rate at which it shrinks as vertices are removed. The above robustness score can be viewed as a generalization of the robustness score proposed in [28].

2.4   Scale-Free Networks

By adapting the definition in [24], we call an integer sequence $(d_1, d_2, \ldots, d_n)$ scaling if its elements follow a finite-mean power-law distribution, characterized on the basis of a size-rank relation as $d_i \approx n^{\frac{1}{\gamma}} d_n i^{-\frac{1}{\gamma}}$, where $\gamma > 1, d_n \in \mathbb{N}$ are constants denoting respectively the scaling factor and the minimum value in the sequence.[2] We call a graph scale-free if it realizes a scaling integer sequence. In the following, we define the extremely scaling integer sequence as the integer sequence closest to the respective ideally scaling integer sequence up to a possible difference of at most one in the first index (corresponding to the largest value).

Definition 1. *An integer sequence* $D = (d_1, d_2, \ldots, d_n)$ *is called extremely scaling if*

$$d_i = \begin{cases} \lfloor n^{\frac{1}{\gamma}} d_n i^{-\frac{1}{\gamma}} \rceil + 1 & i = 1 \text{ and } \sum_{i=1}^{n} \lfloor n^{\frac{1}{\gamma}} d_n i^{-\frac{1}{\gamma}} \rceil \text{ is odd} \\ \lfloor n^{\frac{1}{\gamma}} d_n i^{-\frac{1}{\gamma}} \rceil & otherwise \end{cases},$$

where $\gamma > 1, d_n \in \mathbb{N}$ *are constants.*

In the above definition, n, γ, d_n respectively denote the length, the scaling factor, and the minimum value of the extremely scaling integer sequence.

---

[2] This notion of scaling integer sequences refers to ranks rather than frequencies. Therefore, the scaling factor is one less than the exponent in the corresponding power-law distribution [24].

2.5 Cubic Expander Graphs

A graph $G = (V, E)$ is a β-vertex-expander if for every $S \subseteq V$ of size at most $|V|/2$ there are at least $\beta|S|$ vertices in $V \setminus S$ adjacent to a vertex in S. We call G an expander if it is a β-vertex-expander for some constant $\beta > 0$. It is known that all expanders are connected [25].

Sufficiently large random cubic graphs are almost surely expanders [11]. Provided that n is sufficiently large and even, the RANDCUBIC algorithm [30] can generate a random cubic graph with n vertices, using worst-case $O(n)$ time and space [14]. Thus, we can use the RANDCUBIC algorithm with worst-case linear time and space requirements to generate cubic graphs that are almost surely expanders.

For generating a k-regular expander graph with n vertices, a deterministic and polynomial-time algorithm is proposed in [2] under the assumption that k is a constant strictly greater than two, n is sufficiently large, and nk is even. Therefore, we can use this deterministic polynomial-time algorithm to generate cubic graphs that are expanders with certainty.

For any constant $\alpha \in (0, 1)$, the proof of Lemma 2.2 in [6] implies that if G is an expander with n vertices and n is sufficiently large, then $R_G(B) = 1 - o(1)$ for any sequence B of at most n^α vertices. Therefore, sufficiently large cubic expanders are provably robust against any vertex removal strategy.

3 Proposed Method

In this section, we propose RR (Algorithm 1) to realize a sufficiently large and extremely scaling integer sequence $D = (d_1, d_2, \ldots, d_n)$ by a graph G that is almost surely robust against any vertex removal strategy. We assume that n is even, $d_n \geq 3$, and that the scaling factor of D is $\gamma < 7$. In Sect. 3.3 we present a similar algorithm that does not require the assumption on the parity of n.

Algorithm 1: Robust Realization (RR)

Input: The sufficiently large integer sequence $D = (d_1, d_2, \ldots, d_n)$ of even
length that is extremely scaling with a factor of $\gamma < 7$, where $d_n \geq 3$.
Output: The graph G realizing D such that for any constant $\alpha \in (0, 1)$ almost
surely $R_G(B) = 1 - o(1)$ for any sequence B with $|B| \leq n^\alpha$.

1 $D_{\text{res}} \leftarrow (d_1 - 3, d_2 - 3, \ldots, d_n - 3)$
2 $G_{\text{res}} \leftarrow$ HAVEL-HAKIMI(D_{res})
3 $G_{\text{reg}} \leftarrow$ RANDCUBIC(n)
4 **return** COMBINE($G_{\text{res}}, G_{\text{reg}}$)   // See Algorithm 2 in Section 3.2

In Sect. 3.1 we prove that $D_{\text{res}} = (d_1 - 3, d_2 - 3, \ldots, d_n - 3)$ is graphical and a suitable implementation of the Havel-Hakimi algorithm can realize it in linear time and space. We denote this realization by G_{res}.

We use the RANDCUBIC algorithm to generate a random cubic graph on the vertices of G_{res} in $O(n)$ time and space. We denote this cubic graph by G_{reg}.

In Sect. 3.2 we propose COMBINE (Algorithm 2) that modifies G_{res} by degree-preserving edge swaps, until $E(G_{res}) \cap E(G_{reg}) = \emptyset$, whereupon it outputs $G = (V(G_{res}), E(G_{res}) \cup E(G_{reg}))$. Our analysis in Sect. 3.2 demonstrates that COMBINE (Algorithm 2) uses worst-case $O(n)$ space and almost surely $O(n)$ but worst-case $o(n^2)$ time. According to our analysis, these worst-case bounds remain valid even if G_{reg} is replaced by any other size-matching cubic graph.

Note that, by construction, the graph G realizes the integer sequence D and G_{reg} is a spanning subgraph of it. Our discussion in Sect. 2.5 implies that a sufficiently large random cubic graph (e.g., G_{reg}) is almost surely an expander, and expanders are provably robust against any vertex removal strategy. Thus, we can deduce that G is a realization of D that is almost surely robust against any vertex removal strategy.

From the above four paragraphs, we can conclude that RR (Algorithm 1) can realize D by a graph G almost surely in $O(n)$ time and space such that G is robust against any vertex removal strategy. To provide some intuition about the reason for the almost sure robustness of a realization obtained with RR (Algorithm 1), we illustrate such a realization in Fig. 1 and show how it changes when we subject it to a degree-based targeted attack.

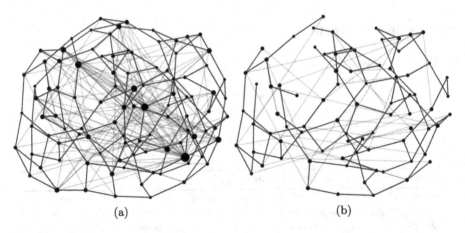

(a)   (b)

Fig. 1. Subfigure (a) shows the graph G realizing an extremely scaling integer sequence $D = (d_1, d_2, \ldots, d_n)$ with parameters $n = 100, \gamma = 2$, and $d_n = 3$. We have obtained G using RR (Algorithm 1). In our illustration of G, the size of each vertex is proportional to its degree, the dark edges correspond to the embedded random cubic graph, and the gray edges represent the other edges. We can observe a higher concentration of gray edges around vertices with higher degrees, but the dark edges have a more uniform distribution. Subfigure (b) shows the graph G after removing 20% of its vertices with the highest initial degrees. We see that G remains fully connected after this targeted attack. The extreme robustness of G against this targeted attack is clearly due to the embedded random cubic graph, in which the edges are almost uniformly distributed.

When provable robustness is desired instead of almost sure robustness, and efficiency is not the main concern, it is sufficient to replace the random cubic graphs used in RR (Algorithm 1) with size-matching cubic expander graphs. As we discussed in Sect. 2.5, such cubic expanders can be constructed in deterministic polynomial time using the approach proposed in [2].

3.1 Graphicality of D_{res}

In this subsection, we state and prove Theorem 1, which indicates that D_{res} as in Algorithm 1 can be realized in linear time and space, when using a suitable implementation of the Havel-Hakimi algorithm. To prove Theorem 1, we use Lemma 1 and Lemma 2, which are introduced below and proved in the appendix to make the main text clearer.

Lemma 1. *Let $(d_1, d_2, \ldots, d_n)$ be an extremely scaling integer sequence with scaling factor γ. If $\gamma < 7$ and $d_n \geq 3$, then $\sum_{i=1}^{n}(d_i - 3) \in \Theta(n)$ and there exists a constant $\kappa \in (0, 1)$ such that $\sum_{i=1}^{d_1} d_i \in O(n^\kappa)$.*

Lemma 2. *Let $(d_1, d_2, \ldots, d_n)$ be a non-increasing integer sequence with even sum. If there exists $k \in \{0, 1, \ldots, d_n\}$ such that $\sum_{i=1}^{d_1}(d_i + k) \leq \sum_{i=d_1+1}^{n}(d_i - k)$ and nk is even, then $(d_1 - k, d_2 - k, \ldots, d_n - k)$ is graphical.*

Equipped with Lemma 1 and Lemma 2, we are now ready to prove the main result of this subsection, stated below in Theorem 1.

Theorem 1. *Let $(d_1, d_2, \ldots, d_n)$ be an extremely scaling integer sequence of even length with scaling factor $\gamma < 7$ and $d_n \geq 3$. If n is sufficiently large, then there exists an implementation of the Havel-Hakimi algorithm that can realize $(d_1 - 3, d_2 - 3, \ldots, d_n - 3)$ in $O(n)$ time and space.*

Proof. Let $D_{res} := (d_1 - 3, d_2 - 3, \ldots, d_n - 3)$. There are implementations of the Havel-Hakimi algorithm that require $O\left(\sum_{i=1}^{n}(d_i - 3)\right)$ time and space to construct a realization of D_{res} if one exists (see Algorithm 1.2.1 in [22] for an example). Therefore, it suffices to prove: (I) There exists a realization of D_{res}, and (II) $\sum_{i=1}^{n}(d_i - 3) \in \Theta(n)$.

First, we prove (II). Note that $(d_1, d_2, \ldots, d_n)$ satisfies the assumptions of Lemma 1. Therefore, by using Lemma 1 we know that $\sum_{i=1}^{n}(d_i - 3) \in \Theta(n)$, and $\sum_{i=1}^{d_1} d_i \in O(n^\kappa)$ for some constant $\kappa \in (0, 1)$. This completes the proof of (II).

Now we prove (I). Considering that n is assumed to be sufficiently large, $\sum_{i=1}^{d_1} d_i \in O(n^\kappa)$ and $\sum_{i=1}^{n}(d_i - 3) \in \Theta(n)$ imply that $2\sum_{i=1}^{d_1} d_i \leq \sum_{i=1}^{n}(d_i - 3)$. A simple rearrangement of the terms shows that $\sum_{i=1}^{d_1}(d_i + 3) \leq \sum_{i=d_1+1}^{n}(d_i - 3)$. The last inequality and the assumptions of the theorem about $(d_1, d_2, \ldots, d_n)$ imply the graphicality of D_{res} by an application of Lemma 2. This completes the proof of (I), since by definition D_{res} is graphical if it has a realization. □

Note that Lemma 2 may be of independent interest because it provides a simple sufficient condition for the graphicality of integer sequences, and in light of Kundu's Theorem [23] we can also interpret it as a simple sufficient condition for the existence of realizations with a k-factor (k-regular spanning subgraph).

3.2   The COMBINE Algorithm

In this subsection, we propose COMBINE (Algorithm 2), which given G_{res} and G_{reg} as in Algorithm 1, performs degree-preserving edge swaps in G_{res} until $E(G_{\text{res}}) \cap E(G_{\text{reg}}) = \emptyset$, and then outputs $G = (V(G_{\text{res}}), E(G_{\text{res}}) \cup E(G_{\text{reg}}))$.

Algorithm 2: COMBINE

    Input: $G_{\text{res}}, G_{\text{reg}}$ `// As in Algorithm 1`

1 $S \leftarrow E(G_{\text{res}}) \cap E(G_{\text{reg}})$
2 **for** $e = \{u,v\} \in S$ **do**
3   **if** u *is still adjacent to* v *in* G_{res} **then**
4         $F_e(G_{\text{res}}) \leftarrow \{\{x,y\} \in E(G_{\text{res}}) | \{x,y\} \cap (N_{G_{\text{res}}}[u] \cup N_{G_{\text{res}}}[v]) \neq \emptyset\}$
5         $H_e(G_{\text{res}}) \leftarrow \{\{x,y\} \in E(G_{\text{res}}) | \{x,y\} \cap (N_{G_{\text{reg}}}(u) \cup N_{G_{\text{reg}}}(v)) \neq \emptyset\}$
6         $e' \sim E(G_{\text{res}}) \setminus (F_e(G_{\text{res}}) \cup H_e(G_{\text{res}}))$
7   degree-preserving-edge-swap(e, e') `// Performed in `G_{res}

8 **return** $G = (V(G_{\text{reg}}), E(G_{\text{res}}) \bigcup E(G_{\text{reg}}))$

In the remainder of this subsection, a conflicting edge or a conflict refers to an existing edge in $E(G_{\text{res}}) \cap E(G_{\text{reg}})$. In the following, we present the detailed analysis of COMBINE (Algorithm 2) after giving an outline of the analysis and clearly explaining the presuppositions for the analysis.

Outline of Analysis: For an arbitrary conflicting edge $e = \{u,v\}$, we denote by $F_e(G_{\text{res}})$ the edges in G_{res} with at least one endpoint in $N_{G_{\text{res}}}[u] := \{u\} \bigcup N_{G_{\text{res}}}(u)$ or $N_{G_{\text{res}}}[v] := \{v\} \bigcup N_{G_{\text{res}}}(v)$. Similarly, we denote by $H_e(G_{\text{res}})$ the edges in G_{res} with at least one endpoint in $N_{G_{\text{reg}}}(u)$ or $N_{G_{\text{reg}}}(v)$.

It is easy to verify that for any $e' \in E(G_{\text{res}}) \setminus (H_e(G_{\text{res}}) \bigcup F_e(G_{\text{res}}))$, a degree-preserving edge swap in G_{res} between e, e' reduces the number of conflicting edges by at least one without changing G_{reg} or the vertex degrees in G_{res} at all.

Based on the above observation, we can prove that COMBINE (Algorithm 2) is correct and has an efficient implementation by showing that for each conflicting edge e, the set $E(G_{\text{res}}) \setminus (H_e(G_{\text{res}}) \bigcup F_e(G_{\text{res}}))$ is non-empty and a member of it can be found efficiently.

Presuppositions for Analysis: Since we assume that G_{res} and G_{reg} are as in Algorithm 1, we know that $(d_1 - 3, d_2 - 3, \ldots, d_n - 3)$ is the degree sequence of G_{res}, where $(d_1, d_2, \ldots, d_n)$ is a sufficiently large extremely scaling integer sequence with scaling factor $\gamma < 7$ and $d_n \geq 3$. Thus, Lemma 1 implies that $\sum_{i=1}^{d_1} d_i \in O(n^\kappa)$ and $\sum_{i=1}^{n}(d_i - 3) \in \Theta(n)$ for a constant $\kappa \in (0,1)$. These asymptotic results and n being sufficiently large are assumptions in our analysis.

In analyzing our proposed implementation of Algorithm 2, we assume that both G_{res} and G_{reg} are represented by adjacency lists. We also implicitly assume that any auxiliary space used is immediately released when it is no longer needed.

Analysis of the Algorithm: The computation in line 3 or 7 of Algorithm 2 needs worst-case $O(d_1)$ time and $O(1)$ space, where $d_1 \leq \sum_{i=1}^{d_1} d_i \in O(n^\kappa)$. The handshaking lemma implies that $|E(G_{res})| = \frac{1}{2} \sum_{i=1}^{n} (d_i - 3) \in \Theta(n)$. Therefore, the computation of $E(G_{res}) \cap E(G_{reg})$ in line 1 of Algorithm 2 can be performed in $O(n)$ time and space, since for each of the $O(n)$ edges in $E(G_{res})$ its existence in G_{reg} can be checked in $O(1)$ time, given the constant degrees in G_{reg}.

We construct $F_e(G_{res})$ by doing a BFS of depth two in G_{res} from the endpoints of e, visiting $|F_e(G_{res})| \leq 2 \sum_{i=1}^{d_1} d_i \in O(n^\kappa)$ edges.[3] We construct $H_e(G_{res})$ by going through the neighbors of the endpoints of e in G_{reg}, visiting the $|H_e(G_{res})|$ edges incident to them in G_{res}, where $|H_e(G_{res})| \leq 2(3d_1) \leq 6 \sum_{i=1}^{d_1} d_i \in O(n^\kappa)$. After constructing $H_e(G_{res})$ and $F_e(G_{reg})$, we sort both of them using merge-sort to ensure the applicability of the binary search algorithm.[4] Overall, implementing lines $4-5$ in Algorithm 2 needs $O(n^\kappa \log n)$ time and $O(n^\kappa)$ space.

Note that, $|E(G_{res})| \in \Theta(n)$ and $|F_e(G_{res})|, |H_e(G_{res})| \in O(n^\kappa)$ for a constant $\kappa \in (0, 1)$. Thus, under our assumption that n is sufficiently large, we know that $E(G_{res}) \setminus (H_e(G_{res}) \bigcup F_e(G_{res}))$ is always non-empty for any conflicting edge e. To find an edge $e' \in E(G_{res}) \setminus (H_e(G_{res}) \bigcup F_e(G_{res}))$, we use an iterative edge traversal algorithm (e.g., BFS) to visit one edge after another in G_{res} until we find one that is neither in $F_e(G_{res})$ nor in $H_e(G_{res})$. Note that $O(n^\kappa)$ edge visits are sufficient since $|H_e(G_{res})|, |F_e(G_{res})| \in O(n^\kappa)$. Since $F_e(G_{res})$ and $H_e(G_{res})$ are sorted, checking the presence of an edge in them needs $O(\log n)$ time. Thus, implementing line 6 in Algorithm 2 requires $O(n^\kappa \log n)$ time and $O(n^\kappa)$ space.

Putting the paragraphs above together, we see that COMBINE (Algorithm 2) requires worst-case $O\left(|E(G_{res}) \cap E(G_{reg})|n^\kappa \log n + n\right)$ time and $O(n)$ space. By using Lemma 3, we infer that $|E(G_{res}) \cap E(G_{reg})|n^\kappa \log n \in O(n)$, almost surely. Therefore, COMBINE (Algorithm 2) almost surely needs only $O(n)$ time and space. We prove Lemma 3 in the appendix in favor of fluency in the main text.

If we replace the random cubic graph G_{reg} with an arbitrary size-matching cubic graph, then COMBINE (Algorithm 2) needs worst-case $o(n^2)$ time and $O(n)$ space. This is because $|E(G_{res}) \cap E(G_{reg})| \leq |E(G_{reg})| \in O(n)$ and $\kappa \in (0, 1)$ is constant, thus $|E(G_{res}) \cap E(G_{reg})|n^\kappa \log n \in o(n^2)$.

Lemma 3. *Let G_{reg} be a random k-regular graph with n vertices, where $k \in \mathbb{N}$ is constant. Furthermore, let G_{res} be a graph with the same vertices as G_{reg}. If $E(G_{res}) \in O(n)$, then there exists a constant $C > 0$ such that*

$$\Pr\left[|E(G_{res}) \cap E(G_{reg})| \geq \frac{n^{1-\kappa}}{\log n}\right] \leq \frac{C \log n}{n^{1-\kappa}},$$

for any $\kappa \in (0, 1)$.

---

[3] Suppose that a BFS of depth two starts from the vertex v_1, where the neighbors of v_1 are $v_2, v_3, \ldots, v_{d_1-2}$, respectively with degrees $d_2 - 3, d_3 - 3, \ldots, d_{d_1-2} - 3$. This hypothetical scenario provides an upper bound of $\sum_{i=2}^{d_1-2} (d_i - 3) \leq \sum_{i=1}^{d_1} d_i$ for the number of visited edges in any BFS of depth two, starting from any vertex in G_{res}. Therefore, $|F_e(G_{res})| \leq 2 \sum_{i=1}^{d_1} d_i$ follows by an application of the union bound.

[4] In G_{res} we fix a vertex order $v_1, v_2, \ldots, v_n$ and assume for any edges e, e' that $e \leq e'$ holds if and only if $f(e) \leq f(e')$, where $f(\{v_i, v_j\}) := (n-1) \max\{i, j\} + \min\{i, j\}$.

3.3   Relaxing the Assumption on the Parity of n

In this subsection, we propose GRR (Algorithm 3) to realize a sufficiently large and extremely scaling integer sequence $D = (d_1, d_2, \ldots, d_n)$ by a graph G that is almost surely robust against any vertex removal strategy. We assume that $d_n \geq 3$, and that the scaling factor of D is $\gamma < 7$. Note that GRR (Algorithm 3) relaxes the assumption on the parity of n, which RR (Algorithm 1) required.

Algorithm 3: General Robust Realization (GRR)

Input: The sufficiently large integer sequence $D = (d_1, d_2, \ldots, d_n)$ that is extremely scaling with a factor of $\gamma < 7$, where $d_n \geq 3$.

Output: The graph G realizing D such that for any constant $\alpha \in (0, 1)$ almost surely $R_G(B) = 1 - o(1)$ for any sequence B with $|B| \leq n^\alpha$.

1 **if** n *is even* **then**
2 | $G \leftarrow \mathsf{RR}(D)$
3 **else**
4 | $\hat{D} = (\hat{d}_1, \hat{d}_2, \ldots, \hat{d}_{n-1})$ where $\begin{cases} \hat{d}_i = d_{i+1} - 1 & i \in \{1, 2, \ldots, d_1\} \\ \hat{d}_i = d_{i+1} & \text{otherwise} \end{cases}$.
5 | $\hat{G} \leftarrow \mathsf{RR}(\hat{D})$ // $\deg_{\hat{G}}(v_i) = \hat{d}_i$ for all $i \in \{1, 2, \ldots, n-1\}$
6 | $V \leftarrow V(\hat{G}) \cup \{v_n\}$
7 | $E \leftarrow E(\hat{G}) \cup \{\{v_n, v_1\}, \{v_n, v_2\}, \ldots, \{v_n, v_{d_1}\}\}$
8 | $G \leftarrow G(V, E)$
9 **return** G

For the case when n is even and sufficiently large, the correctness of GRR (Algorithm 3) follows from the analysis of RR (Algorithm 1). When n is odd and sufficiently large, the definition of extremely scaling integer sequences can be used to easily prove that $\hat{D} = (\hat{d}_1, \hat{d}_2 \ldots, \hat{d}_{n-1})$, as defined in GRR (Algorithm 3), is a non-increasing integer sequence where $\hat{d}_{n-1} \geq 3$. Since $\sum_{i=1}^{\hat{d}_1} \hat{d}_i \leq \sum_{i=1}^{d_1} d_i$ and $\sum_{i=1}^{n-1}(\hat{d}_i - 3) = \sum_{i=1}^{n}(d_i - 3) - 2d_1$, it follows from applying Lemma 1 that $\sum_{i=1}^{\hat{d}_1} \hat{d}_i \in O(n^\kappa)$ and $\sum_{i=1}^{n-1}(\hat{d}_i - 3) \in \Theta(n)$, for a constant $\kappa \in (0, 1)$. Based on the aforementioned properties of $\hat{D}$, one can easily verify that all our arguments for the correctness of RR (Algorithm 1) are also valid for GRR (Algorithm 3). Finally, GRR (Algorithm 3) asymptotically has the same time and space requirements as RR, since the additional operations within the else condition in GRR (Algorithm 3) have $O(n)$ overhead. Our arguments in this subsection imply Theorem 2.

Theorem 2. *Let $D = (d_1, d_2, \ldots, d_n)$ be an extremely scaling integer sequence with scaling factor $\gamma < 7$ and $d_n \geq 3$. Furthermore, let $\alpha \in (0, 1)$ be any constant. If n is sufficiently large, then GRR (Algorithm 3) can realize D by some graph G almost surely in $O(n)$ time and space such that $R_G(B) = 1 - o(1)$ for any vertex sequence B with $|B| \leq n^\alpha$.*

If desired, we can achieve provable robustness by sacrificing efficiency. To this end, we can replace the random cubic graphs used in RR (Algorithm 1) with size-matching cubic expanders that have a deterministic polynomial-time construction using the approach presented in [2]. This implies Theorem 3.

Theorem 3. *Let $D = (d_1, d_2, \ldots, d_n)$ be an extremely scaling integer sequence with scaling factor $\gamma < 7$ and $d_n \geq 3$. Furthermore, let $\alpha \in (0, 1)$ be any constant. If n is sufficiently large, then there exists a polynomial-time algorithm that can deterministically realize D by some graph G such that $R_G(B) = 1 - o(1)$ for any vertex sequence B with $|B| \leq n^\alpha$.*

4   Experiments

We consider nine extremely scaling integer sequences with parameters $n = 10000$, $\gamma \in \{1.5, 2, 2.5\}$, and $d_n \in \{3, 4, 5\}$. We realize each integer sequence with GRR (Algorithm 3) and illustrate in Fig. 2 how the fraction of vertices in the largest connected component decreases when vertices are removed, based on different strategies. We consider random failure and non-adaptive or adaptive targeted attacks as our vertex removal strategies. In random failure, vertices are removed uniformly at random. In the non-adaptive attack, vertices with higher initial degrees are removed first. In the adaptive attack, vertices are removed using the Generalized Network Dismantling (GND) algorithm proposed in [27].[5]

Note that in Fig. 2, for each pair of γ, d_n and vertex removal strategy, we plot the average behavior over a thousand scenarios to avoid possible biases. To obtain these scenarios, we realize the corresponding extremely scaling integer sequence a hundred times using GRR (Algorithm 3), such that the embedded random cubic graph is generated independently at each realization. We then subject each of the hundred realized networks to ten independent runs of the removal strategy, randomly breaking ties in each run.

The results of our experiments, shown in Fig. 2, demonstrate that scale-free graphs generated by GRR (Algorithm 3) are very robust against non-adaptive and adaptive vertex removal strategies. None of the considered removal strategies cause the generated networks to become noticeably disconnected as long as no more than 20% of their vertices are removed.

If we consider only random failure and targeted attacks based on initial degree, as originally proposed in [1], neither strategy causes the robust instances generated by our algorithm to become noticeably disconnected unless more than 40% of their vertices are removed. Moreover, for the denser robust instances generated by our algorithm with a minimum degree strictly greater than three, there is little difference between these two vertex removal strategies in terms of their performance in network dismantling.

---

[5] We consider the variant of GND where removing each vertex has a unit cost, and the goal is to dismantle the network at the lowest possible cost. The implementation we use for this variant of GND was written by Petter Holme in the Python programming language and is publicly available from https://github.com/pholme/gnd.

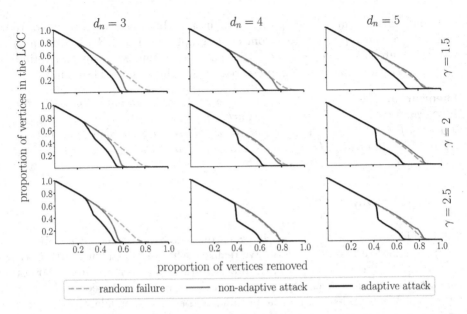

Fig. 2. An illustration of the average reduction in the size of the largest connected component when vertices are removed from the realizations of the extremely scaling integer sequences obtained by our proposed method, namely GRR (Algorithm 3). We consider removal strategies where vertices are removed uniformly at random (random failure), vertices with a higher initial degree are preferred (non-adaptive attack), or the GND algorithm is used as proposed in [27] (adaptive attack). For each pair of γ, d_n and vertex removal strategy, we show the average behavior over a thousand scenarios, i.e., a hundred independent realizations with ten thousand vertices each, exposed to ten independently drawn removal sequences. We see that our realizations maintain near-perfect connectivity during removals unless at least 20% of their vertices are removed.

5   Conclusion

We have shown that sufficiently large, extremely scaling integer sequences have realizations that are provably robust against any vertex removal strategy (see Theorem 3). Moreover, we have shown that such realizations can be obtained almost surely in linear time and space (see Theorem 2). Our proposed proofs are constructive and suggest an algorithmic technique that can be used to obtain similar results for a much broader class of integer sequences.

Our results also suggest that there is no inherent trade-off between robustness against one vertex removal strategy (e.g., targeted attack) and another (e.g., random failure) for the class of scale-free networks. Thus, previous assessments that scale-free networks have a "robust-yet-fragile" nature [9] may be valid as stylized facts pointing to empirical regularities, but not as general statements.

Since the scope of this paper is limited to vertex removal, one potential direction for future work is realizing scaling integer sequences by graphs that are provably robust against other perturbations, such as edge removal or rewiring.

A   Appendix: Omitted Proofs

Lemma 1. *Let $(d_1, d_2, \ldots, d_n)$ be an extremely scaling integer sequence with scaling factor γ. If $\gamma < 7$ and $d_n \geq 3$, then $\sum_{i=1}^{n}(d_i - 3) \in \Theta(n)$ and there exists a constant $\kappa \in (0,1)$ such that $\sum_{i=1}^{d_1} d_i \in O(n^\kappa)$.*

Proof. Note that Definition 1 and the assumptions of the lemma imply that $\gamma \in (1,7)$ and $d_n \geq 3$ are constants. Moreover, based on Definition 1 we have

$$-0.5 < d_i - n^{\frac{1}{\gamma}} d_n i^{-\frac{1}{\gamma}} \leq 1.5, \tag{1}$$

for all $i \in \{1, 2, \ldots, n\}$. Let $\zeta(z)$ be the Euler's generalized constant defined for $z \in (0,1)$[18]. It is shown in [3] that

$$\sum_{i=1}^{t} i^{-\frac{1}{\gamma}} = \frac{t^{1-\frac{1}{\gamma}}}{1 - \frac{1}{\gamma}} + \zeta(\frac{1}{\gamma}) + O(t^{-\frac{1}{\gamma}}). \tag{2}$$

Let $\alpha := \frac{1}{n} \sum_{i=1}^{n}(d_i - n^{\frac{1}{\gamma}} d_n i^{-\frac{1}{\gamma}})$. From (1), we know that $\alpha \in (-0.5, 1.5]$. Thus, we can conclude from (2) that

$$\sum_{i=1}^{n}(d_i - 3) = n^{\frac{1}{\gamma}} d_n \sum_{i=1}^{n} i^{-\frac{1}{\gamma}} - 3n + \alpha n = (\frac{\gamma}{\gamma - 1} d_n - 3 + \alpha)n + o(n) \in \Theta(n). \tag{3}$$

In the last step of the derivation above, we used the fact that $\frac{\gamma}{\gamma - 1} d_n$ is a constant strictly larger than 3.5. Using (1) and (2), we have

$$\sum_{i=1}^{d_1} d_i \leq n^{\frac{1}{\gamma}} d_n \sum_{i=1}^{d_1} i^{-\frac{1}{\gamma}} + 1.5 d_1 \leq (d_1 + 0.5) \sum_{i=1}^{d_1} i^{-\frac{1}{\gamma}} + 1.5 d_1 \in O(d_1^{2 - \frac{1}{\gamma}}). \tag{4}$$

From (1), we know that $d_1 \in O(n^{\frac{1}{\gamma}})$. Therefore, $\sum_{i=1}^{d_1} d_i \in O(n^\kappa)$, where $\kappa := \frac{2}{\gamma} - \frac{1}{\gamma^2} = \frac{\gamma^2 - (\gamma-1)^2}{\gamma^2} \in (0,1)$ is a constant. This concludes the proof. $\square$

Lemma 2. *Let $(d_1, d_2, \ldots, d_n)$ be a non-increasing integer sequence with even sum. If there exists $k \in \{0, 1, \ldots, d_n\}$ such that $\sum_{i=1}^{d_1}(d_i + k) \leq \sum_{i=d_1+1}^{n}(d_i - k)$ and nk is even, then $(d_1 - k, d_2 - k, \ldots, d_n - k)$ is graphical.*

Proof. Based on the lemma's assumptions, $D_k := (d_1 - k, d_2 - k, \ldots, d_n - k)$ is a non-increasing sequence of non-negative integers. Based on a sufficient and necessary condition for graphicality proposed in [7], D_k is graphical if and only if the following conditions are satisfied: (I) $\sum_{i=1}^{n}(d_i - k)$ is even, and (II) $2\sum_{i=1}^{t}(d_i - k) \leq \sum_{i=1}^{n}(d_i - k) + \sum_{i=1}^{t} \min\{d_i - k, t - 1\}$ for all $t \in \{1, \ldots, n-1\}$.

Note that condition (I) is satisfied since $\sum_{i=1}^{n} d_i$ and nk are both even under lemma's assumptions. If $t \geq d_1 - k + 1$, then condition (II) is equivalent to $\sum_{i=1}^{t}(d_i - k) \leq \sum_{i=1}^{n}(d_i - k)$, which is trivial since D_k has non-negative elements.

Therefore, it suffices to show that the inequality in condition (II) is satisfied for all $t \in \{1, \ldots, d_1 - k\}$. For all such t, we know due to the assumptions of the lemma that $\sum_{i=1}^{t}(d_i - k) \leq \sum_{i=1}^{d_1} d_i$ and $\min\{d_i - k, t - 1\} \geq 0$ for all $i \in \{1, \ldots, t\}$. Therefore, it suffices to show that $2\sum_{i=1}^{d_1} d_i \leq \sum_{i=1}^{n}(d_i - k)$, but this is just the rearranged form of $\sum_{i=1}^{d_1}(d_i + k) \leq \sum_{i=d_1+1}^{n}(d_i - k)$, which was assumed in the statement of the lemma. This concludes the proof. $\qquad\square$

Lemma 3. *Let G_{reg} be a random k-regular graph with n vertices, where $k \in \mathbb{N}$ is constant. Furthermore, let G_{res} be a graph with the same vertices as G_{reg}. If $E(G_{\text{res}}) \in O(n)$, then there exists a constant $C > 0$ such that*

$$\Pr\left[|E(G_{\text{res}}) \cap E(G_{\text{reg}})| \geq \frac{n^{1-\kappa}}{\log n}\right] \leq \frac{C\log n}{n^{1-\kappa}},$$

for any $\kappa \in (0,1)$.

Proof. Let m denote the number of edges in G_{res}, where $e_1, e_2, \ldots, e_m$ is an arrangement of them. Moreover, let $X = \sum_{i=1}^{m} X_i$, where $X_i = 1$ if $e_i \in E(G_{\text{reg}})$ and $X_i = 0$ otherwise. It is easy to verify that $X = |E(G_{\text{res}}) \cap E(G_{\text{reg}})|$.

The argument in the proof of Lemma 2.4 in [13] implies that $\mathbb{E}[X_i] = \frac{k}{n-1}$ for all $i \in \{1, 2, \ldots, n\}$, and thus by linearity of expectation $\mathbb{E}[X] = \frac{mk}{n-1}$. Since $m \in O(n)$ and $k \in \mathbb{N}$ is constant, we can derive that $\mathbb{E}[X] \leq C$ for some constant $C > 0$. Since X is by definition non-negative, Markov's inequality implies that

$$\Pr\left[X \geq \frac{n^{1-\kappa}}{\log n}\right] \leq \frac{C\log n}{n^{1-\kappa}}.$$

Since $X = |E(G_{\text{res}}) \cap E(G_{\text{reg}})|$, the above derivation completes the proof. $\qquad\square$

References

1. Albert, R., Jeong, H., Barabási, A.L.: Error and attack tolerance of complex networks. Nature **406**(6794), 378–382 (2000)
2. Alon, N.: Explicit expanders of every degree and size. Combinatorica **41**(4), 447–463 (2021). https://doi.org/10.1007/s00493-020-4429-x
3. Apostol, T.M.: Introduction to analytic number theory. In: Undergraduate Texts in Mathematics, p. 55. Springer, New York (1976)
4. Asano, T.: An $\mathcal{O}(n \log \log n)$ time algorithm for constructing a graph of maximum connectivity with prescribed degrees. J. Comput. Syst. Sci. **51**(3), 503–510 (1995)
5. Barabási, A.L., Albert, R.: Emergence of scaling in random networks. Science **286**(5439), 509–512 (1999)
6. Ben-Shimon, S., Krivelevich, M.: Vertex percolation on expander graphs. Eur. J. Comb. **30**(2), 339–350 (2009)
7. Bollobás, B.: Extremal Graph Theory, dover edition edn., p. 100. Dover Publications, Mineola (2004)
8. Chungphaisan, V.: Construction of Hamiltonian graphs and bigraphs with prescribed degrees. J. Comb. Theory B **24**(2), 154–163 (1978)
9. Doyle, J.C., et al.: The 'robust yet fragile' nature of the internet. Proc. Natl. Acad. Sci. (PNAS) **102**(41), 14497–14502 (2005)

10. Erdős, P.L., Hartke, S.G., Van Iersel, L., Miklós, I.: Graph realizations constrained by skeleton graphs. Electron. J. Comb. **24**(2), P2.47 (2017)
11. Friedman, J.: A proof of alon's second eigenvalue conjecture. In: Proceedings of the Thirty-Fifth Annual ACM Symposium on Theory of Computing, STOC 2003, pp. 720–724. Association for Computing Machinery, New York (2003)
12. Frieze, A., Karoński, M.: Introduction to Random Graphs. Cambridge University Press, Cambridge (2016)
13. Gao, P., Greenhill, C.: Uniform generation of spanning regular subgraphs of a dense graph. Electron. J. Comb. **26**(4), P4.28 (2019)
14. Gao, P., Wormald, N.: Uniform generation of random regular graphs. SIAM J. Comput. **46**(4), 1395–1427 (2017)
15. Hakimi, S.L.: On realizability of a set of integers as degrees of the vertices of a linear graph. I. J. Soc. Ind. Appl. Math. **10**(3), 496–506 (1962)
16. Hasheminezhad, R., Boudourides, M., Brandes, U.: Scale-free networks need not be fragile. In: Proceedings of the 2020 IEEE/ACM International Conference on Advances in Social Networks Analysis and Mining, pp. 332–339. IEEE (2020)
17. Havel, V.: Poznámka o existenci konečných grafů (Czech) [A remark on the existence of finite graphs]. Časopis pro pěstování matematiky **080**(4), 477–480 (1955)
18. Havil, J.: Gamma: Exploring Euler's Constant, pp. 117–118. Princeton University Press, Princeton (2003)
19. Horvát, S., Modes, C.D.: Connectedness matters: construction and exact random sampling of connected networks. J. Phys. Complexity **2**(1), 015008 (2021)
20. Klau, G.W., Weiskircher, R.: Robustness and resilience. In: Brandes, U., Erlebach, T. (eds.) Network Analysis. LNCS, vol. 3418, pp. 417–437. Springer, Heidelberg (2005). https://doi.org/10.1007/978-3-540-31955-9_15
21. Kleitman, D., Wang, D.: Algorithms for constructing graphs and digraphs with given valences and factors. Discret. Math. **6**(1), 79–88 (1973)
22. Kocay, W.L., Kreher, D.L.: Graphs, algorithms, and optimization. In: Discrete Mathematics and its Applications, 2nd edn. CRC Press, Boca Raton (2017)
23. Kundu, S.: The k-factor conjecture is true. Discret. Math. **6**(4), 367–376 (1973)
24. Li, L., Alderson, D., Doyle, J.C., Willinger, W.: Towards a theory of scale-free graphs: definition, properties, and implications. Internet Math. **2**(4), 431–523 (2005)
25. Lountzi, A.: Expander Graphs and Explicit Constructions. Master's thesis, Uppsala University, Algebra and Geometry (2015)
26. Rao, S.B.: A survey of the theory of potentially P-graphic and forcibly P-graphic degree sequences. In: Rao, S.B. (ed.) Combinatorics and Graph Theory. LNM, vol. 885, pp. 417–440. Springer, Heidelberg (1981). https://doi.org/10.1007/BFb0092288
27. Ren, X.L., Gleinig, N., Helbing, D., Antulov-Fantulin, N.: Generalized network dismantling. Proc. Natl. Acad. Sci. **116**(14), 6554–6559 (2019)
28. Schneider, C.M., Moreira, A.A., Andrade, J.S., Jr., Havlin, S., Herrmann, H.J.: Mitigation of malicious attacks on networks. Proc. Natl. Acad. Sci. (PNAS) **108**(10), 3838–3841 (2011)
29. Tyshkevich, R.I., Chernyak, A.A., Chernyak, Z.A.: Graphs and degree sequences. I. Cybernetics **23**(6), 734–745 (1988)
30. Wormald, N.C.: Generating random regular graphs. J. Algorithms **5**(2), 247–280 (1984)

Functional Characterization of Transcriptional Regulatory Networks of Yeast Species

Paulo Dias[1(✉)], Pedro T. Monteiro[1,2], and Andreia Sofia Teixeira[2,3]

[1] Instituto Superior Técnico, Universidade de Lisboa, Lisboa, Portugal
paulo.a.c.dias@tecnico.ulisboa.pt
[2] INESC-ID, Lisboa, Portugal
[3] LASIGE, Departamento de Informática, Faculdade de Ciências,
Universidade de Lisboa, Lisboa, Portugal

Abstract. Transcriptional regulatory networks are responsible for controlling gene expression. These networks are composed of many interactions between transcription factors and their target genes. Carrying a combinatorial nature that encompasses several regulatory processes, they allow an organism to respond to disturbances that may occur in the surrounding environment. In this work, we study transcriptional regulatory networks of closely related yeast species with the aim of revealing which functions or processes are encoded in the regulatory network topology. The first phase of this work consists of the detection of modules followed by their functional characterization. Here, we unveil the functionality of the species by capturing it in functional modules. In the second phase, we move towards a cross-species analysis where we compare the functional modules of the different species to settle the similarities between them. Lastly, we use a multilayer network approach to combine the genetic information of different species. We seek to identify the functional elements conserved across the different organisms by applying a detection of modules in the multilayer network.

Keywords: Complex Networks · Transcriptional Regulatory Networks · Multilayer Networks · Community Detection · Functional Modules

1 Introduction

Gene expression is the biological process that allows a cell to respond to its changing environment. Each cell is the product of specific gene expression events involving the transcription of thousands of genes. The transcription factors (TFs) are the core elements in the control of gene expression. These genes are responsible for activating or inhibiting the genes under their regulation, the target genes (TGs). Normally, the expression level of a target gene is the result of the combinatorial regulation of multiple transcription factors. The hundreds of interactions

© Springer Nature Switzerland AG 2022
P. Ribeiro et al. (Eds.): NetSci-X 2022, LNCS 13197, pp. 140–154, 2022.
https://doi.org/10.1007/978-3-030-97240-0_11

between transcription factors and target genes define a transcriptional regulatory network that underlies cellular identity and function. The morphological differences between species/organisms arise from the gene's differential regulation encoded in the transcriptional regulatory networks. Thus, these networks are of great biological importance since their analysis is fundamental to understanding differential gene expression [1,2]. Therefore, insights from the structure and function of these networks are essential to the study of organisms. However, despite their central role in biology, the structure and dynamics of these type networks are still not completely understood.

In biological networks, communities can share common biological functions, and they are studied in the investigation of cellular systems of organisms. The study of communities have allowed the identification of important protein complexes in protein-protein interaction (PPI) networks [3,4]. In gene regulatory networks, we highlight the discovery of functionally related groups of genes [5] and of groups of genes associated with functions that drive cancer [6].

Cross-species studies have proven to be crucial in modern biology. They are important to study the differences and similarities between species, which is fundamental to understanding their evolution. In PPI networks, cross-species have been used to predict protein-protein interactions (interologues) conserved across species [7,8]. Moreover, the characterization of interspecies differences in gene regulation has already proven to be fundamental for understanding the diversity and evolution of species [9,10]. Multilayer network approaches are useful in studies involving different types of data since it allows its representation and comparison. As examples, already helped to make predictions in protein functions in yeast [11] or to recognize candidate driver cancer genes [12,13].

In this work, we characterize transcriptional regulatory networks of closely related species. In particular, we consider data from YEASTRACT+[14], which provides a set of closely related yeast species with annotated data, both in terms of functional annotation and in terms of mapping between nodes of different species. These networks are represented as graphs, the transcription factors and target genes are represented by the nodes and the interactions between them by the edges. We outline our approach by dividing it into two phases: (1) detection and functional characterization of communities/modules; (2) cross-species comparison. With this approach, we aim to analyze the interplay between structure and function within each species and also between species.

In the first phase, we perform a detection of modules, applying several community detection techniques to understand which one is the most suitable for the considered networks, followed by their functional characterization to divide the networks into functional elements that may represent the different functions of the species. The functional characterization of communities is done using the Gene Ontology[1] [15]. Considering that transcription factors may be associated with multiple regulatory processes, we include the study of overlapping communities, as they allow genes to belong to different functional groups. Moreover, since the regulatory associations are negative (inhibition) or positive (activation), we also consider the division of the network in polarized communities.

---

[1] http://geneontology.org/.

Table 1. Networks Properties. CC stands for Clustering Coefficient and D for Diameter, $\langle k \rangle$ for average degree. In the Diameter field, a value followed by a * represents the value of the Diameter for the largest component of the graph.

Network	#Nodes	#Edges	#TFs	#TGs	$\langle k \rangle$	CC	D
S. cerevisiae	6 886	195 498	220	6 886	56.60	0.47	4
S. cerevisiae B	6 478	45 209	176	6 475	13.93	0.22	5
C. albicans	6 015	35 687	118	6 015	11.83	0.28	5
Y. lipolytica	5 288	9 238	5	5 288	3.49	0.36	4
C. parapsilosis	3 381	6 986	11	3 380	4.13	0.25	4
C. glabrata	2 133	3 508	40	2 116	3.29	0.09	6*
C. tropicalis	665	698	16	663	2.08	0.01	5
K. pastoris	561	581	4	559	2.07	0.01	5
K. lactis	111	126	10	106	2.25	0.15	2*
Z. bailii	32	31	1	31	1.94	0.00	2
K. marxianus	4	3	1	3	1.50	0.00	2

Regarding community detection algorithms, we highlight some of the most recognized. The Girvan-Newman [16] is the most commonly used divisive algorithm. About modularity-optimization-based methods, we underline the Louvain [17], the Clauset-Newman-Moore [18] and Leiden [19] algorithms. The spectral algorithms, such as the Donetti-Muñoz algorithm [20], are also a well-known class of techniques. Enumerating other techniques, we have the Infomap [21], the Label Propagation [22] and the Markov Cluster algorithm [23]. In the detection of overlapping communities, we point to the CFinder algorithm [24]. For more details, we refer to the review from Fortunato *et al.* [25].

Moving to the second stage, we start by settling the similarities among species by comparing the functional modules between these. We also use the connections between species to infer functional elements not previously detected in some organisms. Finally, we use a multilayer network approach combining the genetic information of the species in which we apply a modules detection algorithm to find functional elements conserved across species.

2   Identification of Functional Modules

2.1   Data

We consider data from the YEASTRACT+[2] portal which provides the transcriptional regulatory networks of 10 closely-related yeast species [14]. The characteristics of these networks are presented in Table 1. We can observe that the different species have different levels of documentation, as reflected by the number of nodes and edges. The gene associations may be classified into two major

---

[2] http://yeastract-plus.org.

Table 2. Number of modules obtained for each network using the different algorithms.

Network	GN	Louvain	Leiden	CNM	LP	MC	Infomap	CF	SC
S. cerevisiae	-	5	5	3	1	1	54	-	2
S. cerevisiae B	-	12	11	6	1	78	48	34	2
C. albicans	-	12	12	7	1	11	23	19	-
Y. lipolytica	1	4	4	4	1	1	1	3	-
C. parapsilosis	25	8	8	6	1	2	5	4	-
C. glabrata	17	14	13	12	16	24	29	14	-

groups: (1) DNA binding evidence; (2) expression evidence. Due to the high level of information of *S. cerevisiae*, we consider a new network to our set denoted *S. cerevisiae B*, which consists of filtering the original network keeping only the regulatory associations supported by binding evidence. This filtering aims to clarify the future interpretation of the results for these species. Comparing the characteristics of the original and filtered network, we observe that the number of nodes, transcription factors, and target genes remains close to the original. This indicates that filtering the original network managed to retain most of the genetic evidence of *S. cerevisiae*. Unlike the species mentioned above, there are species whose networks are small and sparse – *C. tropicalis*, *K. pastoris*, *K. lactis*, *Z. bailii* and *K. marxianus*. This lack of genetic evidence suggests that the characterization of these species may not reflect their biological nature. Therefore, we discarded these networks from the current analysis.

2.2   Comparative Analysis of Modules

For the detection of modules, we select a collection of algorithms that exploit the diverse ideas and techniques of Network Science developed over the years. The set is composed of the following algorithms: Girvan-Newman (GN), Louvain, Leiden, Clauset-Newman-Moore (CNM), Label Propagation (LP), Markov Clustering (MC), Infomap, CFinder (CF), and a spectral clustering technique (SC) for modules detection on signed networks. To execute the introduced algorithms, we used libraries where they are already implemented. Some of the considered algorithms are stochastic, i.e., the result may change in each run because their procedure depends on random events. The Louvain, the Label Propagation, and the Infomap are the non-deterministic algorithms we use in our approach. To compare the different outputs of the algorithms, we run these algorithms 1 000 times. Next, to study the different partitions obtained, we compare each pair of different partitions having the number of modules equal to the value of the mode. To make this comparison, we use the package *clusim* [26] that allows us to compare different partitions using similarity measures, in our case we use *Rand Index* [27]. Despite the stochasticity of the algorithms, we obtain high values for the measure of similarity of the considered pairs of partitions and low variance between them, showing that the structural differences between the

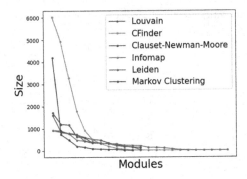

Fig. 1. Modules size distribution for *C. albicans*

partitions are minimal. Thus, regarding stochastic algorithms, we adopt one of the results having the number of modules equal to the mode. Due to the temporal complexity of Girvan-Newman and CFinder algorithms, it was not possible to run them on some of the biggest networks in a reasonable time. Table 2 displays the number of modules obtained for the networks using the different algorithms.

The results in Table 2 show that some of the algorithms fail to detect distinct modules, such as Label Propagation, Girvan-Newman, and Spectral Clustering algorithms in signed networks, which lead us not to choose to study these results. In the *S. cerevisiae*, we detected more modules in the filtered network than in the original network. The applied filter reveals to be essential in the study of the species, the large number of modules found suggests the possibility of discovering a greater diversity of behaviors in the species. Therefore, we decided to use the results of the filtered network to study the respective species. In *Y. lipolytica* few modules were detected, a consequence of the low number of transcription factors. Regarding the other species, it was possible to extract some modules, indicating that these species may contain genetic information about more processes than *Y. lipolytica*. To better understand the division into modules, we decided to study the distribution of their sizes for the different algorithms. In the Fig. 1 we present the distributions for *C. albicans* as example.

A very large gap between the sizes of the modules can make the classification of modules unbalanced since very large modules may aggregate a lot of functionality and small ones may not be associated with any functionality at all. From there, a balanced division of the networks, in which the modules have sizes of the same magnitude, should be the case that better reflects the division of species according to their biological function. The distribution shows that the modularity-based algorithms (Louvain, Leiden and, Clauset-Newman-Moore) have a more balanced division than the others. Infomap, despite having some very small modules, produced others with equivalent size to those mentioned above. CFinder, although it has modules which include almost the entire network, the smaller ones can help us understand if the species benefit from an overlapping communities study. Lastly, the Markov Clustering algorithm gives

Table 3. Significance of the modules obtained for *S. cerevisiae*.

	Louvain		Leiden		Clauset-Newman-Moore	
C	C-score	B-score	C-score	B-score	C-score	B-score
0	1.00	1.00	0.99	1.02e-27	0.97	6.53e-67
1	1.00	1.00	0.99	0.39	1.00	2.07e-69
2	0.99	0.29	1.00	0.01	0.98	1.17e-16
3	1.00	1.00	1.00	0.99	0.99	0.99
4	0.99	1.00	0.99	0.63	0.99	0.01
5	0.99	1.00	0.99	0.01	0.99	0.99
6	0.99	1.00	0.99	1.00	-	-
7	1,00	1.00	0.99	0.83e-9	-	-
8	0.99	1.00	0.99	1,00	-	-
9	0.99	1.00	0.99	0.01	-	-
10	1.00	1.00	0.99	0.32	-	-
11	0.99	1.33e-70	-	-	-	-

us a unbalanced division, having only two modules of same magnitude of those found with the other algorithms, therefore, we decided to discard these results.

To close the first phase of our analysis, we calculated the C-score and B-score [28] for the modules obtained with the modularity-based algorithms. These measures allow us to evaluate the significance of those modules by testing their robustness and stability against random perturbations of the graph structure. These results are presented in Table 3. Looking at the C-score values, none of the algorithms could identify significant modules, consequence of the restrictive null model of the method. The B-score, which uses a less restrictive null model, identifies some modules as significant. According to the B-score values, the Louvain algorithm only produced one significant module, which may be a consequence of its stochasticity. Regarding the other two algorithms, both produced significant modules. Combining the significance of some modules and the balanced division, at that point, Leiden showed to be the one that best captures the structure of the species. Nevertheless, in the functional analysis, we take into account the results of Infomap, CFinder, Louvain, and Clauset-Newman-Moore, which also presented interesting results.

2.3   Functional Analysis of Modules

In this section we provide the functional characterization of the modules previously detected through the label assignment process. These labels represent specific functionalities of the species. The idea is to associate the modules to the most represented and significant Gene Ontology terms among their genes. Given the whole set of terms associated with a module, we perform a three-step filtering of the terms to find the most representative and significant terms: (1)

select only the most global terms (level 2 terms of the Gene Ontology hierarchy); (2) keep only the most over-represented terms of the module using the hypergeometric test (we consider a term as over-represented if is p-value $\in [0; 0.05]$); (3) retain the terms represented in at least 10% of the module.

Algorithms Performance

Using *S. cerevisiae* network as a reference, we compare the performance of the considered algorithms. Beginning with the modularity-based methods, Fig. 2. A first look shows that most modules have more than one label, exposing the functional diversity within these. However, it is observable that not all genes in the modules are linked to functionalities that characterize the modules they belong to. By applying the p-value filtering, we obtain only the most specific terms from each module. Therefore, there are always fractions of genes in the modules that are not associated with any of the terms. These genes correspond to behaviors that end up being captured by other modules.

In Fig. 2, we observe that some functions appear with high representation in the modules. Such as the metabolic process, cellular process, biological regulation, or response to stimulus. In contrast, others seem to be less represented. Being specific functions, these are associated with a smaller set of genes. Reproduction, reproductive process, and transporter activity are good examples of specific functions detected in the modules. The Clauset-Newman-Moore algorithm captured a smaller diversity of functions, failing to identify some functions present in the modules originated by the Louvain and Leiden algorithms. Comparing the results from Louvain and Leiden we can observe that some modules are very similar in terms of functionality. However, Leiden was able to identify functions that Louvain could not, such as the cellular process (usually heavily represented in modules) or reproductive process. Moreover, Leiden was the algorithm in whose modules it was possible to identify more functions of the species, indicating that the division of the species obtained with this algorithm is the one that better reflects the division of functionality of the species.

Regarding the study of overlapping communities, it was possible to retain some new information about the species, such as the presence of functions not previously detected: transcription regulator activity, developmental process, and signaling. However, the study of overlapping communities is not enough to functionally characterize the species, since most communities are small components of larger communities. This results in most communities to be associated with the same behaviors. The performance of the Infomap algorithm lacked consistency. Although it managed to classify some modules of relevant size, it failed to classify the vast majority of modules.

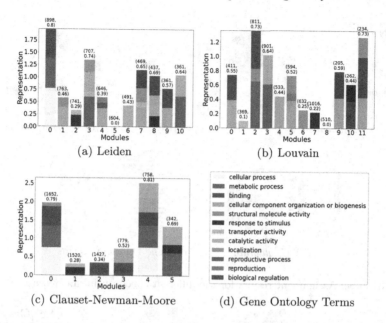

(a) Leiden   (b) Louvain

(c) Clauset-Newman-Moore   (d) Gene Ontology Terms

Fig. 2. Modules and respective functions for modularity-based methods on *S. cerevisiae*. The bar of each term symbolizes its representation in the module. The pair of values at the top of each bar are respectively the size of the module and the fraction of genes of the module related with at least one term (in the module).

Functional Analysis of Remaining Species

Additionally, we analyze the results of the label assignment process for the remaining species. We use the results obtained with the Leiden algorithm, Fig. 3, since it is the algorithm that best captures the functions of *S. cerevisiae*.

Starting with *C. albicans*, we notice the absence of terms in modules *M0*, *M9*, *M10*. In *M0*, since the module encompasses a large part of the species, it is difficult to detect most over-represented terms using the p-value. All the remaining modules are associated with at least one function. Many of those are associated with three or more terms, capturing many of the functions of the species. An interesting point is the association of some modules to functions such as multi-organism process and growth, which are not sufficiently representative/significant to be associated with a module in *S. cerevisiae*. Also in *C. parapsilosis* and *C. glabrata*, some modules are associated with functions not detected in *S. cerevisiae*. Due to the large sizes of *S. cerevisiae* modules, it is difficult for specific terms to have a good representation in these, since they are associated with few genes. In all of these species, general functions already captured in *S. cerevisiae* were also detected, such as metabolic process, response to stimulus, or biological regulation. Revealing once again the central role these have in the functionality of different organisms. It is noticed that the modules of *C. glabrata* are associated with more functionality than the modules of *C.*

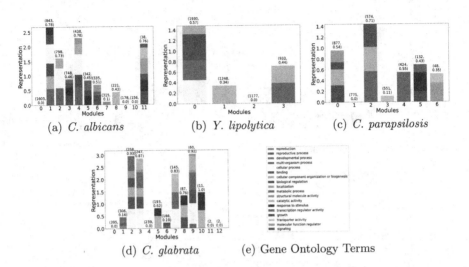

Fig. 3. Label Assignment results for the different species using Leiden algorithm.

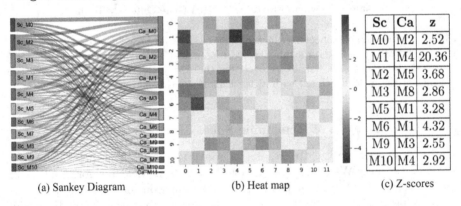

Fig. 4. (a) - Sankey diagram representing the connections between the modules of
S. cerevisiae and C. albicans. (b) - Heat map representing the level of connectivity
between the modules of S. cerevisiae (y axis) and C. albicans (x axis). (c) - Table with
the highest Z-score values.

parapsilosis and Y. lipolytica, although we have more generic evidence on the
last two. Whereas that C. glabrata has more transcription factors, we assume
that the information about this species contains genetic evidence about more
biological processes. This results in a more diversified classification of modules
in comparison to C. parapsilosis and Y. lipolytica.

3   Cross-Species Comparison

3.1   Functional Comparison of Modules

To compare the modules we resort to the homology mappings between species to establish the connections between species. Each link in a homology mapping denotes the connection between two homologous genes. In biology, it is established that the DNA sequence of two homologous genes derives from a common ancestor (may or may not have the same function). For this work, the homology mappings are also obtained from YEASTRACT+ [14].

S. cerevisiae vs *C. albicans*

We now focus on the comparison between *S. cerevisiae* and *C. albicans*. For this purpose, we explore the level of connection between the functional modules obtained with the Leiden algorithm. In Fig. 4(a) we present a Sankey diagram representing the connections between the modules for both species.

To understand the level of connection between modules, we perform an analysis to assess the quality of the mappings. First, we calculate the number of links shared between every pair of modules of the two species. Then, we compare these distributions with 1 000 realizations of the same process in a null model, which consists of maintaining the community structure of both networks but with randomization of the nodes. Consequently, this procedure results in different mappings between species. In Fig. 4(b) we present the heat map of the z-scores representing the level of connection between modules. The analysis of the heat map reveals the existence of some pairs of modules with strong connections (green and blue colors), these pairs are listed in Fig. 4(c).

Next, we consult the functions associated with the modules that are part of strong connections and we verify the sharing of functions between some of the modules. This circumstance points to homologous genes with the same function as the cause for the strong connectivity in some pairs of modules. One good example is the pair of modules *M0* and *M2* of *S. cerevisiae* and *C. albicans* respectively. In both cases, the metabolic and cellular processes are widely represented terms, homologous genes associated with those functions may be the origin for this solid connection. However, in other cases, mutual labels only represent a small part of the genes of the modules. Such as in *M1* of *S. cerevisiae* and *M4* of *C. albicans*, which is by far the strongest connection between the two species. In this case, the mutual functions between modules seem not to be sufficient to justify the strong connection. Thus, this connection may arise from other events, such as the sharing of functions that were only detected in one of the modules (cellular and metabolic process). Thus, this connection may arise from other events, such as the sharing of functions that were only detected in one of the modules (cellular and metabolic process).

Table 4. Strongly connected pairs of modules from different species. For each module, we can consult the percentage of genes that have homologous with the same function in the other module that is part of the connection. A green cell means that the term was found in the module through the label assignment process, a cell in red denotes the opposite (the term was not found in the module).

Connections	Terms					
	GO:0071840	GO:0005198	GO:0008152	GO:0009987	GO:0005488	GO:0065007
M1-Sc	0.10	0.14	0.17	0.18	0.07	
M4-Ca	0.13	0.16	0.21	0.23	0.11	
M0-Sc	0.03		0.09	0.10	0.06	0.04
M0-Yl	0.01		0.04	0.05	0.03	0.02
M0-Ca	0.03		0.10	0.12	0.07	0.04
M0-Yl	0.03		0.09	0.10	0.06	0.04

Terms	Function
GO:0071840	cellular component organization or biogenesis
GO:0005198	structural molecule activity
GO:0008152	metabolic process
GO:0009987	cellular process
GO:0005488	binding
GO:0065007	biological regulation

Detailed Analysis of Connections

We examine the terms associated with the links of the connections between modules of different species. A term is associated with a link if the term is common to the homologous genes in it. In Table 4 we present some of the most relevant connections among species. The detailed analysis of the connections demonstrates that there are functional groups of considerable size in different species formed by homologous genes with the same functions. This evidence reveals the conservation of functional elements across different organisms. Also, using the information of Table 4, we can diagnose functional elements in some modules that were not detected with the previous analysis. Such as the metabolic and cellular processes in *M1* of *S. cerevisiae*. Finally, we look at the connection between *M0* of *C. albicans* and *M0* of *Y. lipolytica*. In this cross-species analysis, we unveil some functional elements present in *M0* of *C. albicans*. With this new information, it is clear that the absence of labels assigned to this module in the label assignment process results from its large size.

3.2   Multilayer Approach for Cross-Species Comparison

In the previous section, we found functional elements conserved across species. However, we did not check if these elements have other associated functions or even if they overlap, since each gene can have more than one function associated to it. Therefore, in this final step, we build a multilayer network between species in which we perform a module detection task using the Infomap algorithm, which is suitable for this type of network. With the detection and functional characterization of the modules, we seek to identify and characterize functional structures conserved across species. In this multilayer network, the inter-layer links are those of the homology mappings between species.

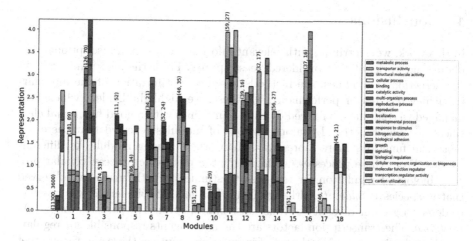

Fig. 5. Comparison of labels between the modules of the multilayer and the respective groups of genes from *S. cerevisiae* and *C. albicans*. The three bars side-by-side respectively describe the labels of the module, of the genes from *S.cerevisiae* and the genes from *C. albicans*. At the top of the first bar of each module is shown the module size and the number of inter-layer links in the module.

Using *S. cerevisiae* and *C. albicans*, we create the multilayer network. From the detection of modules, we could find 19 modules containing genes from both species. Going further with our analysis, we study the contribution of the genes of each species for the classification of the modules in the multilayer network. The comparison between the functions of each module and those of the respective gene groups can be seen in Fig. 5.

We observe that the first module represents a large part of the multilayer network, suggesting that this one may not provide useful information about small functional elements conserved between species. Looking at the classification of this module, we confirm that this one does not have GO terms associated with it, not contributing with relevant results for the analysis. Regarding the rest of the modules, we verify that the number of pairs of homologous genes corresponds to about half the module size, indicating that these modules are mostly composed of pairs of homologous genes. We verify that in some modules the functionalities result from the mutual contribution of the species, such as in *M1*, *M2*, *M4*, *M7*, *M8*, *M11*, *M12*, *M13* and *M16*. These modules result from the combination of homologous genes that are functionally identical and that constitute functional structures conserved among species. Some functions in the modules are equally represented, such as the metabolic and cellular process in *M1* or reproduction and reproductive process in *M7*. This is a consequence of these functions being associated to the same set of genes.

4   Conclusions

In this work, we contribute with relevant information about transcriptional regulatory networks of the considered yeast species. From the algorithms used in the detection of modules, the methods based on optimization of the modularity achieved a better performance. Of these, we highlight Leiden, which best managed to combine a balanced division of modules with a good functional classification. The functional characterization of modules revealed that there are biological functions more represented than others among modules of different species. From these processes, we highlight the metabolic process, cellular process, biological regulation, or response to stimulus. Furthermore, we observed that in species *C. glabrata*, although it has less genetic evidence, it was possible to detect a greater diversity of functions than in species *C. parapsilosis* and *Y. lipolytica*. The transcription factors are the main agents responsible for regulating the behavior of species, the set of interactions between these and their target genes constitute the regulation of certain behaviors. Since *C. glabrata* contains more transcription factors, it contains genetic evidence about more functions.

The cross-species comparison allowed us to establish some similarities between species. As an example, we found that modules from different species contain identical functions due to the presence of functionally identical homologous genes between them. With the creation of the multilayer, we were able to verify that there are functional structures conserved across species that carry identical genetic information.

We highlight some limitations of our approach. Firstly, the difficulty of finding meaningful terms with the p-value approach in large modules. Therefore, in an unbalanced division of the network, it will be difficult to label the large modules. Secondly, the threshold used to consider a term as relevant in a module (10%) may be too restrictive. To overcome this problem, we could test different values for the threshold in a set of modules with different sizes. Then, we could use the relation between the threshold values and the size of the modules to predict the threshold values for each module considering its size.

As future work, we could consider the creation of a measure that would allow us to evaluate the functional characterization of the modules. This one could combine the diversity of functionality found in the modules and the proportion of genes in the modules that are covered by the functions assigned to them. Therefore, modules associated with functions covering almost all of their genes would be considered as well-classified. Moreover, we would like to consider subprocesses, i.e., GO terms at a level greater that 3, to uncover specific regulatory processes within the identified modules. Also, we found some genes in modules not associated with any Gene Ontology terms, we could use the functions of the modules in which these genes belong to predict their functionality.

Acknowledgements. This work was supported by national funds through Fundação para a Ciência e a Tecnologia (FCT) with references PTDC/BII-BIO/28216/2017 and PTDC/CCI-BIO/29676/2017, UIDB/50021/2020 and UIDP/00408/2020 (INESC-ID and LASIGE multi-annual funding, respectively).

References

1. Davidson, E.H., et al.: A genomic regulatory network for development. Science **295**(5560), 1669–1678 (2002)
2. Luscombe, N.M., Madan Babu, M., Yu, H., Snyder, M., Teichmann, S.A., Gerstein, M.: Genomic analysis of regulatory network dynamics reveals large topological changes. Nature **431**(7006), 308–312 (2004)
3. Rives, A.W., Galitski, T.: Modular organization of cellular networks. Proc. Natl. Acad. Sci. **100**(3), 1128–1133 (2003)
4. Spirin, V., Mirny, L.A.: Protein complexes and functional modules in molecular networks. Proc. Natl. Acad. Sci. **100**(21), 12123–12128 (2003)
5. Wilkinson, D.M., Huberman, B.A.: A method for finding communities of related genes. Proc. Natl. Acad. Sci. **101**(suppl 1), 5241–5248 (2004)
6. de Anda-Jáuregui, G., Alcalá-Corona, S.A., Espinal-Enríquez, J., Hernández-Lemus, E.: Functional and transcriptional connectivity of communities in breast cancer co-expression networks. Appl. Netw. Sci. **4**(1), 1–13 (2019). https://doi.org/10.1007/s41109-019-0129-0
7. Matthews, L.R., et al.: Identification of potential interaction networks using sequence-based searches for conserved protein-protein interactions or "interologs". Genome Res. **11**(12), 2120–2126 (2001)
8. Sharan, R., et al.: Conserved patterns of protein interaction in multiple species. Proc. Natl. Acad. Sci. **102**(6), 1974–1979 (2005)
9. Borneman, A.R., et al.: Divergence of transcription factor binding sites across related yeast species. Science **317**(5839), 815–819 (2007)
10. Stuart, J.M., Segal, E., Koller, D., Kim, S.K., et al.: A gene-coexpression network for global discovery of conserved genetic modules. Science **302**(5643), 249–255 (2003)
11. Zhao, B., Sai, H., Li, X., Zhang, F., Tian, Q., Ni, W.: An efficient method for protein function annotation based on multilayer protein networks. Hum. Genomics **10**(1), 1–15 (2016)
12. Cantini, L., Medico, E., Fortunato, S., Caselle, M.: Detection of gene communities in multi-networks reveals cancer drivers. Sci. Rep. **5**(1), 1–10 (2015)
13. Yu, L., Shi, Y., Zou, Q., Gao, L.: Studying the drug treatment pattern based on the action of drug and multi-layer network model. bioRxiv, p. 780858 (2019)
14. Monteiro, P.T., et al.: YEASTRACT+: a portal for cross-species comparative genomics of transcription regulation in yeasts. Nucleic Acids Res. **48**(D1), D642–D649 (2019)
15. Ashburner, M., et al.: Gene ontology: tool for the unification of biology. Nature Genet. **25**(1), 25–29 (2000)
16. Girvan, M., Newman, M.E.J.: Community structure in social and biological networks. Proc. Natl. Acad. Sci. **99**(12), 7821–7826 (2002)
17. Blondel, V.D., Guillaume, J.L., Lambiotte, R., Lefebvre, E.: Fast unfolding of communities in large networks. J. Stat. Mech. Theor. Exp. **2008**(10), P10008 (2008)
18. Clauset, A., Newman, M.E., Moore, C.: Finding community structure in very large networks. Phys. Rev. E **70**(6), 066111 (2004)
19. Traag, V.A., Waltman, L., Van Eck, N.J.: From Louvain to Leiden: guaranteeing well-connected communities. Sci. Rep. **9**(1), 1–12 (2019)
20. Donetti, L., Munoz, M.A.: Detecting network communities: a new systematic and efficient algorithm. J. Stat. Mech. Theor. Exp. **2004**(10), P10012 (2004)

154 P. Dias et al.

21. Rosvall, M., Bergstrom, C.T.: Maps of random walks on complex networks reveal community structure. Proc. Natl. Acad. Sci. **105**(4), 1118–1123 (2008)
22. Raghavan, U.N., Albert, R., Kumara, S.: Near linear time algorithm to detect community structures in large-scale networks. Phys. Rev. E **76**(3), 036106 (2007)
23. Van Dongen, S.M.: Graph clustering by flow simulation. PhD thesis, Faculteit Wiskunde en Informatica, Universiteit Utrecht (2000)
24. Adamcsek, B., Palla, G., Farkas, I.J., Derényi, I., Vicsek, T.: Cfinder: locating cliques and overlapping modules in biological networks. Bioinformatics **22**(8), 1021–1023 (2006)
25. Fortunato, S.: Community detection in graphs. Phys. Rep. **486**(3–5), 75–174 (2010)
26. Gates, A.J., Ahn, Y.Y.: Clusim: a python package for calculating clustering similarity. J. Open Source Softw. **4**(35), 1264 (2019)
27. Rand, W.M.: Objective criteria for the evaluation of clustering methods. J. Am. Stat. Assoc. **66**(336), 846–850 (1971)
28. Lancichinetti, A., Radicchi, F., Ramasco, J.J.: Statistical significance of communities in networks. Phys. Rev. E **81**(4), 046110 (2010)

Competitive Information Spreading on Modular Networks

Satoshi Furutani[1,2(✉)], Toshiki Shibahara[1], Mitsuaki Akiyama[1], and Masaki Aida[2]

[1] NTT Social Informatics Laboratories, Tokyo, Japan
{satoshi.furutani.ek,toshiki.shibahara.de}@hco.ntt.co.jp,
akiyama@ieee.org
[2] Tokyo Metropolitan University, Tokyo, Japan
aida@tmu.ac.jp

Abstract. Information spreading on social networks is one of the most important topics in network science and has long been actively studied. However, most studies only focus on the spread of a single piece of information on random networks, even though information spreading in the real world is much more complicated, involving a complex topology structure and interactions between multiple information. Therefore, in this paper, we model the competitive information spreading on modular networks and investigate how the community structure affects competitive information spreading in two spreading scenarios: sequential and simultaneous. In the sequential spreading scenario, we find that the community structure has little effect on the final prevalence but affects the spreading process (time evolution of the prevalence). In contrast, in the simultaneous spreading scenario, we find that community structure has a strong effect on not only the spreading process but also the final prevalence. Specifically, two competing pieces of information cannot coexist and one drives out the other on a non-modular network, whereas they can coexist in different communities on a modular network. Our results suggest that the effect of community structure cannot be ignored in the analysis of competitive spreading (especially, simultaneous spreading) of multiple information.

Keywords: information spreading · cascade dynamics · modular networks

1 Introduction

In modern information society, social networks are an essential platform for information spreading. Information spreading on social networks has long been actively studied because of its various applications. Traditional analysis of information spreading has been motivated by analogy with disease spreading [1,2]. It assumes that the information is spread stochastically from the infectious (i.e., an individual who has spread the information) to the susceptible (i.e., an individual

P. Ribeiro et al. (Eds.): NetSci-X 2022, LNCS 13197, pp. 155–168, 2022.
https://doi.org/10.1007/978-3-030-97240-0_12

who has not yet spread). A contagion process that spreads through independent interactions between the susceptible and infectious is called *simple contagion* (also known as *biological contagion*). Typical simple contagion models include susceptible-infectious-susceptible (SIS) and the susceptible-infectious-recovered (SIR) models [3,4].

On the other hand, *complex contagion* (also known as *social contagion*) has also been widely studied [5–7]. The complex contagion process is a contagion process in which an individual requires social pressure (or social reinforcement) from multiple individuals to adopt some kind of behavior (e.g., spreading information, memes, and innovations and participating in political protest and signature-collecting campaigns). The spread of information, memes, and behaviors has been found to be better explained by complex contagion rather than by simple contagion [8,9]. Most existing studies have modeled information spreading as either simple or complex contagion. However, in the real world, an individual who has a strong interest in the information may spread it immediately upon receiving it, whereas an individual who has no interest in it may not. Therefore, it is reasonable to assume that the ease of information spreading (i.e., the number of exposures required to adopt spreading information) depends on the characteristics of individuals, such as interest, attitude, and literacy. Indeed, an empirical study that analyzed the spread of social movements on Facebook reported that the characteristics of individuals affect the type of contagion [10]. To imitate the complex contagion in the real world, a generalized contagion model that takes into account both simple and complex contagion has also been proposed [11,12].

In the perspective of network structure, most existing studies consider information spreading on random networks with an arbitrary degree distribution $p(k)$ (i.e., using the configuration model [13]). However, real social networks have modular (or community) structures. A community is, roughly speaking, a group of nodes that are densely connected with nodes within the group, and sparsely connected with nodes between other groups. There are few studies of a complex contagion process on modular networks [14–16]. Galstyan and Cohen studied the dynamics of complex contagion on a random network of two loosely coupled communities and found that when the two communities are sufficiently loosely coupled, the spreading dynamics exhibit a two-tiered structure [14]. Glesson provides a unified framework for theoretical analysis of complex contagion models on networks consisting of two or more communities with arbitrary degree distributions [15]. Nematzadeh et al. used a linear threshold model to investigate the impact of community structure on information spreading and found that there is the optimal network modularity for global information spreading [16].

The above-mentioned studies focus on the spread of a single piece of information. However, when information spreads on a real social network, it often spreads interacting with other information. For example, when false information is spread on a social network, in most cases, the debunking information is also spread and hinders the spread of false information. Therefore, to accurately understand the mechanism of information spreading in the real world, the competitive spreading of multiple information needs to be considered. However, despite its importance, there are very few studies of multiple complex contagion processes on a non-modular network, and none on a modular network. Liu et al. proposed a sequential social contagion model based on susceptible-adopted-recovered (SAR) model [7], which is a complex contagion model in which two behaviors spread sequentially on the same non-modular network [17]. The adoption of the first behavior has an inhibiting or synergistic effect on the adoption of the second behavior. They found that these effects affect the type of phase transition in the second behavior spreading. Min and Miguel studied the role of dual users (i.e., users who adopt both spreading entities) in two complex contagion processes and found that the presence of dual users enables the prevalence of the later entity to override the advantage of the earlier one [18].

On the basis of this background, in this paper, we consider a spreading model of two competing pieces of information (information A and information B) on social networks and investigate how the community structure affects the competitive information spreading. We consider two scenarios of competitive spreading: *sequential spreading* and *simultaneous spreading*. In the sequential spreading scenario, information A spreads first, and information B spreads next while being hindered by information A. In the simultaneous spreading scenario, information A and information B spread simultaneously while interfering with each other. As a result of the analysis, in the sequential spreading scenario, we found that the community structure has little effect on the final prevalence, but affects the spreading process (i.e., the time evolution of the prevalence). However, in the simultaneous spreading scenario, we found that the community structure affects both the final prevalence and the spreading process. Specifically, information A and information B cannot coexist and one drives out the other on a non-modular network, whereas they can coexist in different communities on a modular network. Our results suggest that the effect of community structure cannot be ignored in the analysis of competitive spreading (especially, simultaneous spreading) of multiple information.

2   Models

2.1   Information Spreading Model

In this paper, as the (single) information spreading model, we use the generalized contagion model proposed by Min and Miguel [12]. Let us consider a network consisting of N nodes that can be in a susceptible state and an adopted state. Each node v is assigned an adoption threshold θ_v (randomly drawn from threshold distribution $Q(\theta)$). A susceptible node v adopts the information when the number of exposures to the information is larger than θ_v, and then attempts to spread the information to its neighbors. The information is transmitted with probability λ along each edge. Varying the adoption threshold, this model represents both simple and complex contagion. When $\theta_v = 1$, a susceptible node v becomes adopted by single exposure thus indicating simple contagion. When $\theta_v > 1$, it represents complex contagion since multiple exposures are needed for adoption.

This model can recover some representative contagion models by varying two parameters, λ and $Q(\theta)$. SIR model [3,4] corresponds to $(\lambda, Q(\theta)) = (\lambda, \delta_{\theta,1})$ where $\delta_{i,j}$ is the Kroneckar delta function. Watts' threshold model [5] corresponds to $(\lambda, Q(\theta)) = (1, \delta_{\theta,k_v T})$ where k_v is the degree of node v and T is the threshold. A modified version of Watts' threshold model proposed in [14] corresponds to $(\lambda, Q(\theta)) = (1, \delta_{\theta,n>1})$. In this study, we set threshold distribution to $Q(\theta) = (1-p)\delta_{\theta,1} + p\,\delta_{\theta,n}$ $(n > 1)$. This means that a fraction $(1-p)$ of nodes follows simple contagion and a fraction p of nodes requires n (> 1) exposures for adoption.

2.2   Competitive Information Spreading Model

In this subsection, we present the competitive spreading model of two competing pieces of information (information A and information B). Let us assume that each node spreads information following the generalized contagion model in the previous subsection and can be in three states: the state that adopts information A (state A), the state that adopts information B (state B), and the state that still has not adopted either (state S). Moreover, we assume that each node adopts the information of the majority from its perspective. Specifically, for information B to be spread by a node v, the number of exposures of information B to node v, $\#_v^B$, must be larger than not only the threshold θ_v but also that of information A, $\#_v^A$. Note that the number of exposures of the information to a node is not always equal to the number of neighbors who spread the information if the transmissibility $\lambda < 1$.

We consider two scenarios of competitive spreading: *sequential spreading* and *simultaneous spreading*. In the sequential spreading scenario, information A spreads first, and then information B spreads. When information A spreads, since there is no other information, node v spreads information if $\#_v^A \geq \theta_v$. On the other hand, in the spreading phase of information B, for information B to be spread by node v, the number of exposures of information B must satisfy $(\#_v^B \geq \theta_v) \wedge (\#_v^B > \#_v^A)$. This means that information A hinders the spreading of information B. In the real world, this corresponds to a situation in which the spread of correct information through a social network is hindered due to fake news having already been widely spread and believed. In the simultaneous spreading scenario, information A and information B spread simultaneously while interfering with each other. In the real world, this scenario corresponds to the situation where a hoax starts spreading on a social network, and the debunking information spreads soon.

3   Single Information Spreading on Non-modular and Modular Networks

In this section, for comparison with competitive information spreading, we consider single information spreading on non-modular (random) and modular networks. We analyze the cascade condition (i.e., the condition that causes an information cascade) and how the community structure affects information spreading by using tree-like approximation [19, 20]. The tree-like approximation analyzes information spreading by replacing an infinite random graph with an arbitrary degree distribution $p(k)$ to the non-clustered tree-like structure. Contagion is initiated from seed nodes (level 0) and spreads by level-by-level, that is from level $t-1$ to level t, and then level $t+1$. This approximation gives good results for a network that is not a tree. For the synchronous updating (i.e., all nodes are updated simultaneously), the level t corresponds to the time step t of the contagion process.

3.1   Spreading on Non-modular Networks

We first consider single information spreading on non-modular networks. Note that the results of this case have been already reported by Min and Miguel [12] in detail. Let us consider an infinite locally tree-like network with the degree distribution $p(k)$ and the average degree z. A contagion is initiated from the fraction of randomly chosen seed nodes, ρ_0.

The final cascade size ρ_∞, the fraction of adopted nodes in the network in the steady state, is calculated as

$$\rho_\infty = \rho_0 + (1-\rho_0) \sum_{k=1}^{\infty} p(k) \sum_{m=0}^{k} \binom{k}{m} q_\infty^m (1-q_\infty)^{k-m} F(m) =: h(q_\infty),$$

where q_∞ is the steady state probability that a top level ($t \to \infty$) node is adopted. The probability q_∞ is derived as the fixed point of the recursive equation

$$q_t = \rho_0 + (1-\rho_0) \sum_{k=1}^{\infty} \frac{kp(k)}{z} \sum_{m=0}^{k-1} \binom{k-1}{m} q_{t-1}^m (1-q_{t-1})^{k-m-1} F(m) =: f(q_{t-1}),$$

(1)

with the initial value $q_0 = \rho_0$. Here, $F(m) = F(m; \lambda, Q(\theta))$ is the probability that more than the threshold number of neighbors out of m adopted neighbors succeed in transmission with the probability λ, and defined as

$$F(m) := \sum_{\theta=1}^{\infty} Q(\theta) \sum_{s=\theta}^{m} \binom{m}{s} \lambda^s (1-\lambda)^{m-s}.$$

(2)

Note that, if $p(k)$ is a Poisson distribution and $F(m)$ does not depend on k, it satisfies $\rho_\infty = q_\infty$ [14, 15]. For $\rho_0 \to 0$, the equation $q_\infty = f(q_\infty)$ always has a trivial solution $q_\infty = 0$, and when $f'(0) = \sum_k \frac{k(k-1)}{z} p(k) F(1) > 1$, it has a non-trivial solution $q_\infty > 0$ (i.e., cascades occur). Hence, we have the cascade condition

$$\lambda > \lambda_c = \frac{\langle k \rangle}{(1-p)\left(\langle k^2 \rangle - \langle k \rangle\right)},$$

(3)

where $\langle \varphi(k) \rangle = \sum_k \varphi(k) p(k)$ is the expected value of a random variable $\varphi(k)$. Especially, for the Poisson distribution $p(k) = e^{-z} z^k / k!$, the cascade condition

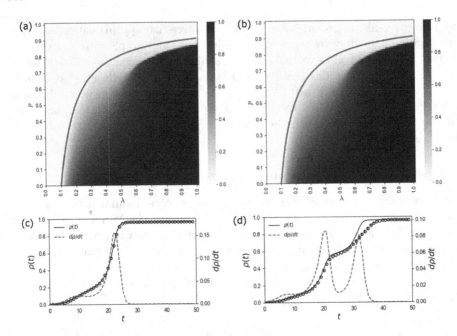

Fig. 1. Phase diagram of the final cascade size for non-modular networks (a) and modular networks with two communities (b). The red line represents the cascade condition computed by the tree-like approximation. The simulations are averaged over 20 runs for each combination of (λ, p) with parameters $N = 2.0 \times 10^4$, $z = 10$, $\rho_0 = 10^{-3}$, $n = 4$. The cascade size ρ_t and its change rate $d\rho/dt$ for non-modular networks (c) and modular networks with two communities (d). The black and red lines respectively represent the theoretical curves of $\rho(t)$ and $d\rho/dt$, and symbols represent the simulation results (almost all error bars are smaller than symbols). The simulations are averaged over 20 runs with parameters $N = 5.0 \times 10^4$, $z = 10$, $\rho_0 = 10^{-3}$, $\lambda = 0.8$, $p = 0.8$, $n = 4$. For modular networks, the percentage of edges between communities is set to 0.1% of all edges, and the seed nodes are chosen from only one community. (Color figure online)

can be written as $\lambda > 1/(z(1 - p))$. For the power-law distribution $p(k) \propto k^{-\beta}$ ($2 < \beta < 3$), the critical threshold λ_c vanishes since $\langle k^2 \rangle \to \infty$ in the thermodynamic limit $N \to \infty$.

The fraction of complex contagion nodes, p, affects the difficulty of the cascade occurrence and the type of phase transition. Figure 1a shows the cascade size ρ_∞ to a combination (λ, p) for a non-modular network with $z = 10$ and $n = 4$. The red curve represents the set of phase transition points $\lambda = 1/(z(1 - p))$. From this figure, we can see that the larger p is, the harder it is for cascades to occur. In addition, for $p < p_c = 0.71$, the continuous phase transition of ρ_∞ occurs with respect to λ, while the discontinuous phase transition occurs for $p > p_c$. For more detail, see [12].

3.2 Spreading on Modular Networks

On the basis of the analysis of [15], we analyze single information spreading on a modular network with N nodes, consisting of d communities $C_1, \ldots, C_d$. Let $z^{(i)}$ and $p^{(i)}(k)$ be the average degree and degree distribution of nodes in the community C_i, respectively. Then, $\rho_0^{(i)}$ denotes a fraction of seed nodes in C_i, satisfying $\rho_0 = \sum_{i=1}^{d} \frac{N^{(i)}}{N} \rho_0^{(i)}$ where $N^{(i)} = |C_i|$. Let γ_{ij} be the probability that the endpoints of a certain edge randomly chosen from the network are nodes belong to C_i and C_j. Note that γ_{ij} satisfies the following equations:

$$\sum_{j=1}^{d} \gamma_{ij} = \frac{N^{(i)} z^{(i)}}{\sum_{i'=1}^{d} N^{(i')} z^{(i')}}, \quad \sum_{i=1}^{d} \sum_{j=1}^{d} \gamma_{ij} = 1.$$

We define the probability $q_t^{(i)}$ that a random node at level $t - 1$ in C_i is adopted, conditional on its parents (level t) being susceptible. The recursive equation of $q_t^{(i)}$ can be written as

$$q_t^{(i)} = \frac{1}{\sum_{j=1}^{d} \gamma_{ij}} \sum_{j=1}^{d} \gamma_{ij} \left[\rho_0^{(j)} + (1 - \rho_0^{(j)}) \sum_{k=1}^{\infty} \frac{k p^{(j)}(k)}{z^{(j)}} \right.$$

$$\left. \times \sum_{m=0}^{k-1} \binom{k-1}{m} (q_{t-1}^{(j)})^m (1 - q_{t-1}^{(j)})^{k-m-1} F(m) \right] =: \phi_i(q_{t-1}^{(1)}, \ldots, q_{t-1}^{(d)}).$$

$$(4)$$

We have the fixed point $\boldsymbol{q}_{\infty} = (q_{\infty}^{(1)}, \ldots, q_{\infty}^{(d)})$ by iteratively calculating Eq. (4) with the initial values $q_0^{(i)} = \rho_0^{(i)}$ for $i = 1, \ldots, d$. Eq. (4) can be linearized around the trivial fixed point $\boldsymbol{q}_{\infty} = \boldsymbol{0}$ as $\boldsymbol{q}_t = \boldsymbol{J} \boldsymbol{q}_{t-1}$ where $\boldsymbol{J} \in \mathbb{R}^{d \times d}$ is the Jacobi matrix whose (i, j)-component is

$$\left. \frac{\partial \phi_i}{\partial q^{(j)}} \right|_{q=0} = \frac{\gamma_{ij}}{\sum_{j'=1}^{d} \gamma_{ij'}} \sum_{k=1}^{\infty} \frac{k(k-1)}{z^{(j)}} p^{(j)}(k) F(1). \tag{5}$$

Thus, we obtain the cascade condition by evaluating the largest eigenvalue of $\boldsymbol{J}$.

For a special case, if communities are symmetric (i.e. $\forall j$, $N^{(j)} = N/d$, $p^{(j)}(k) = p(k)$, and $z^{(j)} = z$), the Jacobi matrix becomes

$$\boldsymbol{J} = \sum_{k=1}^{\infty} \frac{k(k-1)}{z} p(k) F(1) \tilde{\boldsymbol{\Gamma}}, \quad \text{where} \quad (\tilde{\boldsymbol{\Gamma}})_{ij} = \frac{\gamma_{ij}}{\sum_{j'=1}^{d} \gamma_{ij'}}.$$

Since the largest eigenvalue of the stochastic matrix $\tilde{\boldsymbol{\Gamma}}$ is 1, the cascade condition of information spreading on modular networks coincides with that on non-modular networks (3).

Indeed, Figs. 1a and 1b show that the final cascade size on non-modular and modular networks are nearly the same, indicating that the community structure has little effect on how much information is finally spread. On the other hand, the community structure affects the time evolution of the cascade size (i.e., how the information spreads). Figures 1c and 1d show the cascade size $\rho_t = \sum_{i=1}^{d} \frac{N^{(i)}}{N} q_t^{(i)}$ and its change rate $d\rho/dt \approx \rho_{t+1} - \rho_t$ for each time step t on non-modular and modular networks. On a non-modular network, a cascade initiated from seed nodes first activates simple contagion nodes and then progressively spreads throughout the network, thus its change rate forms small and large peaks. On a modular network, the cascade first spreads and saturates in one community, and then spreads in another community. Hence, the spreading peaks in different communities are separated in time. This phenomenon is called *two-tiered dynamics* [14]. Note that, it is easy to assume that the gap between peaks becomes smaller and disappears as the connection between communities becomes stronger. Similar results were reported in previous studies [14,15], although the spreading model considered is different.

4   Competitive Information Spreading on Non-modular and Modular Networks

When information spreads on a real social network, other information often spreads, which hinders the spread. Hence, to accurately understand the mechanism of information spreading in the real world, it is necessary to consider a situation where two competing pieces of information spread. In this section, we analyze the spreading of two competing pieces of information, information A and information B, in sequential and simultaneous spreading scenarios.

4.1   Sequential Spreading Scenario

In the sequential spreading scenario, we analyze the cascade condition of information B in a network where information A has already been spread. Let a_t and b_t respectively be the probabilities that a node at level t is in state A and state B, conditional on its parents at level $t+1$ not being in state A or state B. Since the spreading of information A is no different from the spreading of single information discussed in Sect. 3.1, we have the probability that a node is state A in steady state, a_∞, by iteratively updating the recursive Eq. (1) starting from $a_0 = \rho_0^A$. On the other hand, since the spread of information B is affected by information A, the updating equation of b_t is given as follows by using a_∞:

$$b_t = \rho_0^B + (1 - \rho_0^B) \sum_{k=1}^{\infty} \frac{kp(k)}{z} \sum_{m+l=0}^{k-1} \frac{(k-1)!}{m!\, l!\, (k-m-l-1)!}$$
$$\times a_\infty^m\, b_{t-1}^l\, (1 - a_\infty - b_{t-1})^{k-m-l-1} G(m,l) =: g(b_{t-1}). \tag{6}$$

The first term on the right-hand side of the above Eq. (6) represents the probability that a node at level t is initially in state B (i.e., is a seed node with probability ρ_0^B) and the second term represents the probability that a node at level t is not a seed node but is activated by its neighbors in state B. Here, $G(m, l) = G(m, l; \lambda_A, \lambda_B, Q(\theta))$ is the probability that a node with m neighbors who spread information A and l neighbors who spread information B adopts information B, defined as

$$G(m, l) := \sum_{\theta=0}^{\infty} Q(\theta) \sum_{u=\theta}^{l} \binom{l}{u} \lambda_B^u (1 - \lambda_B)^{l-u} \sum_{s=0}^{S} \binom{m}{s} \lambda_A^s (1 - \lambda_A)^{m-s}, \quad (7)$$

where $S := \min(u-1, m)$. Assuming that $\rho_0^B \to 0$, for a given a_∞, the fixed point equation $b_\infty = g(b_\infty)$ always has a trivial solution $b_\infty = 0$ and has non-trivial solution $b_\infty > 0$ if $g'(0) > 1$. Thus, by calculating $g'(0) > 1$, we have the cascade condition of information B as follows:

$$\lambda_B > \frac{z}{(1 - p)\frac{d^2}{d\alpha^2}\langle \alpha^k \rangle}, \quad (8)$$

where $\alpha := 1 - \lambda_A a_\infty$.

Especially, if $p(k)$ is the Poisson distribution, the cascade condition can be written as $\lambda_B > e^{z\lambda_A a_\infty}/(z(1 - p))$ since $\langle \alpha^k \rangle = e^{(\alpha-1)z}$. The exponent in the numerator, $z\lambda_A a_\infty$, can be interpreted as the node's expected exposure to information A and when $z\lambda_A a_\infty > \log z(1 - p)$, the spreading of information B becomes impossible in principle.

In the same way as in Sect. 3.2, we can analyze the cascade condition for a modular network. For a given $(a_\infty^{(1)}, \ldots, a_\infty^{(d)})$ calculated by Eq. (4), $b_t^{(i)}$ of community C_i is given by

$$b_t^{(i)} = \frac{\sum_{j=1}^d \gamma_{ij} g(b_{t-1}^{(j)})}{\sum_{j=1}^d \gamma_{ij}} = \psi_i(b_{t-1}^{(1)}, \ldots, b_{t-1}^{(d)}), \quad \forall i = 1, \ldots, d \quad (9)$$

By linearizing $b_\infty^{(i)} = \psi_i(b_\infty^{(1)}, \ldots, b_\infty^{(d)})$ around the trivial fixed point $b_\infty^{(i)} = 0$, we obtain the cascade condition. As in the case of the single information spreading, for symmetric communities, the cascade condition is the same as in Eq. (8).

Figures 2a and 2b show the final cascade size of information B, ρ_∞^B, for non-modular and modular networks with two communities. These figures indicate that even in the sequential spreading scenario, the community structure does not affect the final prevalence as in the case of the single information spreading. Figures 2c and 2d show the time evolution of the cascade size of information B at each time step t with $p = 0.6$. For $p = 0.6$, the critical point is $\lambda_c = 0.25$. Thus, the result for $\lambda_A = 0.2$ represents a state with little interference from information A, while the result for $\lambda_A = 0.3$ represents a state with interference from information A. From these figures, we can see that the existence of prior information has the effect of delaying the spreading of subsequent information.

4.2   Simultaneous Spreading Scenario

Next, we consider the simultaneous spreading of two competing pieces of information. For a non-modular network, the probabilities a_t and b_t are calculated

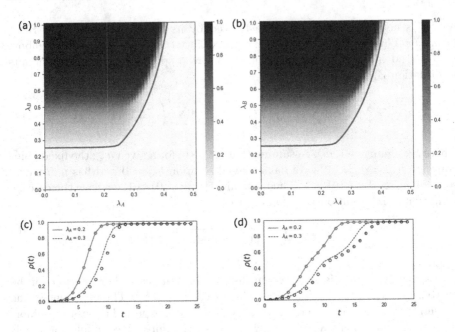

Fig. 2. Phase diagram of the final cascade size ρ_∞^B for non-modular networks (a) and modular networks with two communities (b) in the sequential spreading scenario. The red line represents the cascade condition computed by the tree-like approximation. The simulations are averaged over 20 runs for each combination of (λ_A, λ_B) with parameters $N = 2.0 \times 10^4$, $z = 10$, $\rho_0^A = \rho_0^B = 10^{-3}$, $p = 0.6$, $n = 4$. The cascade size ρ_t and its change rate $d\rho/dt$ for non-modular networks (c) and modular networks with two communities (d) in the sequential spreading scenario. The simulations are averaged over 20 runs with parameters $N = 5.0 \times 10^4$, $z = 10$, $\rho_0^A = \rho_0^B = 10^{-3}$, $\lambda_B = 0.8$, $p = 0.6$, $n = 4$. For modular networks, the percentage of edges between communities is set to 0.1% of all edges, and the seed nodes are chosen from only one community. (Color figure online)

as

$$a_t = \rho_0^A + (1 - \rho_0^A) \sum_{k=1}^{\infty} \frac{kp(k)}{z} \sum_{m+l=0}^{k-1} \frac{(k-1)!}{m!\,l!\,(k-m-l-1)!}$$
$$\times a_{t-1}^m b_{t-1}^l (1 - a_{t-1} - b_{t-1})^{k-m-l-1} F(m,l) =: f(a_{t-1}, b_{t-1}), \quad (10)$$

$$b_t = \rho_0^B + (1 - \rho_0^B) \sum_{k=1}^{\infty} \frac{kp(k)}{z} \sum_{m+l=0}^{k-1} \frac{(k-1)!}{m!\,l!\,(k-m-l-1)!}$$
$$\times a_{t-1}^m b_{t-1}^l (1 - a_{t-1} - b_{t-1})^{k-m-l-1} G(m,l) =: g(a_{t-1}, b_{t-1}). \quad (11)$$

where $F(m,l) = F(m,l;\lambda_A, \lambda_B, Q(\theta))$ is the probability that a node with m neighbors who spread information A and l neighbors who spread information B adopts information A, and is defined in the same way as Eq. (7).

For a modular network, the probabilities $a_t^{(i)}$ and $b_t^{(i)}$ of the community C_i are calculated by using $f(a_{t-1}, b_{t-1})$ and $g(a_{t-1}, b_{t-1})$ of Eqs. (10) and (11) as follows:

$$a_t^{(i)} = \frac{\sum_{j=1}^{d} \gamma_{ij} f(a_{t-1}^{(j)}, b_{t-1}^{(j)})}{\sum_{j=1}^{d} \gamma_{ij}} = \phi_i(a_{t-1}^{(1)}, \ldots, a_{t-1}^{(d)}, b_{t-1}^{(1)}, \ldots, b_{t-1}^{(d)}), \qquad (12)$$

$$b_t^{(i)} = \frac{\sum_{j=1}^{d} \gamma_{ij} g(a_{t-1}^{(j)}, b_{t-1}^{(j)})}{\sum_{j=1}^{d} \gamma_{ij}} = \psi_i(a_{t-1}^{(1)}, \ldots, a_{t-1}^{(d)}, b_{t-1}^{(1)}, \ldots, b_{t-1}^{(d)}). \qquad (13)$$

Unfortunately, in the simultaneous spreading scenario, it is difficult to derive the meaningful cascade condition of information B by the linear stability analysis. We now assume that $p(k)$ is the Poisson distribution. By linearizing Eqs. (10) and (11) around the trivial fixed point $(a_\infty, b_\infty) = (0, 0)$, we obtain the (trivial) cascade condition $\lambda_B > \lambda_c = 1/(z(1-p))$. Furthermore, for a fixed λ_A ($> \lambda_c$), by linearizing them around $(a_\infty, b_\infty) = (a_\infty, 0)$, we obtain $\lambda_B > e^{z\lambda_A a_\infty}/(z(1-p))$. However, unlike Sect. 4.1, this condition is meaningless since a_∞ depends on λ_B. Therefore, we focus on the nullclines of these equations, which are the curves such that $a = f(a, b)$ and $b = g(a, b)$ on the (a, b)-phase plane. The nullcline analysis enables us to analyze the qualitative behaviors of a_∞ and b_∞.

Figure 3 shows the nullclines of Eqs. (10) and (11) for $\lambda_A \ll \lambda_B$ and $\lambda_A = \lambda_B$. When considering a trajectory on the phase plane, a_t increases horizontally in the region $a < f(a, b)$, while a_t decreases in the region $a > f(a, b)$. Similarly, in the region $b < g(a, b)$, b_t increases vertically, while in the region $b > g(a, b)$, b_t decreases. Hence, we can roughly predict in which direction the solution starting from $(a_0, b_0) = (\rho_0^A, \rho_0^B)$ will go. Intersection points of these curves represent the possible final states (fixed points) of the system described by Eqs. (10) and (11).

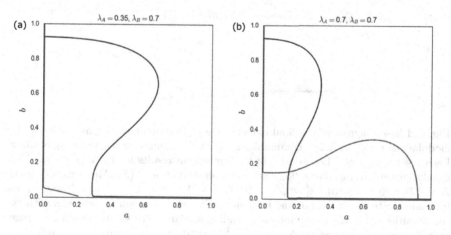

Fig. 3. Nullclines of Eqs. (10) and (11) on the (a, b)-phase plane for $\lambda_A \ll \lambda_B$ and $\lambda_A = \lambda_B$. The red and blue curves respectively represent $a = f(a, b)$ and $b = g(a, b)$. The parameters are $z = 10$, $\rho_0^A = \rho_0^B = 0$, $p = 0.6$, $n = 4$. (Color figure online)

In this system, the number of fixed points varies depending on λ_A and λ_B. First, if λ_A and λ_B are smaller than the critical threshold λ_c, the system has a trivial fixed point $(a, b) = (0, 0)$. For $\lambda_A \gg \lambda_B$, the system has the only stable fixed point $(a, b) = (a^*, 0)$, and conversely for $\lambda_B \gg \lambda_A$, the system has only the stable fixed point $(a, b) = (0, b^*)$. For $\lambda_A \approx \lambda_B$, the system has two stable fixed points $(a, b) = (a^*, 0)$ and $(0, b^*)$, and one unstable fixed point $(a, b) = (a^*, b^*)$. Therefore, in this system, it is expected that information A and information B will never coexist in a steady state, and one drives out the other.

Indeed, as shown in Fig. 4a, the simulation results of the final cascade size of information B, ρ_B^∞, on non-modular networks show that for $\lambda_B > \lambda_A$, information B spreads throughout the network, whereas information B becomes extinct for $\lambda_A > \lambda_B$. Even for $\lambda_A = \lambda_B$, the two cannot coexist, and either information A or information B widely spreads due to slight fluctuations of the network structure. This result is known in ecology as the *competitive exclusion principle* [21].

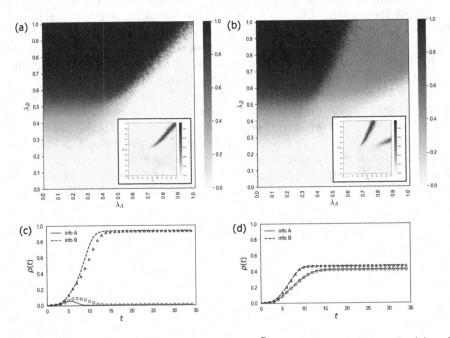

Fig. 4. Phase diagram of the final cascade size ρ_∞^B for non-modular networks (a) and modular networks with two communities (b) in the simultaneous spreading scenario. Each inset represents the variance of the simulation results for the cascade size. The simulations are averaged over 20 runs for each combination of (λ_A, λ_B) with parameters $N = 2.0 \times 10^4$, $z = 10$, $\rho_0^A = \rho_0^B = 10^{-3}$, $p = 0.6$, $n = 4$. The cascade size ρ_t and its change rate $d\rho/dt$ for non-modular networks (c) and modular networks with two communities (d) in the simultaneous spreading scenario. The simulations are averaged over 20 runs with parameters $N = 5.0 \times 10^4$, $z = 10$, $\rho_0^A = \rho_0^B = 10^{-3}$, $\lambda_A = 0.6$, $\lambda_B = 0.7$ $p = 0.6$, $n = 4$. For modular networks, the percentage of edges between communities is set to 0.1% of all edges, and the seed nodes are chosen from only one community.

On the other hand, when the network has a community structure, information A and information B coexist in the region $\lambda_A \approx \lambda_B$ (Fig. 4b). Indeed, it is also known in ecology that the spatial heterogeneity of competitive environments breaks the competitive exclusion principle and allows coexistence [22].

Figures 4c and 4d show the time evolution of the cascade size of information A and information B at each step t for $\lambda_A \approx \lambda_B$. For non-modular networks, information A initially spreads but is soon driven out by information B and becomes extinct (Fig. 4c). On the other hand, for modular networks, information A and information B coexist (Fig. 4d).

5   Conclusion

In this study, we modeled the spreading of two competing pieces of information on a non-modular and modular network and analyzed how the community structure affects the competitive spreading in the sequential and simultaneous spreading scenarios under the majority assumption (i.e., assumption that each node spreads the majority information from its perspective). In the sequential spreading scenario, we found that the community structure has little effect on the final prevalence but affects the spreading process; that is, the spreading peaks in different communities are separated in time. In contrast, in the simultaneous spreading scenario, we found that community structure has a strong effect on not only the spreading process but also the final prevalence. On a non-modular network, two competing pieces of information cannot coexist and one drives out the other. However, on a modular network, they avoid competition and coexist in different communities even though the majority assumption is a strong assumption that prevents coexistence. These results suggest that the effect of community structure cannot be ignored in the analysis of competitive spreading (especially, simultaneous spreading) of multiple information. Further studies are needed to analyze the spreading dynamics in other scenarios (e.g., cooperative scenario) and/or under looser assumptions than the majority assumption.

References

1. Goffman, W., Newill, V.: Generalization of epidemic theory. Nature **204**(4955), 225–228 (1964)
2. Bettencourt, L.M., Cintrón-Arias, A., Kaiser, D.I., Castillo-Chávez, C.: The power of a good idea: quantitative modeling of the spread of ideas from epidemiological models. Phys. A Stat. Mech. Appl. **364**, 513–536 (2006)
3. Anderson, R.M., May, R.M.: Infectious diseases of humans: dynamics and control. Oxford University Press, Oxford (1992)
4. Keeling, M.J., Rohani, P.: Modeling Infectious Diseases in Humans and Animals. Princeton University Press, Princeton (2011)
5. Watts, D.J.: A simple model of global cascades on random networks. In: The Structure and Dynamics of Networks, pp. 497–502. Princeton University Press (2011)

6. Granovetter, M.: Threshold models of collective behavior. Am. J. Sociol. **83**(6), 1420–1443 (1978)
7. Wang, W., Tang, M., Zhang, H.-F., Lai, Y.-C.: Dynamics of social contagions with memory of nonredundant information. Phys. Rev. E **92**(1), 012820 (2015)
8. Centola, D.: The spread of behavior in an online social network experiment. Science **329**(5996), 1194–1197 (2010)
9. Mønsted, B., Sapieżyński, P., Ferrara, E., Lehmann, S.: Evidence of complex contagion of information in social media: an experiment using twitter bots. PLoS ONE **12**(9), e0184148 (2017)
10. State, B., Adamic, L.: The diffusion of support in an online social movement: evidence from the adoption of equal-sign profile pictures. In: Proceedings of the 18th ACM Conference on Computer Supported Cooperative Work & Social Computing, pp. 1741–1750 (2015)
11. Karampourniotis, P.D., Sreenivasan, S., Szymanski, B.K., Korniss, G.: The impact of heterogeneous thresholds on social contagion with multiple initiators. PLoS ONE **10**(11), e0143020 (2015)
12. Min, B., San Miguel, M.: Competing contagion processes: complex contagion triggered by simple contagion. Sci. Rep. **8**(1), 1–8 (2018)
13. Newman, M.E., Strogatz, S.H., Watts, D.J.: Random graphs with arbitrary degree distributions and their applications. Phys. Rev. E **64**(2), 026118 (2001)
14. Galstyan, A., Cohen, P.: Cascading dynamics in modular networks. Phys. Rev. E **75**(3), 036109 (2007)
15. Gleeson, J.P.: Cascades on correlated and modular random networks. Phys. Rev. E **77**(4), 046117 (2008)
16. Nematzadeh, A., Ferrara, E., Flammini, A., Ahn, Y.-Y.: Optimal network modularity for information diffusion. Phys. Rev. Lett. **113**(8), 088701 (2014)
17. Liu, Q.H., Zhong, L.F., Wang, W., Zhou, T., Eugene Stanley, H.: Interactive social contagions and co-infections on complex networks. Chaos Interdisc. J. Nonlinear Sci. **28**(1), 013120 (2018)
18. Min, B., San Miguel, M.: Competition and dual users in complex contagion processes. Sci. Rep. **8**(1), 1–8 (2018)
19. Gleeson, J.P., Cahalane, D.J.: Seed size strongly affects cascades on random networks. Phys. Rev. E **75**(5), 056103 (2007)
20. Gleeson, J.P., Porter, M.A.: Message-passing methods for complex contagions. In: Lehmann, S., Ahn, Y.-Y. (eds.) Complex Spreading Phenomena in Social Systems. CSS, pp. 81–95. Springer, Cham (2018). https://doi.org/10.1007/978-3-319-77332-2_5
21. Hardin, G.: The competitive exclusion principle. Science **131**(3409), 1292–1297 (1960)
22. Amarasekare, P.: Competitive coexistence in spatially structured environments: a synthesis. Ecol. Lett. **6**(12), 1109–1122 (2003)

HyperNetVec: Fast and Scalable Hierarchical Embedding for Hypergraphs

Sepideh Maleki[1]([✉]), Donya Saless[2], Dennis P. Wall[3], and Keshav Pingali[1]

[1] The University of Texas at Austin, Austin, TX, USA
{smaleki,pingali}@cs.utexas.edu
[2] The University of Tehran, Tehran, Iran
donya.saless@ut.ac.ir
[3] Stanford University, Stanford, CA, USA
dpwall@stanford.edu

Abstract. Many problems such as node classification and link prediction in network data can be solved using graph embeddings. However, it is difficult to use graphs to capture non-binary relations such as communities of nodes. These kinds of complex relations are expressed more naturally as hypergraphs. While hypergraphs are a generalization of graphs, state-of-the-art graph embedding techniques are not adequate for solving prediction and classification tasks on large hypergraphs accurately in reasonable time. In this paper, we introduce HyperNetVec, a novel hierarchical framework for scalable unsupervised hypergraph embedding. HyperNetVec exploits shared-memory parallelism and is capable of generating high quality embeddings for real-world hypergraphs with millions of nodes and hyperedges in only a couple of minutes while existing hypergraph systems either fail for such large hypergraphs or may take days to produce the embeddings.

Keywords: Hypergraph embedding · Network embedding

1 Introduction

A *hypergraph* is a generalization of a graph in which an edge can connect any number of nodes. Formally, a hypergraph H is a tuple (V, E) where V is the set of *nodes* and E is a set of nonempty subsets of V called *hyperedges*. Nodes and hyperedges may have weights. Graphs are a special case of hypergraphs in which each hyperedge connects exactly two nodes.

Hypergraphs arise in many application domains. For example, Giurgiu et al. [11] model protein interaction networks as hypergraphs; nodes in the hypergraph represent the proteins and hyperedges represent *protein complexes* formed by interactions between multiple proteins. The DisGeNET knowledge platform [24] represents a disease genomics dataset as a hypergraph in which nodes represents genes and hyperedges represent diseases associated with certain collections of genes. Algorithms for solving hypergraph problems are then used to predict new protein complexes or to predict that a cluster of genes is associated with an as-yet undiscovered disease.

© Springer Nature Switzerland AG 2022
P. Ribeiro et al. (Eds.): NetSci-X 2022, LNCS 13197, pp. 169–183, 2022.
https://doi.org/10.1007/978-3-030-97240-0_13

1.1   Hypergraph Embedding

Bengio et al. [1] show that one way to solve prediction problems in graphs is to find an embedding of the graph using *representation learning*. Formally, an embedding of a network is a mapping of the vertex set into $\mathcal{R}^d$ where n is the number of nodes in the network and $d \ll n$. There is a rich literature on graph embedding methods that use a variety of techniques ranging from random walks [13,22,27] to matrix factorization [25] and graph neural networks [14,30]. Graph embedding techniques can be extended to hypergraphs in two ways but neither of them is satisfactory.

One approach is to represent the hypergraph as a graph by replacing each hyperedge with a clique of edges connecting the vertices of that hyperedge, and then use graph embeddings to solve the prediction problems. This approach has been explored in HGNN [9] and HyperGCN [31]. However, the clique expansion is lossy because the hypergraph cannot be recovered from the clique expansion in general. This information loss persists even if the dual of the hypergraph is considered [17].

Zien et al. [36] show that another approach is to work with the *star expansion* of the hypergraph. Given a hypergraph $H = (V, E)$ where V is the set of nodes and E is the set of hyperedges, we create a bipartite graph $H^* = (V^*, E^*)$ by (i) introducing a node v_e for each hyperedge $e \in E$ so in final graph $V^* = V \cup E$, and (ii) introducing an edge between a node $u \in V$ and a hyperedge node $v_e \in E$ if $u \in e$ in the hypergraph, so *i.e.*, $E^* = (u, v_e) : u \in e, e \in E$. Unlike the clique expansion of a hypergraph, the star expansion is not lossy provided nodes representing hyperedges are distinguished from nodes representing hypergraph nodes. However, graph representation learning approaches do not distinguish between the two types of nodes in the bipartite graph, which lowers accuracy for prediction problems as we show in this paper.

These problems motivated us to develop *HyperNetVec*, a *parallel multi-level framework for constructing hypergraph embeddings*. HyperNetVec leverages existing graph embedding algorithms and it performs hypergraph embedding in a much faster and more scalable manner than current methods. We evaluate HyperNetVec on a number of data sets for node classification and hyperedge prediction. Our experiments show that our hierarchical framework can compute the embedding of hypergraphs with millions of nodes and hyperedges in just a few minutes without loss of accuracy in downstream tasks, while all existing hypergraph embedding techniques either fail to run on such large inputs and or take days to complete.

Our main technical contributions are summarized below.

- **HyperNetVec:** We describe *HyperNetVec*, a hierarchical hypergraph embedding framework that is designed to handle variable-sized hyperedges.
- **Node features:** Unlike many other systems in this space, **HyperNetVec** can exploit the topology of the graph as well as node features, if they are present in the input data.
- **Unsupervised hypergraph embedding system:** To the best of our knowledge, HyperNetVec is the first unsupervised hypergraph embedding

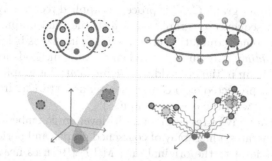

Fig. 1. Multi-level embedding. **Top left:** original hypergraph. **Top right:** contracting nodes of a hypergraph to create a coarser hypergraph. **Bottom left:** initial embedding. **Bottom right:** iterative refinement of embeddings.

system. The embeddings obtained from this framework can be used in downstream tasks such as hyperedge prediction and node classification.

– **Scalability:** HyperNetVec is the first hypergraph embedding approach that can generate embeddings of hypergraphs with millions of nodes and hyperedges.

Our approach can significantly reduce run time while producing comparable and in some cases, better accuracy than state-of-the-art techniques.

2   Related Work

There is a large body of work on graph and hypergraph embedding techniques so we discuss only the most closely related work.

2.1   Network Embedding

There are relatively few efforts on hypergraph embedding that treat hyperedges as first-class entities. As mentioned above, one popular approach to hypergraph embedding is to convert the hypergraph to a graph and then use a graph embedding technique [9,29,33]. For example, each hyperedge can be replaced with a clique connecting the nodes of that hyperedge to produce a graph representation. Other approaches such as HyperGCN [31] use a graph convolution on a modified clique expansion technique where they *choose* what edges to keep in the graph representation. While this method keeps more structure than methods based on the clique expansion of a hypergraph, existing methods fail to scale to large networks as we show in this paper.

Multi-level Embedding. Multi-level (hierarchical) approaches attempt to improve the run-time and quality of existing or new embedding techniques. Multi-level graph embedding consists of three phases: coarsening, initial embedding, and refinement. *Coarsening:* A coarsened graph G' is created by merging pairs of nodes in input graph G. This process is applied recursively to the coarser graph, creating a sequence of graphs. In which the final graph is the coarsest graph that meets some termination criterion (*e.g.*, its size is below some threshold). *Initial embedding:* Any unsupervised embedding methods for networks can be used to generate an initial embedding. *Refinement:* For graphs G' and G, the embedding of G' is projected onto G and then refined, starting from the coarsest graph and finishing with the original graph.

There is a large body of research on multi-level *graph* embedding. For example, *HARP* [4] generates a hierarchy of coarsened graphs and perform embedding from the coarsest level to the original one. MILE [19] uses heavy edge matching [3] to coarsen the graph and leverages GCN as a refinement method to improve embedding quality. However, training a GCN model is very time consuming for large graphs and leads to poor performance when multiple GCN layers are stacked together [18]. These multi-level embedding methods only utilise structural information (topology) of a graph. However, in many datasets such as citations, nodes of a graph have attributes. For a high quality embedding, it is important to exploit node attributes as well as structural information of a graph. GraphZoom [6] first performs graph fusion to generate a new graph that encodes the topology of the original graph and the node attribute information and then uses a coarsening algorithm that merges nodes with high spectral similarity. Finally, they apply a local refinement algorithm. While GraphZoom outperforms previous multi-level embedding systems, it still takes hours, in some cases days, to generate embeddings for a graph with millions of nodes and edges.

In general, hypergraphs are a more complicated topic and the corresponding algorithms are typically more compute and memory intensive. Multi-level approaches for *hypergraphs* have been used mainly for hypergraph partitioning [7,16,20]. In principle, ideas from multi-level graph embedding approaches can be adopted for hypergraphs. For example, for the coarsening algorithm, we can merge pairs of nodes that have a hyperedge in common (heavy edge matching). While this approach is able to produce coarser hypergraphs, it reduces the number of hyperedges in the coarser graphs only for those pairs of matched nodes that are connected by a hyperedge of size two. As a result, the coarsest hypergraph is still large in terms of the size of the hyperedges which increases the running time of the overall algorithm. In our experience, the coarsening and refinement algorithms proposed in multi-level graph embedding systems are not adequate for solving inference problems on hypergraphs, as we discuss in this paper. These limitations led us to design HyperNetVec, which scales to hypergraphs with millions of nodes and hyperedges while producing high-quality embeddings.

3   Methodology

Given a hypergraph $H = (V, E)$, the algorithms described in this paper use the star expansion of the hypergraph and assign a vector representation h_u to each $u \in (V \cup E)$. Intuitively, these embeddings attempt to preserve *structural similarity* in the hypergraph: if two hyperedges have many nodes in common or if two nodes are in many of the same hyperedges, the algorithm attempts to assign the two hyperedges/nodes to points that are *close* in the vector space. *Closeness* can be computed using distance or other measures of vector similarity. Embedding should also exploit the *transitivity* property of similarity: if a and b are similar, and b and c are similar, we want the embedding of a and c to be close to each other as well. Finally, if nodes have features, the embeddings should also exploit *functional similarity* between nodes.

Figure 1 illustrates the high-level idea of multi-level hypergraph embedding. This framework consists of three phases: (i) *Coarsening*, which iteratively merges nodes of the hypergraph to shrink the size of the hypergraph until the hypergraph is small enough that any network embedding algorithm can quickly obtain the embedding of the smallest hypergraph; (ii) *Initial embedding*, in which a network embedding algorithm is used on the coarsest hypergraph to generate the embedding, and (iii) *Refinement*, in which the embedding vectors of the coarser hypergraph are projected onto a finer hypergraph and a refinement algorithm is used to refine these embedding vectors. In the rest of this section, we describe these phases in more detail. HyperNetVec is a parallel implementation of the multilevel approach.

3.1   Coarsening

Intuitively, coarsening finds nodes that are *similar* to each other and merges them to obtain a coarser hypergraph. To obtain a high quality embedding, we need to explore both structural similarity and functional similarity. The connectivity of nodes and hyperedges of a hypergraph determines structural similarity while node features determine functional similarity.

The first step in coarsening a hypergraph is to find nodes that are similar to each other and merge them. This is accomplished by "assigning" each node to one of its hyperedges, and then merging all nodes $\{n_1, n_2, ..., n_k\}$ assigned to a given hyperedge to produce a node n' of the coarser hypergraph. We refer to n' as the *representative* of node n_i in the coarse hypergraph, and denote it as $\text{rep}(n_i)$. If all nodes of a hyperedge h_j are merged, we remove that hyperedge from the hypergraph. Otherwise, we add the hyperedge to the next level and refer to it as $\text{rep}(h_j)$. If a node n_i is contained in hyperedge h_j in the finer hypergraph and h_j is present in the coarse hypergraph, then $\text{rep}(n_i)$ is made a member of $\text{rep}(h_j)$.

If nodes of a hypergraph have features, this information can be used to find similar nodes and merge them together. In a hypergraph with node features, the feature vector of a hyperedge is the mean aggregation of the features of its nodes. In this scenario, metrics of vector similarity or distance between a feature vector of a hyperedge and a node can be used for assigning nodes to hyperedges. However, if the hypergraph has no features, HyperNetVec can use other measures such as weights or degrees of a hyperedge to assign nodes to hyperedges. The datasets used in experiments in this paper for node classification are citation networks and the node feature vectors come from bag-of-words encoding. In these datasets, *cosine similarity* aligns well with class labels. However, other metrics of vector similarity or distance such as L2 norm, correlation distance, etc. can also be used.

In summary, at each level of coarsening, HyperNetVec computes a feature vector for a hyperedge by finding the mean aggregation of the feature vectors of its nodes. Then it assigns each node v in the current hypergraph to a hyperedge $c(v)$, defined (for cosine similarity) as $c(v) = \text{argmax}_{e \in \mathcal{N}(v)} \dfrac{f(e) \cdot f(v)}{|f(e)| \cdot |f(v)|}$ where $\mathcal{N}(v)$ is the set of hyperedges that node v belongs to, $f(e)$ is the feature vector of hyperedge e and $f(v)$ is the feature vector of node v.

Nodes that are assigned to the same hyperedge are merged together and the resulting node is added to the coarse hypergraph. In case of a tie, HyperNetVec randomly chooses a hyperedge in the neighborhood of the node.

3.2 Initial Embedding

We coarsen the hypergraph until it is small enough that *any* unsupervised embedding method can generate the embedding of the coarsest hypergraph in just a few seconds. We use the edgelist of the coarsest bipartite graph (star expansion) as the input to this embedding method.

3.3 Refinement

The goal of this phase is to improve embeddings by performing a variation of Laplacian smoothing [28] that we call the *refinement* algorithm. The basic idea is to update the embedding of each node u using a weighted average of its own embedding and the embeddings of its immediate neighbors $\mathcal{N}(u)$. Intuitively, smoothing eliminates high-frequency noise in the embeddings and tries to assign similar embeddings to nodes that are close to each other in the graph, which improves the accuracy of downstream inference tasks. A simple iterative scheme for smoothing is: $\tilde{z}_u^i = \sum_{v \in \mathcal{N}(u)} \left(\frac{w_{uv}}{\sum_{v \in \mathcal{N}(u)} w_{uv}} \right) z_v^{i-1}$. In this formula, z_u^i is the embedding of node u in iteration i, and w_{uv} is the weight on the outgoing edge from u to v; if there no weights in the input hypergraph, a value of 1 is used and the denominator is the degree of node u. This iterative scheme can be improved by introducing a hyper-parameter ω that determines the relative importance of the embeddings of the neighboring nodes versus the embedding of the node itself, to obtain the following iterative scheme: $z_u^i = (1-\omega)z_u^{i-1} + \omega \tilde{z}_u^i$. The initial embeddings for the iterative scheme are generated as follows. For the coarsest graph, they are generated as described in Sect. 3.2. For the other hypergraphs, if a set of nodes S in hypergraph H_{i-1} was merged to form a node n in the coarser hypergraph H_i, the embedding of n in H_i is assigned to all the nodes of S in H_{i-1}.

Abstractly, this iterative scheme uses *successive over-relaxation* (SOR) with a parameter ω to solve the linear system $Lz = 0$ where L is the Laplacian matrix of H^*, the bipartite (star) representation of the hypergraph. The Laplacian is defined as $(D - A)$ where D is the diagonal matrix with diagonal elements d_{uu}

Algorithm 1: Refinement

1: **Input:** Bipartite graph representation $H^* = (V^*, E^*, W)$ of hypergraph
   $H = (V, E, W)$, vector representation z_u for all $u \in (V^*)$, neighborhood function
   $\mathcal{N}(u)$, parameter ω, parameter k for max iteration
2: **Output:** Refined vector representation h_u, $\forall u \in (V^*)$
3: $z_u^0 \leftarrow z_u, \forall u \in (V^*)$
4: $iter = 0$
5: **while** $iter < k$ **do**
6:    **for** $u \in V^*$ in parallel **do**
7:       $\tilde{z}_u^i \leftarrow \sum_{v \in \mathcal{N}(u)} w_{uv} z_v^{i-1} / \sum_{v \in \mathcal{N}(u)} w_{uv}$
8:       $z_u^i \leftarrow (1 - \omega) z_u^{i-1} + \omega \tilde{z}_u^i$
9:    **end for**
10:   $iter += 1$
11: **end while**
12: $h_u \leftarrow z_u^k, \forall u \in (V^*)$

---

equal to the degree of node u for unweighted graphs (for weighted graphs, the sum of weights of outgoing edges), and A is the adjacency matrix of H^*. To avoid oversmoothing, we do not compute the exact solution of this linear system but if we start with a good initial embedding z^0, a few iterations of the iterative scheme lead to significant gains in the quality of the embedding, as we show experimentally in Sect. 4.

Algorithm 1 shows the psuedocode for refinement. The inputs to this algorithm are H^*, the bipartite representation of the hypergraph, z_u, the initial embedding for each node and hyperedge, and a relaxation parameter ω between 0 and 1. Embeddings of the hyperedges are updated using the embeddings of the nodes, and the embeddings of nodes are updated using the embeddings of hyperedges. Note that if u represents a hyperedge, $\mathcal{N}(u)$ is the set of nodes in that hyperedge, and if u represents a node in the hypergraph, $\mathcal{N}(u)$ represents the set of hyperedges that u is contained in. Each iteration of the refinement algorithm has a linear time complexity in the size of the bipartite representation of the hypergraph.

4   Experiments

HyperNetVec provides an unsupervised method for representation learning for hypergraphs. We show these representations perform well for both node classification and hyperedge prediction. Prior works such as HyperGCN and Hyper-SAGNN have been evaluated for one or the other of these tasks but not both.

Experimental Settings. We implement *HyperNetVec* in Galois 6.0 [23]. All experiments are done on a machine running CentOS 7 with 4 sockets of 14-core Intel Xeon Gold 5120 CPUs at 2.2 GHz, and 187 GB of RAM. All the methods used in this study are parallel implementations and we use the maximum number of cores available on the machine to run the experiments. The embedding dimension is 128. The hyperparameter ω in the refinement algorithm is set to 0.5 for all experiments. Once node embeddings are obtained, we apply logistic regression with cross-entropy loss for our downstream tasks.

Table 1. Datasets used for node classification.

Dataset	Nodes	Hyperedges	Edges	Classes	Features
Citeseer	1,458	1,079	6,906	6	3,703
PubMed	3,840	7,963	69,258	3	500
DBLP	41,302	22,363	199,122	6	1,425

4.1 Node Classification

Given a hypergraph and node labels on a small subset of nodes, the task is to predict labels on the remaining nodes. We used the standard hypergraph datasets from prior works, and these are listed in Table 1. We are given 4% of node labels and predict the remaining 96%.

Methods Compared. We explore a number of popular methods for graph embedding. We also compare our results with hypergraph convolutional networks approaches for semi-supervised classification.

Random-Walk Methods: We select node2vec [13] (high performance implementation [12]) for this group. This method is properly tuned. We explored window size {10,20}, walk length {20, 40, 80, 120}, number of walks per vertex {10,80,40}, p {1,4,0.5}, and q {1,4,0.5}. The results reported in the paper are for the best hyper-parameter values, which are 10,80,10,4,1 respectively.

Graph Convolutional Network: We compare with GraphSAGE [14]. We use GraphSAGE in unsupervised manner with the mean aggregator model.

Multi-level Based Embedding Methods: We compare against unsupervised approaches MILE [19], and GraphZoom [6]. MILE is a multi-level graph embedding framework. We used the default refinement technique, MD-gcn. GraphZoom is also a multi-level graph embedding framework. For the coarsening, we used *simple*.

Semi-supervised Classification on Hypergraphs. We compare with HyperGCN. Given a hypergraph, HyperGCN [31] approximates the hypergraph by a graph where each hyperedge is approximated by a subgraph. A graph convolutional network (GCN) is then run on the resulting graph. We used 200 epochs and learning rate of 0.01. For the multi-level approaches, we use node2vec, and GraphSAGE as the initial embedding methods. Since MILE cannot utilise node features, we do not run GraphSAGE as an initial embedding method for MILE. We report the mean test accuracy and standard deviation over 100 different train-test splits. We optimize hyperparameters of all the baselines. For HyperNetVec, we use 80 iterations of refinement. Alternatively, other stopping criteria such as epsilon difference between two consecutive iterations can be used.

Running Time. For HyperNetVec and other multi-level approaches, running time includes all three phases: coarsening, initial embedding, and refinement. For the rest of the baselines, we use the time for hypergraph embedding. For each approach to computing the initial embeddings (node2vec, GraphSAGE), we have a row showing the accuracy and running times when that approach is used, and rows below those showing the accuracy and running times if that approach is used in conjunction with HyperNetVec or other multilevel approaches. For example, the first row in Table 2 shows the running times and accuracy when node2vec is used on the star expansion of the hypergraph, while the second row (HyperNetVec + nv *(l=0)*) shows the total running time and accuracy if HyperNetVec is used without coarsening but with the output of node2vec being post-processed using our refinement algorithm. The line below that *(l=2)* shows the results if two levels of coarsening are used in addition.

Datasets. We used the following standard hypergraph datasets in our study. Nodes not connected to any hyperedge, as well as hyperedges containing only one node, were removed. *Citeseer (co-citation):* scientific publications classified into six classes. All documents cited by a document are connected by a hyperedge. [10]. *PubMed (co-citation):* scientific publications from PubMed Diabetes database. All documents cited by a document are connected by a hyperedge [10]. *DBLP (co-authorship):* scientific publications consist of 6 conference categories. All documents co-authored by an author are in one hyperedge [5].

Table 2. Node classification. Accuracy in % and time in seconds. *l* is the number of coarsening levels. 0 means without coarsening.

	Citeseer		PubMed		DBLP	
	Accuracy	Time	Accuracy	Time	Accuracy	Time
node2vec (nv)	51.3 ±1.	14	65.3 ± 2.	66	64.3 ± .4	470
HyperNetVec + nv *(l=0)*	59.1 ±1.	16	79.7 ±1.	70	72.4 ± .4	490
HyperNetVec + nv *(l=2)*	60.6 ±1.	17	80.7 ±1.	69	78.9 ±.5	216
GraphZoom + nv *(l=2)*	54.4 ±1.	15	74.9 ± .1	100	70.2 ± .5	434
MILE + nv *(l=2)*	52.2 ±1.	14	68.7 ± .2	60	71.8 ±1.	402
GraphSAGE (gs)	45.6 ±1.	1,167	60.7 ± .2	277	67.7 ± .1	925
HyperNetVec + gs *(l=0)*	60.3 ±3.	1,170	80.4 ±.1	296	79.9 ±.1	1,055
HyperNetVec + gs *(l=2)*	60.2 ±1.	843	80.8 ±.1	120	79.4 ±.4	530
GraphZoom + gs *(l=2)*	52.7 ±1.	853	72.4 ± .1	137	75.6 ± .4	593
HyperGCN	54.1 ±10	12	64.3 ± 10	60	63.3 ± 10	480

These are the main takeaways from Table 2. HyperNetVec generates the highest quality embeddings for the node classification task. HyperNetVec outperforms HyperGCN in terms of quality for all datasets by up to 15%. The refinement algorithm improves the quality of embeddings for all the datasets by up to 23%. This can be seen by comparing the statistics for HyperNetVec without coarsening ($l = 0$) with those for node2vec, and GraphSAGE. The initial embedding for HyperNetVec is obtained from node2vec, and GraphSAGE so differences in the statistics arise entirely from the fact that HyperNetVec performs refinement. HyperNetVec outperforms prior multi-level graph embedding approaches (MILE and GraphZoom) for all the datasets by up to 11% for MILE and up to 9% for GraphZoom. Coarsening reduces the overall running time of the embedding for larger hypergraphs. Since coarsening reduces the size of the hypergraph, the initial embedding and refinement can be done faster. This can be seen by comparing the statistics for HyperNetVec with 2 levels of coarsening ($l = 2$) with those for slower initial embedding approach such as GraphSAGE.

4.2 Hyperedge Prediction

In hyperedge prediction, we are given a hypergraph with a certain fraction of hyperedges removed, and given a proposed hyperedge (i.e. a set of nodes) our goal is to predict if this is likely to be a hyperedge or not. Formally, given a k-tuple of nodes $(v_1, v_2, ..., v_k)$, our goal is to predict if this tuple is likely to be a hyperedge or not.

We compare our method with the *supervised hyperedge prediction method* Hyper-SAGNN [34] on four datasets listed in Table 3, and with the graph method node2vec. Hyper-SAGNN is a self-attention based approach for hyperedge prediction. We used their encoder-based approach with learning rate of 0.001 and 300 epochs.

Table 3. Datasets used for hyperedge prediction.

	Nodes	Hyperedges	Edges
GPS	221	437	1, 436
MovieLens	17, 100	46, 413	47, 957
Drug	7, 486	171, 757	171, 756
Wordnet	81, 073	146, 433	145, 966
Friendster	7, 458, 099	1, 616, 918	37, 783, 346

Datasets. We used the following datasets in our study. *GPS:* a GPS network. Hyperedges are based on (user, location, activity) relations [35]. *MovieLens:* a social network where hyperedges are based on (user, movie, tag) relations, describing peoples' tagging activities [15]. *Drug:* a medicine network. The hyperedges are based on (user, drug, reaction) relations [8]. *Wordnet:* a semantic network from WordNet 3.0. The hyperedges are based on (head entity, relation, tail entity), expressing the relationships between words [2]. *Friendster:* an on-line gaming network. Users can form a group on Friendster social network which other members can then join. These user-defined groups are considered as communities. Communities larger than 500 were removed [32].

We used the same training and test data setups as Hyper-SAGNN (except for Friendster, which Hyper-SAGNN could not run). For this task, they randomly hide 20 percentage of existing hyperedges and use the rest of the hypergraph for training. The negative samples are 5 times the amount of positive samples. We downloaded their code and datasets from their GitHub repository. We used the encoder-based approach to generate the features.

For HyperNetVec, we use two levels of coarsening and two levels of refinement. We first obtain the embedding of the hypergraphs with node2vec as the initial embedding technique. To train our classifier, we used the same positive samples as Hyper-SAGNN. For negative samples we used only the negative samples of a *single* epoch of Hyper-SAGNN. We then use the vector of the variances of each dimension of the embedding for hyperedge prediction. The intuition is that if nodes are spread out (high variance in the embedding), then they probably do not form a hyperedge whereas nodes that are close to each other are likely to constitute a hyperedge. Various operators such as average, min, and max can be used instead of variance.

Experimental Results. Table 4 summarizes the hyperedge prediction results for HyperNetVec, node2vec, and Hyper-SAGNN. HyperNetVec achieves the best AUC and running time compared to Hyper-SAGNN. Hyper-SAGNN took almost a day for wordnet whereas HyperNetVec completed the task in less than a minute. HyperNetVec achieves better AUC compared to node2vec on all datasets except drug, and it is always faster.

HyperNetVec for Large Hypergraphs. We study the scalability of HyperNetVec on a large hypergraph (Friendster) and compare HyperNetVec's accuracy and running time with that of MILE, and DeepWalk (a random-walk based method [22]). (Hyper-SAGNN, GraphZoom and node2vec failed to generate results for Friendster). We randomly hide 20% of existing hyperedges and use the rest of the hypergraph to generate the embeddings for the nodes of the hypergraph and finally, use the variance operator for prediction. Since the hypergraph is large, we used five levels of coarsening and ten levels of refinement. The other baseline that was able to run Friendster was MILE with 15 levels of coarsening, and it failed for smaller numbers of coarsening levels. It took MILE 8 h to generate embeddings for Friendster with an accuracy of 90.4 while it took HyperNetVec only fifteen minutes to do the same task with better accuracy (92.3%). DeepWalk was also able to generate the embeddings for Friendster after 17 h with accuracy 84.9%.

Figure 2 compares MILE, DeepWalk, and HyperNetVec in terms of accuracy for different levels of coarsening for HyperNetVec (for MILE, we used 15 levels of coarsening). The main takeaway from Fig. 2 is that using more levels of coarsening reduces the running time of the overall algorithm, as one would expect. However, a large number of coarsening levels may reduce the accuracy. While this is a fact in most multi-level approaches, Fig. 2 shows that the loss of accuracy for HyperNetVec is negligible and we are able to get more than 13x speed up by using 5 levels of coarsening instead of 3 levels, while losing less than 3% in accuracy.

Table 4. Area Under Curve (AUC) scores. Time in seconds.

	GPS		MovieLens		Drug		Wordnet		Friendster	
	AUC	Time	AUC	Time	AUC	Time	AUC	Time	AUC	Time
HyperNetVec	94.5	1	94.8	6.4	96.5	295	93.0	43.4	93.2	897
Hyper-SAGNN	90.6	1,800	90.8	11,160	95.9	39,540	87.7	82,800	-	-
node2vec	94.0	10	79.8	19	97.4	895	89.0	940	-	-

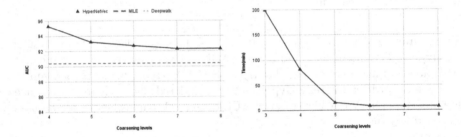

Fig. 2. Performance on Friendster

We also study the behaviour of HyperNetVec for the largest hypergraph, Friendster. In Table 5, we see the effect of the coarsening on the size of the hypergraph as well as accuracy and running time. Without coarsening, initial partitioning using DeepWalk takes 17 h (61,260 s) but with 8 levels of coarsening, the end-to-end running time is only 474 s. Therefore, using 8 levels of coarsening improves running time by 130X. The table also shows the breakdown of time in different kernels of HyperNetVec. If the coarsest hypergraph is small, most of the time is spent in refinement whereas if the coarsest hypergraph is large, the time is spent mostly in initial embedding.

Table 5. Behavior of HyperNetVec at different levels of coarsening on Friendster. COARSE-N is the number of levels of coarsening, time is in seconds.

COARSE-N	0	3	4	5	6	7	8
Hyperedges	1,616,918	564,262	460,830	419,588	404,857	399,194	396,333
Nodes	7,458,099	436,099	154,418	85,371	67,682	61,669	59,359
Coarse time	0	31	34	36	43	41	39
Init time	61,260	11,760	4,620	600	120	51	29
Refine time	0	181	237	261	261	349	406
Accuracy	84.9	95.8	95.3	93.2	92.7	92.3	92.3

5 Ongoing Work

In our ongoing research, we want to automatically learn the values of important hyper-parameters such as the number of coarsening levels and the value of ω that should be used in refinement. For very large hypergraphs, it may be necessary to use distributed-memory machines, which requires partitioning the hypergraph between the memories of the machines in the cluster. Our prior work on BiPart can be used for this task [20, 21, 26].

References

1. Bengio, Y., Courville, A., Vincent, P.: Representation learning: a review and new perspectives. IEEE Trans. Pattern Anal. Mach. Intell. **35**(8), 1798–1828 (2013). https://doi.org/10.1109/TPAMI.2013.50
2. Bordes, A., Usunier, N., Garcia-Durán, A., Weston, J., Yakhnenko, O.: Translating embeddings for modeling multi-relational data. In: Proceedings of the 26th International Conference on Neural Information Processing Systems (2013)
3. Bui, T.N., Jones, C.: A heuristic for reducing fill-in in sparse matrix factorization. In: SIAM Conference on Parallel Processing for Scientific Computing, March 1993
4. Chen, H., Perozzi, B., Hu, Y., Skiena, S.: Harp: Hierarchical representation learning for networks (2017)
5. dataset, D.: citation dataset dblp. https://www.aminer.org/lab-datasets/citation/DBLP-citation-Jan8.tar.bz
6. Deng, C., Zhao, Z., Wang, Y., Zhang, Z., Feng, Z.: Graphzoom: a multi-level spectral approach for accurate and scalable graph embedding (2020)
7. Devine, K.D., Boman, E.G., Heaphy, R.T., Bisseling, R.H., Catalyurek, U.V.: Parallel hypergraph partitioning for scientific computing. In: Proceedings of the 20th International Conference on Parallel and Distributed Processing (2006). http://dl.acm.org/citation.cfm?id=1898953.1899056
8. FAERS: drug dataset. https://www.fda.gov/Drugs/
9. Feng, Y., You, H., Zhang, Z., Ji, R., Gao, Y.: Hypergraph neural networks (2019)
10. Getoor, L.: Cora dataset. https://linqs.soe.ucsc.edu/data
11. Giurgiu, M., et al.: CORUM: the comprehensive resource of mammalian protein complexes-2019. Nucl. Acids Res. (2019)

12. Grover, A.: High performance implementation of node2vec. https://github.com/snap-stanford/snap/tree/master/examples/node2vec
13. Grover, A., Leskovec, J.: node2vec: Scalable feature learning for networks (2016)
14. Hamilton, W.L., Ying, R., Leskovec, J.: Inductive representation learning on large graphs (2018)
15. Harper, F.M., Konstan, J.A.: The Movielens datasets: history and context. ACM Trans. Interact. Intell. Syst. 5(4) (2015). https://doi.org/10.1145/2827872
16. Karypis, G., Aggarwal, R., Kumar, V., Shekhar, S.: Multilevel hypergraph partitioning: applications in VLSI domain. IEEE Trans. Very Large Scale Integr. Syst. (1999)
17. Kirkland, S.: Two-mode networks exhibiting data loss. J. Complex Netw. 6(2), 297–316 (2017). https://doi.org/10.1093/comnet/cnx039
18. Li, Q., Han, Z., Wu, X.M.: Deeper insights into graph convolutional networks for semi-supervised learning (2018)
19. Liang, J., Gurukar, S., Parthasarathy, S.: Mile: a multi-level framework for scalable graph embedding (2020)
20. Maleki, S., Agarwal, U., Burtscher, M., Pingali, K.: Bipart: a parallel and deterministic hypergraph partitioner. SIGPLAN Not. (2021). https://doi.org/10.1145/3437801.3441611
21. Mateev, N., Pingali, K., Stodghill, P., Kotlyar, V.: Next-generation generic programming and its application to sparse matrix computations. In: Proceedings of the 14th International Conference on Supercomputing. ICS 2000, pp. 88–99. Association for Computing Machinery, New York (2000)
22. Perozzi, B., Al-Rfou, R., Skiena, S.: Deepwalk: online learning of social representations. In: Proceedings of the 20th ACM SIGKDD International Conference on Knowledge Discovery and Data Mining. KDD 2014. ACM, New York (2014)
23. Pingali, K., et al.: The tao of parallelism in algorithms. In: PLDI 2011, pp. 12–25 (2011)
24. Piñero, J., et al.: The DisGeNET knowledge platform for disease genomics: 2019 update. Nucl. Acids Res. 48(D1), D845–D855 (2019)
25. Qiu, J., Dong, Y., Ma, H., Li, J., Wang, K., Tang, J.: Network embedding as matrix factorization. In: Proceedings of the Eleventh ACM International Conference on Web Search and Data Mining (2018). https://doi.org/10.1145/3159652.3159706
26. Rogers, A., Pingali, K.: Compiling for distributed memory architectures. IEEE Trans. Parallel Distrib. Syst. 5(3), 281–298 (1994)
27. Tang, J., Qu, M., Wang, M., Zhang, M., Yan, J., Mei, Q.: Line. In: Proceedings of the 24th International Conference on World Wide Web (2015)
28. Taubin, G.: A signal processing approach to fair surface design. In: Proceedings of the 22nd Annual Conference on Computer Graphics and Interactive Techniques (1995). https://doi.org/10.1145/218380.218473
29. Tu, K., Cui, P., Wang, X., Wang, F., Zhu, W.: Structural deep embedding for hyper-networks (2018)
30. Xu, K., Hu, W., Leskovec, J., Jegelka, S.: How powerful are graph neural networks? (2019)
31. Yadati, N., Nimishakavi, M., Yadav, P., Nitin, V., Louis, A., Talukdar, P.: Hyper-GCN: a new method of training graph convolutional networks on hypergraphs (2019)
32. Yang, J., Leskovec, J.: Defining and evaluating network communities based on ground-truth (2012)
33. Zhang, M., Cui, Z., Jiang, S., Chen, Y.: Beyond link prediction: predicting hyperlinks in adjacency space. In: AAAI, pp. 4430–4437 (2018)

34. Zhang, R., Zou, Y., Ma, J.: Hyper-SAGNN: a self-attention based graph neural network for hypergraphs. In: International Conference on Learning Representations (ICLR) (2020)
35. Zheng, V.W., Cao, B., Zheng, Y., Xie, X., Yang, Q.: Collaborative filtering meets mobile recommendation: a user-centered approach. In: Proceedings of the Twenty-Fourth AAAI Conference on Artificial Intelligence (2010)
36. Zien, J.Y., Schlag, M.D.F., Chan, P.K.: Multilevel spectral hypergraph partitioning with arbitrary vertex sizes. IEEE Trans. Comput. Aided Des. Integr. Circuits Syst. (1999). https://doi.org/10.1109/43.784130

Author Index

Printed in the United States
by Baker & Taylor Publisher Services